D0330875

FREEDOM FOR SALE

ALSO BY JOHN KAMPFNER

Blair's Wars

FREEDOM FOR SALE

Why the World Is Trading Democracy for Security

JOHN KAMPFNER

BASIC
BOOKS

A Member of the Perseus Books Group
New York

Published by Basic Books,
A Member of the Perseus Books Group

Books published by Basic Books are available at special
discounts for bulk purchases in the United States by
corporations, institutions, and other organizations. For more
information, please contact the Special Markets Department
at the Perseus Books Group, 2300 Chestnut Street, Suite 200,
Philadelphia, PA 19103, or call (800) 810-4145, ext. 5000, or
e-mail special.markets@perseusbooks.com.

Designed by Brent Wilcox

Library of Congress Cataloging-in-Publication Data
Kampfner, John.
    Freedom for sale : why the world is trading democracy for
security / John Kampfner.
        p.   cm.
    Includes bibliographical references and index.
    ISBN 978-0-465-01539-9 (alk. paper)
    1. Authoritarianism—Cross-cultural studies.
2. Capitalism—Cross-cultural studies.   3. Capitalism—Political
aspects—Cross-cultural studies.   4. Liberty—Cross-cultural
studies.   I. Title.
    JC480.K36 2009
    320.53—dc22
                                            2009032379

10 9 8 7 6 5 4 3 2 1

To Constance, Alex, and Lucy

CONTENTS

Introduction

Why is it that so many people around the world appear willing to give up freedoms in return for either security or prosperity? From John Stuart Mill to Jeremy Bentham, from Sigmund Freud to Franklin Roosevelt, various thinkers have posed this question through the generations. Invariably we are told that it is obvious that freedom is the higher good, and that those who choose otherwise are being deceived. "Those who would give up essential liberty to purchase a little temporary safety deserve neither liberty nor safety," declared Benjamin Franklin in 1755.

If only it were that simple. During the first part of my journalistic career, in the 1980s, I spent a lot of time in the former Soviet Union and in other countries that were generally described as dictatorships. Freedom of expression, freedom of movement, and freedom of association were heavily curtailed. Although these restrictions varied from country to country and from regime to regime, they always affected people's day-to-day lives. The lack of private freedoms was as problematic as the more politically charged restrictions on the press and politics. Citizens could not decide for themselves where to live, what to buy, and in some cases, even what relationships to enter into. The dividing lines with the West, with democracies, no matter how imperfect, were clear.

Having witnessed the fall of the Berlin Wall and the collapse of the USSR firsthand, I have been struck by the changes in the lives of some of the people I knew who lived through these momentous times. I remember spending the evening of December 25, 1991, in the company of Lev Kerbel, a much-decorated sculptor, in his Moscow studio, its every inch of wall space occupied by a model of a Soviet hero. Kerbel was uncertain about the future as we sat before the small, flickering TV, watching as the Soviet flag that had waved atop the dome of the Kremlin for decades came down, and the tricolor of the new Russia took its place. A proud and sprightly man, his demeanor belying his age, Kerbel had been born on the day of the Bolshevik revolution in 1917. During his long career he had made a name for himself creating giant monuments to Lenin and Marx from Prague to Pyongyang. I had first met him in the autumn of 1985, just as his last great offering to the people of Moscow—the marble and granite monument to Lenin dominating October Square—was being unveiled. Now, six years later, the floor space of his studio was crammed with Lenins and Marxes, along with a Stalin lying in state, Italian Communists, Bashkirian poets, composers, soldiers, and female collective farm workers with headscarves. The wall in his kitchen had become a visitors' book, and I added my signature. When I returned many years later, I saw that Boris Yeltsin had signed his name close to mine.

Over tea and brandy, Kerbel reminisced about a system to which he and millions of others had grown accustomed. For more than thirty years, the system had provided security and stability for the vast majority of a people who did not have the consumer expectations of their counterparts in the West. All they needed to do to enjoy a quiet life was to keep their heads down, to avoid causing trouble. Kerbel did more than that. He became one of the public faces of the Soviet Union. Despite his fears about the new way of living after the collapse of the Soviet Union, over the coming months he settled into the new world of the *rynok*, the market, with reasonable ease. He learned about commercial contracts and started producing sculptures for the new generation of oligarchs, either of themselves or of their wives or mistresses. His daughters began to work for American television, and Lev went on holiday to the Canary Islands.

The battle between liberalism and autocracy that had split Europe apart in the twentieth century, part of an enduring ideological divide that had grown out of the Enlightenment, had been won. Francis Fukuyama, the U.S.-based author who initially seemed to personify the optimism of the new globalized world, predicted that the end of the Cold War and the collapse of communism would lead to the "end of history" and "the universalisation of Western liberal democracy as the final form of human government."[1] Although Fukuyama's argument was complex, for more than a decade the debate about democracy and democratization was reduced to a simple matrix. Throughout this period it was assumed that freedom, liberty, and human rights were intertwined with democracy, and that democracy was inextricably linked to the free market. They not only thrived together, but they needed each other to survive.

The West's "victory" in the Cold War appeared to confirm the supremacy of both its ideology and its business model. As Margaret Thatcher had once said, it did not matter whether you started with political freedom or economic freedom: You would end up sooner or later with both. Thatcher was tapping into a rich vein of Anglo-Saxon thinking that saw free markets and liberal democracy as mutually reinforcing. Capitalism is "compatible only with democracy," wrote the American Christian social theorist Michael Novak in 1982. "While bastard forms of capitalism do seem able for a time to endure without democracy, the natural logic of capitalism leads to democracy."[2] Under communism, neither the Soviet Union, nor China, nor their satellites had posed an economic threat, let alone a meaningful ideological one, to the West. The assumption was that post-Communist Russia and China would move warmly into the West's economic and political embrace.

The number of countries embracing multiparty elections and other facets of democracy had already begun to increase. By the time the "third wave" of democratization began in 1974 in Portugal, barely a quarter of the world's states met the minimal test of a democracy: to be a place where the people were able, through universal suffrage, to choose and replace their leaders in regular, free, and fair elections. Over the course of the next two decades, dictatorships gave way to freely elected governments in southern Europe, Latin America, and East Asia. Finally, an explosion of freedom in the early 1990s liberated Eastern Europe and spread democracy from Moscow to Pretoria. This shift coincided with an unprecedented moment of U.S. military, economic, and cultural dominance. Arguably, the movement reached its peak in June 2000 at the first meeting, in Warsaw, of the grandly titled Community of Democracies, spearheaded by the administration of U.S. president Bill Clinton. There, 106 states, including some as disparate as Chile, the Czech Republic, India, Mali, Portugal, and South Korea, vowed "to respect and uphold core democratic principles and practices" of free and fair elections, freedom of speech and expression, equal access to education, rule of law, and freedom of peaceful assembly.[3]

Representative democracy expanded rapidly after that evening I spent with Lev Kerbel in 1991; by 2000, 120 out of the 192 nation-states of the UN could broadly be defined as democratic. For the first time in modern history, democracy had acquired majority status in the world. Yet, as Paul Ginsborg, professor of contemporary European history at the University of Florence, has pointed out, at the very time it appeared to be dominant, liberal democracy had actually entered a profound crisis. "This was not a crisis of *quantity*; quite the opposite. The crisis, rather, was one of *quality*," Ginsborg wrote. "While formal electoral democracy expanded with great rapidity all over the world, disaffection grew in democracy's traditional heartlands. It was expressed in a number of different ways—declining voter turnout, declining political participation (more people were likely to be members of civil action groups like Greenpeace than of a mainstream party) and a loss of faith in democratic institutions and in the political class in general."[4] A new German word, *Politikverdrossenheit*, meaning disenchantment with politics, officially entered the lexicon in 1994. The concept was expressed in a variety of dramatic ways, such as in antiglobalization protests at the meetings of the World Trade Organization in Seattle in 1999 and at the Group of Eight Summit in Genoa in 2001, where hundreds were arrested or injured. Tellingly, the gulf between rulers and ruled was treated by the elites with relative equanimity. Politicians made speeches about the democrat deficit but appeared comfortable with a status quo that rendered to them notional constitutional legitimacy—or, in the case of George W. Bush in the U.S. presidential election of 2000, a dubious judicial legitimacy.

By the start of the twenty-first century, the rise of China and the resurgence of Russia posed a new and immediate challenge. Capitalism had been embraced beyond the West and adapted to purpose. As a mechanism for the acquisition of wealth, it was proving remarkably malleable. Authoritarian capitalism was becoming a formidable adversary. The market had been decoupled from democracy; more than that, it was embraced with alacrity by those very elites whom the West thought it had defeated. The forces of globalization and unrestricted transfers of wealth and assets reinforced the hubris of capitalists both new and old.

Having seen its economic hegemony challenged, the West was also about to suffer a fundamental attack on its confidence. The terrorist attacks of 9/11 shattered comfortable assumptions about the balance between security and liberty. The resurgent autocrats drew strength from two forces playing out simultaneously—the inherent weaknesses of democratic systems, and the actions of Western leaders in their "war on terror." The new authoritarian capitalists exploited the mismatch between the rhetorical exhortations of the Bush administration, as it pursued its agenda of "democratization" around the world, and the tawdry practices it indulged in—from the manipulation of evidence leading up to the Iraq War to the humiliation of prisoners at Abu Ghraib, the systematic use of torture in secret jails around the world, illegal "rendition flights," and the extraterritorial incarceration of hundreds of terrorist suspects at Guantánamo Bay.

In order to succeed in this moral void, the new authoritarians made a pact with their respective peoples. Although the precise rules varied from country to country, the template was always the same. Repression was selective, confined to those who openly challenged the status quo.

The number of people who fell into that category was actually very small—journalists who criticized the state or published information that cast the powerful in a negative light, lawyers who defended these agitators, and politicians and others who publicly went out of their way to "cause trouble." The remaining members of the population could freely travel and could live more or less as they wished; moreover, they could make and spend money—and they gladly did so. A distinction had been created between *public* freedoms and *private*, or privatized, freedoms. For many people this way of dividing things up presented an attractive proposition. After all, how many members of the public, going about their daily lives, really wish to challenge the structures of power? Especially if there is food on the table and cell phones, or per-haps iPods, in their pockets? One can more easily than one realizes be lulled into thinking that one is *sufficiently* free.

In the pages that follow, I look at several examples of how this new kind of authoritarian capitalism has played out in different countries. The patterns are puzzling, sometimes dispiriting, for what they say about human nature and the extent to which our acquiescence to the state is a voluntary act. I begin with Singapore, the state in which I was born, and which has long intrigued me. I am constantly struck by the number of people there—people I know who are very well traveled with long stints at Western universities—who are keen to defend a system that requires an almost complete abrogation of freedom of ex-pression in return for a very good material life. This is the pact. In each country the exact terms of the pact are unique; citizens hand over dif-ferent freedoms in accordance with their own customs and priorities. In some it is press freedom; in others it is the right to vote out their government, to have an impartial judiciary, or simply to get on with their lives without being spied upon. In many it is a combination of these and more.

In the global order of the past two decades, the alliance of polit-ical leaders, business, and the middle classes was the key. The arrangement was built on a clear but usually unstated set of under-standings. What mattered in all these societies was that the number of people who benefited from the deal gradually increased, and that the states remained flexible enough to provide the legal infrastructure needed for a thriving commercial environment, as well as the kinds of freedoms that make people feel as if they can do as they please, so long as they do not challenge those in power. Thus they ensured property rights, provided for contract law and environmental protection, allowed different lifestyle choices, granted the right to travel, and gave people the right to earn money—and keep it. The people who mattered—the wealthy and the aspiring wealthy—were to be protected against the use of arbitrary state power. But could such protection be provided without the tools of conventional democracy, such as free elections and an open media? That was the conundrum that authoritarian capitalists faced.

The most obvious practitioners were countries such as China and Russia, where a critical mass of people (perhaps a minority, but a sizable one nonetheless) believed that an excess of freedoms could damage economic growth, political stability, or social harmony. Such a state, if it was clever, would provide limited but visible outlets for dissent—the arts, perhaps, or newspapers with small circulations— while maintaining its grip on mass audiences. Its most important task was to co-opt vested interests, the most important of which was business, both domestic and international. As Chris Patten recalled from his experience as governor of Hong Kong, the most persistent critics of his attempts to instill an element of democracy to the colony before its handover to China were U.S. and U.K. business leaders in the region. Why rock the boat, they asked him?

I remember hearing similar voices of resistance in Russia in the 1990s. I lost count of the number of Western bankers and others who were genuinely disdainful of the democratic changes that were being introduced throughout the decade. Why, they wondered, jeopardize potentially lucrative contracts for the sake of an experiment inimical to Russian society and history?

Western business found common cause with a new generation of Western-educated counterparts in Russia and China. Many would insist that an authoritarian regime, as long as it was stable, provided an attractive proposition for the creation of wealth. The corporate elite helped sustain the political elite. This was Deng Xiaoping's compact with the post-Tiananmen generation. The debate on political reform of the 1980s gave way to consideration of how best to open up the ruling Communist Party to greater scrutiny and accountability without "destabilizing" a political structure that had delivered three decades of high growth.

The pact belonged not just to states in transition such as these, however, and not just in faraway places across continents and oceans. It belonged also far closer to home, to the democracies themselves. The same kinds of trade-offs played out in different circumstances and cultures, and at different speeds, in the West, though perhaps not to the same degree. We all did it. We are still doing it. We each choose different freedoms we are prepared to cede. Citizens in both systems—in the democracies as well as in the authoritarian states—have colluded, but those in the West have colluded the most. They had the choice to demand more of their governments, to rebalance the pact between liberty, security, and prosperity, but as long as the going was good, they chose not to exercise it.

The context changed in 2008 as years of steady growth ended spectacularly. The collapse of the banks not only led to economic crisis but called into question the future of governments that had derived their legitimacy through securing sustained well-being for their peoples. Yet far from unraveling the pact, the global financial collapse enhanced it. Western countries that had dismissed the idea of the state as an economic force were forced to rehabilitate it. In conditions of insecurity, and with the state once again intervening wherever it saw fit, it was a propitious time for it to assume even greater control over other aspects of people's day-to-day lives. The clamor for security that was exploited after the terrorist attacks on New York and Washington in 2001 was adapted for the new "emergency."

In this book I do not look at tyrannical regimes that rule by the barrel of a gun, where families and parents denounce each other, where the state is an unambiguously malevolent force and there is no element of consent. This is not about Zimbabwe or North Korea or Burma. In those countries there is no pact between the government and the people, but an instinct simply to survive. Nor do I focus on countries with their own particularities, such as Israel, or Hugo Chavez's Venezuela, or post-apartheid South Africa.

Instead, in the course of a year's travels, and in these chapters, I have focused on countries that, whatever their political hue, have accepted the terms of globalization. As a result, in spite of their cultural and circumstantial differences, they have adopted a similar set of priorities, a similar trade-off of liberties in their quest for material wealth. I talked to intellectuals, journalists, lawyers, cultural figures, politicians, and ordinary people, asking them the same question that I framed at the start of this chapter: Why have freedoms been so easily traded in return for security or prosperity?

Singapore, the subject of a remarkable socioeconomic experiment under Prime Minister Lee Kuan Yew from 1959 to 1990, is often perceived as a one-dimensional consumer paradise. It may in part be that, but it also asks more fundamental questions about priorities. Upon its independence from Britain, it had the same per capita gross domestic product (GDP) as Ghana. But in the past forty years it has grown to become one of the world's economic miracles, an island of stability in a region of upheaval. In Chapter 1 I look at the vicious defamation culture, in which the authorities prosecute local citizens and foreigners alike for the slightest criticism, and assess an electoral system in which constituency boundaries are rigged and opposition activists are regularly jailed. Yet the achievements are also striking. Previously fractious ethnic groups—the majority Chinese, Malays, and Indians—live in relative harmony, and through remarkable social housing and public services, the entire population is well cared for at the level of physical needs. The pivot is a middle class that, with some exceptions, is comfortable with a pact in which their private space is unimpeded, as long as they do not interfere with the public realm.

In China, the officially described "century of humiliation" at the hands of foreigners was followed by the Maoist era of uniformity and seclusion. Progress has been remarkable in the past three decades and has taken place within a system that interprets the theory of democracy in accordance with its needs. As I describe in Chapter 2, Corruption, human rights abuses, and environmental degradation have accompanied a one-party structure that has depended on economic growth to keep itself in power. Yet, during my various trips, I noted the porous nature of the pact. Free speech, even if formally circumscribed in China, particularly on the Internet, is alive and well on the street and in semiprivate situations. The government is trying to manage and channel it through a combination of technology, modern-day "spin" techniques, and brute force. However, the middle classes have no vested interest in granting the vote to hundreds of millions of poorer people with different political priorities. The lack of democracy is, for the moment at least, part of the deal. The government knows that the delivery of comforts to the private realm will ensure its success.

In Chapter 3 I move on to Russia, a place I've been visiting regularly for thirty years. I focus on people I have known from a time when the expression best translated as "to get hold of" was more important than the verb meaning "to buy," a time when foreign travel was allowed only through officially sanctioned groups. These friends celebrated the failure of the coup of 1991 and the subsequent collapse of their autocratic system. They discovered new freedoms, and reveled in them, before Boris Yeltsin consolidated his power by manipulating an election with the tacit approval of the West. Democracy gradually and inexorably became associated with chaos and sleaze. The ascent of Vladimir Putin in 2000 brought a security clampdown coinciding with a surge of wealth, thanks to the global price of oil and gas. As their country became richer and more assertive, my friends would recite a slogan of the only three Cs that were important to the New Russians—Chelsea, Courchevel, and Cartier. While doughty journalists and human rights campaigners continued to ask questions, the vast majority acquiesced in the pact. These jet-setters continued to fear that their fortunes and their properties might at any point be seized. That is why they took their money abroad. But they enjoyed the fruits of their private freedoms, leaving the *siloviki*—the politicians who hailed from the security elite—to rule unimpeded.

Next I look at perhaps the most curious, and certainly the most colorful, symbol of the global pact—the United Arab Emirates, specifically, the brazen and gaudy city of Dubai and the oil-rich, but less pretentious, Abu Dhabi. A saying during the boom times on the floors of finance houses went: "Shanghai, Mumbai, Dubai, or goodbye." The ruling sheikhs of the UAE offered steady wealth to everyone from young British financiers to Russian mobsters and B-list celebrities in the form of property deals and tax-free salaries—in return for keeping out of trouble while in the country, either making money or enjoying what money could buy. In Dubai the sheikhs were even more accommodating, putting religious concerns to one side to allow Westerners to lead their lives as they wished, prosecuting them for sexual or drunken displays only *in extremis*. Monuments to conspicuous wealth sprung up all over as hotels and apartment blocks vied with each other for luxury. As I explain in Chapter 4, the sheikhs believed their model was immune to the Western economic crisis. Dubai, in particular, took a major hit. So what will come out of a pact that was built purely on a mutual interest in money?

In the remainder of the book I look at the countries that profess adherence to democracy, beginning, in Chapter 5, with India, a nation that takes pride in having the world's most populous multiparty system. With China's economy soaring ahead, parts of India's corporate elite wondered whether their form of governance was an impediment to prosperity. India's rich devised their own pact, asking only to be left alone to make money, to have the poor kept away from their door, and to be assured the basic services the state had failed to deliver in the past. This arrangement was challenged less by the global economic crash than by the terrorist attacks in Mumbai in late 2008. For the first time, the affluent classes were caught up en masse in the violence that has long afflicted India, and they demanded protection.

From India, I turn in Chapter 6 to Italy. But of all the countries in
the world, why choose Italy? Italy matters, not because of any geostrategic relevance, but because it serves as an example of a sham
democracy. In terms of its institutions, Italy fails on almost every
count. The three checks on the executive—parliament, the media, and
the judiciary—have seen their independence and authority eroded over
the past twenty years. Corruption is rampant in Italy, and yet its voters have chosen Silvio Berlusconi, a man noted for his financial irreg-
ularities, his affection for autocrats such as Vladimir Putin, and his
general vulgarity, three times. He has outwitted his opponents with
consummate ease, and he is seeking to expand his powers. It is easy to
dismiss Berlusconi and his antics. But his enduring popularity among
a large swathe of the Italian population highlights the extent to which
notional democracies can thrive and even depend on the same exercise
of arbitrary power that authoritarian states are criticized for.

In 1997, the accession of a center-left government in the United
Kingdom that prided itself on its liberties should have been an inspiring moment. Yet, in a decade, Britain has gone a long way to disman-
tling its liberties. It now possesses a fifth of the world's closed-circuit
television cameras; it has some of the world's most punitive libel laws,
and has recently imposed a law, under the guise of antiterrorism, that
allows for the arrest of anyone taking photographs of the police or
members of the armed forces. A government that was seeking one of
the longest terms of pretrial custody for terrorist suspects proudly
brandishes its authoritarian credentials, arguing that they are generally
well received by the public. In many cases, they are, particularly by
those who do not put them under close scrutiny. In Chapter 7, I look
at a government that confused the benign role of the state in producing a more equitable society with the malign role of seeking to clamp
down on public freedoms. I am keen to understand how British society seems so ready to acquiesce in the erosion of those freedoms until
rather late in the day.

My last destination is the United States, where the pact has been
played out most visibly. In Chapter 8, I trace the effects on society, at

home and abroad, of 9/11, the Iraq War, and the abuses that surrounded the "war on terror." Former president George W. Bush's neoconservative mission grew out of a mixture of hubris and frustration. The removal of Saddam Hussein was to be the catalyst for the birth of democracy in the Middle East, a harbinger of liberation for those oppressed by dictatorships in the region. The failure of this mission helped to show just how misguided it was to begin with, resulting not just from double standards but from a deeper confusion about the promotion of democracy around the world. Was democracy an end in itself? Or was it a means to an end? Should multiparty elections be encouraged in states where the outcome might produce regimes hostile to the West and to the concept of liberal democracy, or internally produce ethnic or political instability? Domestically, Bush presided over a security clampdown that was rarely challenged by mainstream politicians or public opinion. The U.S. media showed itself to be supine, failing to hold power to account on many of the gravest issues.

To what extent would the arrival of Barack Obama reverse the democratic erosion at home and America's loss of democratic credibility abroad? Certainly, the nature of his election victory provided a much-needed boost to the credentials of America's constitutional democracy. Yet hopes for a fresh start were offset by the dramatic collapse in the U.S. and global financial systems. The cruel irony was that a new administration, in which many around the world had pinned their faith, began its work just at a time of eroding American power.

In a different age, the German historian and philosopher Oswald Spengler famously predicted that "the era of individualism, liberalism and democracy, of humanitarianism and freedom is nearing its end." His book *The Decline of the West* was written some ninety years ago, in the fallout from World War I and in the midst of the humiliations of the Treaty of Versailles. The masses, he wrote, "will accept with resignation the victory of the Caesars, the strong men, and will obey them."[5] Global markets are now in the throes of fresh decline, and many of the old certainties are being destroyed: Does this mean that the Spengler vision is about to haunt us again? The challenge this time around is more subtle and sophisticated; the world is less fiercely differentiated between opposing systems. For twenty years, the "Washington Consensus" proselytized the mutually reinforcing creeds of free markets and liberal democracy. The rise of authoritarian capitalism removed the link between them. Then, from mid-2007, the collapse of the neoliberal Anglo-Saxon financial school became as much a crisis for the Western political system as it did for economics.

The events of the past decade have surely undermined the claim that the enrichment of a country, or the growth of a middle class, provides an impulse toward greater liberty. The American political sociologist Barrington Moore, Jr.'s, theories of "no bourgeoisie, no democracy" have surely been refuted by the past twenty years of materialist aspiration.[6] During this period, people in all countries found a way to disengage from the political process while living in comfort. Consumerism provided the ultimate anesthetic for the brain. What happens when the wealth disappears and the anesthetic wears off?

My discoveries are discomforting, but I believe it is more useful to understand than to judge. It has always been the instinct of the politician to seek power and to hold onto it, by fair means or foul. Less understood are the reasons why so many of us—in authoritarian and democratic states alike—succumb, and why so few of us ask why we do it. Whatever systems we happen to live under, our priorities are more similar than we would ever want to admit.

CHAPTER 1

Singapore
Comfortable Model

Understanding the limits to freedom
is what makes freedom possible.

CHUA BENG HUAT,
professor at the National University of Singapore

"Singapore is quite simply the most successful society in the history of humanity." I scratch my head and take a large gulp of my ice-cold water. I am sitting in the office of Professor Kishore Mahbubani, Singapore's leading public intellectual, a man who travels the world telling doubters that countries can be harmonious and prosperous without succumbing to Western liberal democracy. Dean of the Lee Kuan Yew School of Public Policy at the National University, Mahbubani is always a good person to visit to test the political temperature. He plays host to a stream of visitors from around the world. Before me a delegation of Chinese breezes past. After me comes the Swiss ambassador. They are all keen to learn the secret of the success of an island state that is both economic miracle and social test bed.[1]

I am taken aback by the hubris of my host. But I am wary of being dismissive, of falling into the trap of the "Western mindset," a term used to dismiss criticisms leveled by foreigners. For me it is more than idle curiosity. I was born in Singapore, and although I left when I was young, my parents lived in the city-state for fifteen years. Each time I return I invest in a new map, as numerous streets inevitably have been torn down and replaced by ever higher monuments to money and one version of progress. Nostalgia for the past is one of the few luxuries people here cannot afford. I have also kept up with a number of sons and daughters of my parents' friends, some Indian, some Malay, most Chinese. They are established doctors, lawyers, financiers, musicians. They went to universities in Britain, the United States, or Australia, but most came back. They treat Singapore's gleaming Changi airport as a bus stop, hopping on and off planes without thinking twice. In their day-to-day lives they are able to do whatever they please. They enjoy their private freedoms, but free speech and political activism are things they express when they are abroad. I remember, as a student, going on demonstrations with several of my friends when they were in London. Back home, they button their lips. They can take it or leave it, they say. They do it out of choice.

The term "pact" was made for Singapore. The state's per capita GDP is one of the highest in the world, equivalent to the best in the West. In return, members of the citizenry avoid causing trouble. The city-state has become a monument to wealth creation. Its economic progress is both beguiling and alarming. Everything works spectacularly well. The rich are exceedingly rich. The poor are exceedingly comfortable. The Singapore experiment has been conducted by Lee Kuan Yew, its prime minister for thirty years and supreme leader since relinquishing that office. Although Lee dominates the stage, the Singapore pact is about much more than one man. It requires, and receives, the willing cooperation of the vast majority of the people.

It is easy to forget, when one surveys the skyline of Singapore, the glistening office buildings, the state-of-the-art hospitals, and the efficient social housing, that it could have turned out very differently. Singapore was a backwater, a swampy island populated by a few fishermen, when it was founded in 1819 by Stamford Raffles, a British trader looking for a new foothold for the East India Company along the spice route. As the free port became more successful, traders and their coolies from around the region began to appear—up to 10,000 new arrivals in the first five years. Singapore became a melting pot for Chinese, Malays, Indians, Armenians, Europeans, and anyone else keen to make money. British control effectively came to an end with the invasion by the Japanese in 1942. Over the next three years, up to 50,000 Chinese were killed in the "purification through purge" campaigns.

The young Lee was a clerk during the Japanese occupation, and he, like others of his generation, was profoundly influenced by that experience. At the end of the war, he went to Cambridge University to study law. From there he was called to the bar. During his time in England, he was heavily influenced by anticolonial politics as well as by the Fabian socialism of the Labour Party. He studied the Fabians' thinking on the role of the state as an engineer of social change and provider of services, and he became a believer in the "socialization" of land. On his return to Singapore in 1949, he became involved in the fledgling independence movements that had taken hold across Southeast Asia. In Malaya this took the form of armed resistance. The British declared an emergency and for twelve years were engaged in protracted fighting in the jungle. Although Lee considered himself of the left, he argued that more would be achieved through negotiation, and he founded the People's Action Party (PAP) in 1954 as a mixture of democratic socialism and nationalism.

Three years later, Singapore gained full self-government from Britain, and in 1959 Lee became its first prime minister. In 1963, in a bid to provide greater security and tackle economic hardship, Singapore joined the Federation of Malaya. But the union was immediately threatened by ideological division and ethnic tension. Twenty-three people were killed and hundreds injured during race riots the following year. Lee hurriedly withdrew his tiny city-state from the federation and started out on his own. His task was unenviable. With few resources, and in the middle of an unstable region, Singapore faced acute unemployment, housing shortages, and intercommunal strife that threatened to escalate. Most of the population lived in ramshackle wooden *kampong* (village, in Malay) houses. Many of the streets were dirty and squalid. The country had no advantages beyond the position of its port and the enterprise of its population.

Lee sought to invent a new nation as a geographical and cultural entity. While his Southeast Asian neighbors lurched between dictatorship and brief flirtations with democracy, never quite succeeding at either, he created something in between. He saw state-funded regeneration as key, introducing laws that annexed large swathes of land for social housing and other infrastructure projects such as roads, schools, and hospitals. At the time of independence, more than half the workers had no formal education; by 1990, two-thirds had completed secondary education. Between 1965 and 1995 the economy grew a remarkable 9 percent per year, three times as fast as the U.S. economy. Per capita income grew at 7 percent, on average, doubling roughly every decade. Gross national income went from US$1 billion to US$86 billion. Across the city, new schools and colleges quickly produced spectacular results. Singapore's health care became the envy of Asia. Lee took to calling his small country a "first world oasis in a third world region."

For half a century, he has micromanaged his state, seeking to determine outcomes down to the smallest detail. He has personally vetted the suitability of marriage partners for government servants (usually on the basis of IQ) and decreed the number of children they should have. Through public-information campaigns, he has exhorted his citizens to behave in accordance with his strictures. Instructions were issued on everything from hygiene to courtesy. In the 1970s, the "stop at two" campaign proved so successful in curbing the birthrate that it had to be followed by a reverse campaign entitled "Have three or more if you can afford it."

I have lived in, and traveled to, many dictatorships over the years, places where you look under the tables for bugging devices and assume that the man in the reflector shades lurking at the street corner is out to get you. In Singapore, the surveillance is more subtle, but it is a system that few people are sufficiently bothered about to change. It is easy to understand why. Three-quarters of the workforce does not have to pay income tax, and nobody pays more than 20 percent. Such is the demand for real estate, as foreign companies continue to pour in, that many people appear content to have their block of flats knocked down so that higher buildings can go up. And why not? They reap the profits. Almost none of the traditional Singapore remains. The very last village, Kampong Buangkok, consisting, as of this writing, of just twenty-eight houses hidden away in the north of the island, is being gobbled up.

Nothing in Singapore is allowed to stand in the way of wealth creation—and being part of that process, whether by making or by spending money, is the ultimate patriotic duty. Shopping has become the national pastime. Every time I wander down Orchard Road, the main shopping drag, I see happy consumers and happy eaters. This is a foodies' paradise where you can find some of the most inventive cuisine anywhere, fusions of different cultures alongside high-quality basic foods at hawker centers dotted around the city. While there, I ate Sichuan, different types of Japanese, South Indian (eating with my hands, off of a banana leaf), and North Indian. I stopped in food courts (cheap and cheerful). I was invited to formal English surroundings (the Singapore Cricket Club, of course). I even managed German sausages washed down with Riesling. Then there are the tennis and swimming clubs, and the drinking haunts, in the artificially created "entertainment zones" of Clarke Quay and Robinson Quay. Surely, people, especially those who know the world, cannot be bought off as easily as this?

To understand the other Singapore, the less affluent Singapore, you have to visit any of the high-rise developments in the "heartland." Since the 1960s, almost 90 percent of the population has been moved into well-maintained and scrupulously clean apartments in government-built blocks. The Housing and Development Board (HDB) was granted wide powers of compulsory purchase and forced resettlement. One of its missions was to break up communities that were ethnically separated between Chinese, Malays, and Indians. In the brave new world that followed, the ethnic composition of every apartment block was required to mirror the country as a whole. People of different nationalities were instructed to share the same stairwells, community centers, swimming pools, and bus stops. Given the intercommunal strife of the 1960s, the enforced harmony that followed produced results that were nothing short of remarkable. Intercommunal differences are simply not allowed to happen.

Everything is set out in law. Citizens receive priority if they seek an apartment within a mile of their parents; this is to make it easier to look after the elderly. People can buy on the primary market—at below-market rates, with easy access to interest-free loans—but only if they are married. Once they are assigned to HDB housing, they must keep the flat for ten years, in order to cut down on speculation; then they can sell it on at market prices to anyone they wish. Rents are heavily subsidized and linked to earnings. Such is the demand that most people are pleased to secure whatever is available. Toa Payoh is the second oldest of these experiments. From the top floor of one block, forty stories high, I enjoy a panoramic view of the city—a series of high rises as far as the eye can see. Everything one could hope to purchase is available in the surrounding streets—there are little fabric stalls, tiny kiosks selling the latest 46-inch plasma TV screens, people touting the features of floor-to-ceiling fridges. By the lifts of one building—no graffiti or urine smells—I walk past a citizens' notice board. One flyer reminds residents that they can join a group walk at the nearby Chinese garden. Another announces a bird-singing competition—a popular pastime in which local people pit their herons, barn owls, kingfishers—there are said to be seventy-nine species of birds with fine voices—against each other in a sort of localized *American Idol* contest for birds. Some enthusiasts spend up to a month's salary on caged birds for this purpose. Another notice advertises for volunteers for a neighborhood watch scheme in which citizens are encouraged to snitch on anyone who may be guilty of antisocial behavior. The complex boasts excellent sporting facilities, including a stadium, an indoor sports hall, and the country's best swimming pool, where national competitions are held.

On the main walkway I watch a group of old men, Chinese, Malay, and Indians, boisterously playing checkers. It is Friday afternoon, and I suspect they have downed a whisky or two. They invite me to join them. We chat. I struggle to understand their Singlish, the curious hybrid that is most frequently spoken. I ask them about their lives, their aspirations. They have no complaints, they say. Thanks to the global crash, the economy is not what it was, but it will improve. They would, in any case, rather be here than anywhere else in Asia. At least that's what they tell me; it's hard to be sure whether they mean it. People confide only in their good friends here; meaningful opinion polls do not exist. It is invariably difficult to work out whether people are minding what they say, knowing that criticism will land them in trouble, or expressing genuine appreciation. I suspect, in the case of these men, that both suppositions are true.

The longer he stayed in office, the more convinced Lee became that he had found the model for Asia's progress. From his earliest days, he saw public criticism as an impediment. He brought the media under the control of two state companies, Singapore Press Holdings Limited (which runs the newspapers) and MediaCorp (which deals with broadcasting). Elections are held every five years, and opposition parties are theoretically allowed to compete. However, any politician or journalist who says anything controversial about those in power risks arrest and defamation charges. When those defending themselves against such charges run out of money, they are declared bankrupt and may be sent to jail.

Even the minimalist democratic procedures that have existed since independence have been "modified" on several occasions. The PAP tends to be the beneficiary. Constituencies that vote in significant numbers for opposition candidates tend to disappear at the next election. The reasons are not hard to miss: When they do opt for the wrong candidate, the voters are reminded of the errors of their ways, and usually, they dutifully mend them. Not far from loyal Toa Payoh, the neighborhood of Potong Pasir was for many years an anomaly in that it did not have an operating mass rapid transit underground station. The station did exist, but it was kept closed. Various "technical" reasons were given, but the locals knew the real reason. Potong Pasir is notorious for being the longest-held opposition ward in one-party-dominant Singapore, and dissent is not rewarded. Chiam See Tong, of the Democratic Party, has held the ward since 1984, staving off PAP candidates for six successive elections by the sheer power of his personality. No amount of inducements or threats has deterred local voters from irritating the powers that be. Locals are understandably reluctant to give their reasons for voting for Chiam, but it seems to be mainly out of long-standing loyalty. The more the government tries both carrot and stick to coax them from him, the more defiant they become. This small episode is an example of what makes Singapore's claims to being a democracy such a curiosity. Usually it is not a democracy, but very occasionally it is.

The PAP has been in power since 1959 and currently holds 82 of the 84 seats in parliament, even though at the last elections, in May 2006, it captured only 67 percent of the vote. In other words, a more representative form of democracy should not be beyond the grasp of a highly educated electorate. By voting for the opposition, people are choosing to complain. Yet at the same time they know their vote will not make the slightest difference, and they do not seem unduly concerned. Is everyone going through the motions for the sake of "democracy"?

Those who actually represent the opposition know what will happen to them. Chee Soon Juan and J. B. Jeyaretnam were harassed for years. Jeyaretnam became the country's first opposition member of parliament (MP) in 1981, for the Workers Party, and ended up serving two five-year terms. On each occasion he was charged with an array of offenses, ranging from slander to misuse of funds. After his second victory in 1997, he was served with eleven defamation suits, forcing him eventually to declare himself bankrupt. In his final years, Jeyaretnam—once a wealthy, flamboyant, and high-profile lawyer—

took to standing on street corners and outside metro stations to peddle his own books about Singapore politics because no retailer would stock them. He said he had lost count of the number of times he had been sued for defamation. He died in September 2008, aged ninety-two, and the government sent his family polite but cold condolences. The blogosphere commented on his fate, with several people providing sympathetic assessments. The rest of the public quickly moved on. In the world's media the event passed with barely a mention. For all its efforts, Singapore's opposition has been almost completely ignored by Western governments. They choose to berate the Chinese or the Russians for their treatment of critics, but in Singapore there is too much money to be made to bother about such issues.

The longest-serving prisoner of conscience was Chia Thye Poh, who spent nearly twenty-three years in jail, making his term of incarceration for this type of "crime" second only to Nelson Mandela's at the international level. Dubbed the "gentle revolutionary," he was arrested in 1966 under the Internal Security Act (ISA) and spent much of the next two decades in solitary confinement, without being charged. For most of that time, the government gave no explanation for his imprisonment; it eventually accused him of having led a call for the violent overthrow of the leadership. On his release in 1989, Chia was placed under internal exile on Sentosa, Singapore's "holiday" island to the south. The ISA, which gives the security forces the right to make arrests without having warrants, was one of several repressive laws bequeathed to Singapore by the British. Others have been created more recently. They all share colorfully Orwellian titles. There is the Criminal Law Temporary Provisions Act, which allows for the jailing of dissidents, for example; the Undesirable Publications Act, which clamps down on free speech; and the Public Entertainments and Meetings Act, which proscribes any unauthorized gathering of more than four people. Little is left to chance. In 2007 the Workers Party, the opposition group previously led by Jeyaretnam, was refused permission to celebrate its fiftieth anniversary with a bicycle party in a public park.

Although capital punishment figures are regarded as secret, according to Amnesty International 420 people were hanged in Singapore between 1991 and 2005, mainly for murder and drug trafficking. This gives the country the highest execution rate in the world relative to population. During 2007, more than 6,000 convicted persons were sentenced to caning. The criminal code allows caning for more than thirty offenses, including robbery, vandalism, and rioting. The practice is a mandatory prison punishment for rapists, drug traffickers, and visiting foreigners who overstay their visas. The regulations are published, presumably as a deterrent. They stipulate that the cane should be made out of rattan. It is soaked in water beforehand to prevent it from splitting when it comes into contact with the prisoner's buttocks, as well as to make it more flexible. It is treated with antiseptic before use to prevent infection. A lighter cane is used for juvenile offenders.

It is not just human rights groups that highlight Singapore's record. The U.S. State Department identifies, among other things, preventive detention, executive influence over the judiciary, infringement of citizens' privacy rights, restriction of speech and press freedom, and self-censorship by journalists. Its annual reports are available to the public, but they are not discussed in Singapore, nor are they advertised by American administrations that have long seen the city-state as a reliable strategic partner. The British government's annual human rights report does not usually mention the performance of its former colony. As ever, realpolitik sets the terms for the West's critique of the state of democracy and civil liberties in nations around the world.

It is midday, and I am standing on a patch of grass near City Hall. A sign tells me that this is "Speakers Corner." It was established in 2001 to counter international criticism that Singapore is a dictatorship. The government insists that people can say whatever they want here, but they must stay inside the law. That is not so easy. The instructions on the notice board list the following rules: Someone wishing to speak must register at the police station around the corner, fill out forms, and wait for permission; if it is granted, he or she may speak, but the speech will be recorded. The recording will be kept by the government for six years, and it can be used against the speaker in any defamation or other trials. In addition, some topics are off-limits. One may not speak about issues relating to religion or race, for example, or insult anyone in authority. Just in case anyone might be tempted, the sign then helpfully lists the provisions of all the various laws that might be infringed. I pop into the police station to ask the officer when the next speaker is likely to appear. Not for some time, the man tells me. Nor can he remember the last person who applied.

The views of most people I know in Singapore range from mild disapproval at the state of affairs to something a little stronger. But they do not agitate publicly. For many people, it would be risqué even to forward an e-mail, without comment, containing links to opposition activities on the Internet. However, there are those who go so far as to create the websites, while staying anonymous. Indeed, the absence of an open media or political discourse has bred a flourishing rumor mill. Singapore-based websites are vibrant, often with video or audio clips of tiny gatherings that were broken up, or criticisms of the regime. Popular subjects for debate are aired. What exactly is the U.S. military up to in the giant Changi naval base? Does it contain submarine nuclear missiles? What happened to an Indonesian terrorist who disappeared from a high-security jail? How far do Singapore's financial links extend with Burma's ruling junta? Is it true Singapore provides communications equipment for the Burmese army? Is it true the elderly junta leader, Than Shwe, was secretly given cancer treatment at a Singapore governmental hospital? How many of the Burmese generals move their money through Singapore? The discussions are vigorous on the sites of the Workers Party, the more recently formed Singapore Democratic Party (SDP), and a number of online citizens' forums.

The authorities trawl the Internet looking for potential troublemakers but have been reluctant to shut down offending sites. Several of the websites, including the SDP's, have posted a video about free expression and dictatorship entitled *One Nation Under Lee*. According to the opposition, the forty-minute film has been viewed more than 40,000 times on YouTube and has been screened at festivals in other countries, including neighboring Malaysia. It was actually first screened in Singapore at the Excelsior Hotel. Even though the event was a private one and only invited guests were allowed, officials from the Media Development Authority made their way into the function and demanded that the film and the projector be handed over. The incident was caught on camera, and the resulting clip is also available for viewing.[2] *One Nation Under Lee*, a primer for young oppositionists, is somewhat innocent but determined in tone. It cites Burma's detained opposition leader, Aung San Suu Kyi, as a model, extolling the virtues of civil disobedience. The Singapore government, it says, incessantly warns of the "havoc and chaos" that would result from protest, and potential dissidents may be fearful. But Singaporeans do have power to bring about change. Then it goes to the heart of the matter: "The only question is: Do we want to exercise it?"

That question, for the moment, seems rhetorical. Demonstrations are extremely rare, and when they do take place, the gaggle of protesters (usually fewer than ten) offers no resistance as they are quickly swept up into police vans. Seah Chiang Nee, a veteran political commentator, charts political dissent, or lack of it, in his cyber journal, littlespeck.com. He decried the priorities of his countrymen and women when referring in March 2009 to a tiny rally in favor of Burma's pro-democracy movement: "I cannot foresee 2,000 students carrying Armani handbags and iPods marching around Orchard Road throwing Molotov cocktails."[3]

In the newspapers, and particularly on television, none of these issues is mentioned. The press does broach some social and economic problems. It is reasonably open about foreign crises; it exhorts communities and individuals to behave better. But the motivation must be self-improvement or patriotism. I remember a few years ago a government notice in the *Straits Times*, Singapore's most important paper, advising citizens of the punishments they would incur if they failed to trade in their old air-conditioners for new ones by a certain date. Criticism of the government, particularly of named ministers and officials, is frowned upon. It is deeply unacceptable for foreigners to make such criticisms. International newspapers that criticize Lee or his underlings are hounded in the courts. Under new rules, in order to operate in Singapore foreign media must submit a hefty deposit and appoint a local representative who could be answerable in court. The list of illustrious international publications that have incurred the wrath of the authorities includes the *Far Eastern Economic Review*, the *Wall Street Journal*, and the *Financial Times*. At various points they have been forced to apologize for running critical articles about Singapore. To do anything else would make no business sense.

One think-tank, officially sanctioned or at least officially tolerated, so far, is Think Centre, which was approved in October 2001 as an independent nongovernmental organization (NGO). Its president, Sinapan Samydorai, sets out the ground rules: "You can talk about government policies, you can criticise government-linked companies for not being transparent or accountable, but if you talk about an individual within them and say he has family members there, and describe him by name, then you will be in danger of being sued for defamation."[4]

Sometimes individual controversies are aired. In 2005, parliament approved a plan to legalize casino gambling, paving the way for the construction of two multibillion dollar resorts—one in Marina Bay, in the center of the city, and one on Sentosa Island. Many people were furious, arguing that they did not want Singapore to become a mini Las Vegas or a rival to Macau. They did not want the low life that they feared would arrive with gambling. For a while the debate was aired, until it was decreed that it was time to stop. On one of my visits, I went to see the construction site for myself. Accompanied by a photographer, I made my way past the cement mixers and heavy trucks as they plunged through the mud. No sooner had we started taking pictures than we were "invited" into the site office to explain ourselves. A

Scotsman who did not introduce himself asked for our permits, and we were politely escorted off the site.

Occasionally, major crises take place that cannot be kept from public view. In 2004 one of the top charities, the National Kidney Foundation, was discovered to be paying its chief executive for first-class flights, maintenance of his Mercedes, and gold-plated fixtures for his private office bathroom. This came on top of an annual salary of nearly £200,000. The patron of the charity, who happened to be the wife of the former prime minister, declared that she couldn't understand what all the fuss was about, as his salary was "peanuts." When the story was run by the normally cautious *Straits Times*, the foundation inevitably began proceedings for defamation, but the case collapsed amid a rare display of public outrage. The chief executive and the board of the foundation resigned. The Singapore version of the pact requires that top officials maintain an appearance of acting with probity. In this case, that appearance was shattered, and there were serious consequences. Still, government officials would prefer that such things not be leaked in the first place.

Singapore is proud of the amount it pays its top officials. At last count, the prime minister earned US$2.6 million per year, while the most junior member of the cabinet took a mere US$1.3 million. To get the best to serve as administrative service officers, the government pays as much as the private sector. In April 2007, the head of the civil service received US$1.5 million per year, more than the salaries of the U.S. president and British prime minister combined. It is, I am told, a small price to pay if a country wants to progress. The idea is to ensure that the most talented, including potentially the most outspoken, can be absorbed, or co-opted, by the state.

The search for talent is conducted according to officially sanctioned policies. The government does whatever it takes to attract new blood into Singapore, as long as it fills a skills gap. Officials are sent to small towns in Malaysia and India to recruit. Increasingly, they are scouring China. The Singapore government regards ethnic cohesion as one of its top goals. Any remarks considered racially inflammatory are expressly banned; however, the domination of the Chinese over the large Malay and Indian minorities is maintained in subtle ways. The recent arrival of thousands of people from "the mainland," many of whom cannot speak English, which remains Singapore's lingua franca, is making its mark.

There is a second reason for treating government servants so well: to ensure that, at every link in the chain, corruption is fought off. Theoretically, with such high earnings, the benefit of lining one's own pockets is not worth the risk. But with so little investigative journalism, the absence of large-scale corruption is something the people have to take on trust. As for nepotism, this would be regarded negatively only if the person concerned were seen as unworthy of the job. Indeed, the appointment of Lee Hsien Loong, Lee Kuan Yew's oldest son, as prime minister in 2004 was portrayed as playing well to Confucian values. "Familialism," as it is called, or *guan xi*, the Chinese notion of personal relationships or connections, does not, officials say, equate to cronyism.

In the course of 2008, Singapore became the first country in the region to go into recession. Its reliance on exports had left it particularly vulnerable. But, in my sparring sessions at the National University and elsewhere, I saw little sign that the downturn was challenging the fundamental trade-off on which society is ordered. Mahbubani went further, arguing that Asia is better placed economically and politically than the West to rebuild after the crisis. Asia, he said, is making progress toward its eventual goal of practicing democracy more harmoniously than the West, largely because of its emphasis on collectivist rather than individualist endeavor. It is a variation on the theme, a results-based form of democracy that he was defending. The demands of the individual are subordinated to those of the collective, and yet the individual is free in most areas of life. Anyone with any talent is co-opted into the system. "Why are Brazilians best at football [i.e., soccer]? They look in the barrios for six-year-old talent. We do the same with the state. We cherry-pick the best," Mahbubani said. "If you think you can run something better, we give you the chance to prove it. We absorb dissent. The stupidest thing is to crush it. No brain is wasted. The political competence of our founding fathers was extraordinary. I find that very rarely in my travels around the world." Mahbubani's thesis, which he has set out in a recent book, has gone down well in Asia, less so in Europe and America. He was not surprised. "The West is becoming the problem," he said. "You don't want to give up the space. You're also proving increasingly incompetent at government." He concluded: "By every indicator Singapore is the most successful nation. It is not just the wealth we have created; it is how we take care of people at the bottom of the pile."[5]

One of the most intriguing aspects of Lee's authoritarian blend is his eagerness to defend it wherever he goes around the world, particularly on the lecture circuit. In a debate with Harvard's Lawrence Summers in 2006, he insisted that his aim was not to sustain the PAP in power, but to ensure stability more broadly long after he has gone. "At the end of the day," he declared, "we offer what every citizen wants—a good life, security, good education, and a future for their children. That is good governance." The responsibility of the government is therefore a largely technical one of delivering the good life in return for the endorsement of the electorate. Elections are, in essence, a report card. I promise, I deliver, you vote for me. Democracy is used to legitimize the formula. Democracy has been shifted away from any liberal assumptions, without apologies, from representation to trusteeship, from individual rights to collective well-being. This is what it boils down to.

Singaporeans defend their own version of democracy by comparing and contrasting it with the governments of their neighbors. Some countries in the region may in theory have more democratic systems, but in most areas of life, from the economy to security, they have tended to fare worse. Take the Philippines, they say, a country that in political terms is one of the freest in the region. Guns are freely available; terrorism is rife; and the economy is in a shambles, though it was one of the most promising in the region in the 1950s. There is still not one functioning liberal democracy in Southeast Asia. Burma's

tragic story is well known. Vietnam, Cambodia, and Laos are only beginning to recover from the decades when Communists of various
shades, supported by both China and the USSR, wreaked havoc
throughout Indochina; Vietnam and Laos are still nominally Communist, and Cambodia's prime minister is a former member of the
Khmer Rouge. Thailand continues its well-worn pattern of oscillat-
ing between tentative democracy and army-led coups, with the monar-
chy all-powerful but also unaccountable, thanks to stifling *lèse-majeste*
laws, which declare it a crime to say or do anything that offends the
dignity of a reigning monarch. In Malaysia, opposition leader Anwar
Ibrahim was sentenced in 2000 to nine years in prison on charges of
sodomy. He insisted all the way through that he had been framed
when his challenge became too much for the governing coalition to
bear, and many Western politicians and human rights groups accepted
his view. Anwar, a one-time deputy prime minister, had accused the
ruling party of long-serving Prime Minister Mahathir Mohamad of
corruption and cronyism. The incident highlighted the rigidity of
Malaysia's political system and the absence of a human-rights culture.
In Indonesia, supposedly a democracy since the fall of General
Suharto, elections are so marred by corruption and vote-rigging that it
would be a joke to suggest they merit the description "free and fair."

Now, from Indonesia to Malaysia, from Kazakhstan to Russia to
the United Arab Emirates, governments are seeking to learn from Singapore. The most important pupil is China. Progress, coupled with
order and limited freedom, has been the maxim of those who have
ruled since Mao's death; it is a philosophy whose modern origins have
their roots in Singapore. With their horror of chaos, or *luan*, China's
leaders have come to learn and admire Singapore's approach, and their
first port of call is invariably Mahbubani's department, which has become a center for the country's public diplomacy. The party boss in
Jiangsu province sent all of his local party secretaries, around seventy
of them, for a fortnight's stay.

Lee has frequently insisted that the Singapore model is not available for export, as it is applicable only to small countries or city-states.

In the detail, he is clearly right. Obviously, no system can be ordered off the shelf. He contradicts himself, however, by making the case for "Asian values," a concept that was very much in vogue in the 1990s and is still popular in some quarters today. It promotes notions of collective well-being over individualism, social harmony over dissent, and socioeconomic progress over human rights. Lee set out his thinking on this issue in Tokyo in 1992: "With few exceptions, democracy has not brought good government to new developing countries. What Asians value may not necessarily be what Americans, or Europeans, value; Westerners value the freedoms and liberties of the individual. As an Asian of Chinese cultural background, my values are for a government which is honest, effective and efficient."[6]

The counterpoint has been put most eloquently by the economist and philosopher Amartya Sen, who argued that Asian values are invoked to justify authoritarianism that is not specific to Asia. "The championing of Asian values is often associated with the need to resist Western hegemony. The linkage of the two issues, which has increasingly occurred in recent years, uses the political force of anti-colonialism to buttress the assault on civil and political rights in post-colonial Asia. This linkage, though quite artificial, can be rhetorically quite effective," Sen wrote in 1997.[7]

What if the model of material authoritarianism is neither the product of postcolonial reaction nor an Asia-specific phenomenon? What if it can be applied universally? I came across the following compelling observation by a young Israeli academic and antiglobalization activist, Uri Gordon. He likens Lee's Asian values to Machiavelli's *virtù*. "Just as Machiavelli set Roman Virtue in opposition to his contemporary Christian morality, thus Lee can be seen as having chosen Asian values for Singapore as an alternative to the West's liberal democracy. Subduing the population to a comfortable life of self-censorship, Lee and his aides can be seen as devout disciples of the Florentine."[8]

Rather than creating a greater sense of emancipation and self-awareness, Singapore has led the way in persuading the middle class to remove itself from the public realm. Why cause trouble when you have so many comforts to lose? Keen to develop this thinking with other professors in Mahbubani's department, I asked Professor Wang Gungwu, head of the East Asia Institute, to explain the philosophical underpinnings of the Singapore experiment. He described it as a "Hobbesian contract." According to Thomas Hobbes's theory of social contract, unrestricted freedoms produce a "war of all against all." We need, we want, restrictions to save ourselves from our dark sides. "People in Singapore have mastered a range of skills. These include control and freedom," Wang said. Chinese officials, he added, are impressed. "They want their cities run like this. They have a strong fear of mass revolt that would not take much to galvanize in China."[9]

I next turned to a sociologist. "In Singapore, democratization theories and activists meet their nemesis," said the National University's Professor Chua Beng Huat. "Singapore could not have done it without some restrictions on free speech. It would not have worked with a set of adversarial institutions." He disputed my notion of a conscious pact. Personal freedom, he said, "improves through the alleviation of poverty. Therefore you don't feel you're making a bargain." The PAP has been attempting to establish a "political culturalism," he noted, that promotes the notion of the individual as a "cultural citizen," in contrast to the "liberal citizen" associated with liberal democracies. In this way, the PAP has redefined the structures of political representation and participation. At stake is nothing less than the shaping of the boundaries and meaning of politics. A genial and highly articulate man, he left me to ponder this thought: "Understanding the limits to freedom is what makes freedom possible. The greater good is impossible without some constraint on individualism. The weakness of liberalism is the unwillingness to pay the cost of membership."[10]

Perhaps it depends on which freedoms and which limits. It is in the social realm, the battle between the traditional and the modern, that the Singapore pact is most vulnerable. Lee spent years creating a state in his image. Consumer comforts do not appear to have instilled yearnings for major political change. The pressure is taking a different form. In return for ceding the public realm entirely to the government, citizens are now seeking complete control of the private sphere. The promised social liberalism has come in fits and starts, and it is here that the boundaries are being most actively tested. Lee's more proscriptive views on marriage, sex, and other issues are not shared by others in government. Here is a genuine divide, largely along generational lines, that is hard to conceal. I smiled when I was told that the limits on free expression are commonly known as "out-of-bounds markers." In Singapore the obsession with golf, tennis, and other harmless forms of recreation is strong.

Since Lee went into "retirement" in 1990 (he is now called the "minister mentor"), some of the more idiosyncratic restrictions have been toned down. Old laws, such as the one determining the length of men's hair, have been abolished, although others punishing public spitting and failure to flush toilets remain in place. The law outlawing the chewing of gum was "relaxed" in 2004 to allow the use of "therapeutic" gum in order to comply with a free trade agreement with the United States. Cultural life is loosening—a little. An Audience Development Fund has been established to "educate" public taste in art, to encourage artistic risk-taking, within limits. Design, particularly fashion, is booming. At the La Salle arts school, a glass and steel structure in Little India, I saw a group of students rehearsing a play in Mandarin on a piece of artificial turf in the main lobby. Grace, the director, told me they had been allowed to choose from a pool of scripts. The short play they had selected was about meeting different people on a bus. Grace said it was a metaphor for life. One of the actors was wearing a T-shirt that said: "We make money, not art." He asked me if I appreciated the irony.

Occasionally, candid conversations do take place, usually with people who are not worried about their career development in the private or public sector. I discussed nepotism, corruption, secrecy, and sex with a writer named Gerrie Lim. He used to live in Los Angeles, where he wrote books about art and sex. He told me about "NUTS," an acronym that stands for the "No U-Turn Syndrome." Unlike drivers in other countries, Singaporeans will not turn their cars around at inter-sections unless there is a sign telling them they can. They assume that something is forbidden unless expressly told otherwise. When he sub-mitted his most recent book—on the sex industry—to the Media De-velopment Authority, the censor did not respond for over a month. Lim had no idea where he stood, but eventually he was given the go-ahead. "I've never come under overt pressure, but there's always a sense that you're waiting for the call," he said. "People always ask me how I get away with it. I suppose I'm harmless."[11]

As each year goes by, the out-of-bounds markers on moral issues become harder to locate. After it came out in 1998, the American television series *Sex and the City* was banned, but when the film was released in 2008, advertisements for it adorned billboards across Sin-gapore's shopping streets. In 2005, Singapore hosted its first "Sexpo" exhibition. The authorities justified it by arguing that there was much to be gained by couples spicing up their sex lives; they were not, however, encouraging promiscuity. Strict rules were applied and enforced. Nothing was allowed that bore a "resemblance to any gen-italia" or that encouraged oral or anal sex, both of which are strictly prohibited.

In October 2007, parliament rejected a proposal to repeal a law that outlaws private and consensual sexual relations between men. Al-though prosecutions have been rare, those found in violation can be jailed for up to two years on charges of "gross indecency." Homosex-uality is banned on television. One station was fined for showing two fully clothed men in the same bedroom in a home furnishing program. And yet the censors did allow the film *Brokeback Mountain* to be shown in the cinema. "Many of my colleagues in parliament were keenly aware of Singapore's reputation as a nanny state and would have readily relaxed the restrictions," a former member of parliament, who preferred to remain anonymous, told me. But they were wary of loosening restrictions for fear of antagonizing the "heartlanders," such as those I had met in Toa Payoh. This, she emphasized, was surely an example of "consultative democracy" in action.[12]

With Lee in his mid-eighties, Singaporeans know he will not always be there to help keep things running, but they find it hard to
imagine life without the man who has guided them all the way since
independence. The vast majority of his subjects—including people
who are in a position to make informed comparisons—have accepted
his argument that Singapore's prosperity could not have been achieved
any other way. Such is the emphasis on consumer comfort that the
previous economic downturns—the 1997 Asian crash and the difficulties spawned in 2003 by the Severe Acute Respiratory Syndrome
(SARS) virus—were regarded as deeply shocking. If anything, they
reinforced the yearning for political stability. Many people speak of
wanting the newspapers to be more open, their politicians to be less
proscriptive, but at the same time they do not wish to sacrifice any of
the good life—the endless shopping, the cornucopia of excellent
restaurants and bars, the tennis and swimming clubs, their Mercedes
and BMWs.

The government is caught in a bind. It is worried by the number of
Western-educated students who choose to live abroad for long periods
after graduation. It is constantly replenishing them with graduates
from China and elsewhere, but it would keenly like to entice back its
own citizens. It knows that a limited loosening up of society would
help. At the same time, it is frightened of what that might unleash,
and it is seeking to confine any liberalization to specific economic and
cultural issues. It does not want to relax its control of the political or
public realm.

The use of defamation suits has actually increased in recent years.
Singapore is constantly seeking international acceptance for its institutions, and therefore it came as a welcome sign when it invited the
International Bar Association (IBA) to hold its annual conference in
the city in October 2007. A few months later, the IBA's Human
Rights Institute issued a report criticizing the use of defamation suits
by the PAP to silence the opposition and the press, and expressing
concerns about the independence and impartiality of Singapore's
judges. The authorities resorted to their customary mix of legal sanc-

tion and fury. Lee accused human rights organizations of orchestrating "a conspiracy to do us in." He said that the West realized that Russia and China had been studying Singapore's success and increasingly regarded it as a threat.

The debate about the Singapore model, such as it is, is often reduced to easy points' scoring on both sides. Many writers focus on the obsessive state and the obsessive consumer, seeing little beyond. When in 1993 the writer William Gibson coined the phrase "Disneyland with the death penalty," it jarred. The phrase is cited by detractors of Singapore as a good summary of its human rights record and by supporters of the country as an example of foreign high-handedness. Gibson's label is neat and witty. But Singapore itself is much more complicated than that.

Will Lee's passing lead to a relaxation of both the private and the public realm, or will the government seek to crack down even harder? One argument for loosening up is economic self-interest. In a rare public criticism made from inside the country in May 2008, Juan José Daboub, managing director of the World Bank, warned that Singapore would suffer economically if it did not loosen up. "One such challenge is the tricky task of balancing a desire for social order and stability—for many years a defining quality of Singapore's growth—with a need to allow more innovation and creativity to produce high-value goods and services in a more competitive global economy," he said. "Innovation and creativity are, by definition, not orderly and not regulated. As Singapore looks to a growing and prosperous future, striking the right balance will call for some skilled stewardship and probably some risk-taking."[13]

As Singapore's economy nose-dived (growth plunged by nearly 20 percent in the first quarter of 2009, the largest fall ever recorded there), some began to argue more forcefully that the very nature of its authoritarian politics would act as an impediment to recovery. Taking their cue from experts such as Daboub, these critics said that Singapore's state-guided economy was more vulnerable than was officially admitted and that a lack of open debate had exacerbated the problem.

The heavily controlled media had also failed to act as a check on the state's two main investment funds, Temasek and GIC, which ended up with billions of losses from poor acquisitions.

The chances of the crisis leading to a new candor appear, for the moment at least, illusory. Shortly after returning from one trip to the country, I penned a blog for the *Guardian* introducing discussion of the "pact." Entitled "The New Authoritarianism," the blog entry mentioned several of the countries I discuss in this book. My references to Singapore, though, were brief. I spoke of the Singaporeans I knew, adding that they were "well versed in international politics, but . . . perfectly content with the situation back home." I added: "I used to reassure myself with the old certainty that this model was not applicable to larger, more diverse states. I now believe this to be incorrect." After talking about increased threats to civil liberties in countries ranging from Russia to Italy to the United Kingdom, I concluded: "A modern form of authoritarianism, quite distinct from Soviet Communism, Maoism or Fascism, is being born. It is providing a modicum of a good life, and a quiet life, the ultimate anaesthetic for the brain."[14] The following day the *Guardian* called. The Singaporean government was demanding a right of reply. I had no objection to a response to my piece—that, after all, is what commentary is all about—but I could not for the life of me imagine what I had done to earn the ire of Singaporean officials. Indeed, my main concern was that I might be attacked by bloggers for being too generous to the country of my birth.

The reply duly appeared, in the name of the high commissioner to the United Kingdom, Michael Teo. It was mainly a restatement of the philosophy of Singapore's political system. Teo concluded: "Every society has to strike its own balance between individual liberties and the common good. Some in the west like John Kampfner feel a calling to go forth and convert the heathen to western liberal democracy. But the true test is what works in the real world, with real societies. To worship a western model as the only way, and dismiss all other solutions as authoritarian or undemocratic, is surely the ultimate anaesthetic for the brain."[15] On the following day, the *Straits Times* carried

Teo's article in full under the captivating headline, "Singapore Ticks Off British Writer."

The spat left me with a series of conflicting emotions. One was fear: Would I be refused entry into the country—or perhaps locked up on my arrival? Another was concern for my Singaporean friends. Several had forwarded me the various blog references, usually without comment. Another was surprise. I was more concerned that the article would be seen as too soft on Singapore, rather than the opposite. That gave rise to disappointment. Why, I wondered, cannot Singapore engage? Six months later I was back at Changi airport, with just a hint of trepidation, for an academic conference. I was allowed in, with a speedy smile from the immigration officer. Everyone I met— politicians, academics, journalists, and financiers—mentioned, awkwardly, that they had read the piece. We all laughed it off. I talked, publicly, about my views of the "pact," which led to vigorous but friendly sparring. At the Raffles Bar I spent an enjoyable evening with a senior newspaper executive. He, too, mentioned it, embarrassedly, but assured me there had been nothing special in my treatment. This kind of thing, he said, happens all the time. By way of reassurance, he suggested that the Foreign Ministry must have gone into one of its "habitual bouts of group think" in which an order is handed down from on high and is obeyed without discussion. What does it say about the fragility of a regime if it goes into paroxysm of fury about a blog? Regimes on the verge of falling are often the most extreme in their response to criticism, so maybe change is on its way. It might be, but I saw little sign of any major shift toward public activism. Rather, it seems that any liberalizing change will be confined to the private realm. That is the kind of change that most of the people I spoke to in Singapore were seeking, if they admitted to seeking change at all.

I asked my drinking partner at Raffles if he saw any prospect of a softening of the defamation culture. No chance, he said. The law of contempt had been designed to protect public confidence in state institutions, in good times and in bad. Most people in Singapore— citizens, people there on international business, representatives of foreign governments—had a vested interest in preserving the status quo. Why else, he suggested, would Singapore have done so well for so long? For me, someone who has spent much of his career seeking to cause trouble for politicians, this was an unpalatable thought.

Even more horrifying is the thought that plenty more people around the world, irrespective of their political culture, have also been contentedly anesthetized. Singapore may be the home of the trade-off in its purest form, but are we all more Singaporean than we realize?

CHAPTER 2

China
Discreet Player

> With the vote in the wrong hands, the wrong people
> get selected who then manipulate the electorate.

KEVIN AO,
entrepreneur

What could be more pleasant than spending a bright morning sitting by a lake drinking an espresso and listening to the chiming of church bells? I was in Portofino, so that might explain my tranquil demeanor. Except this wasn't the Italian port frequented by the rich and famous. This Portofino was an artificial village built around a lake in Shenzhen, a southern city in China that is a monument to the free market. More precisely, I was in an area called OCT, Overseas Chinese Town. The lake I was looking at was manmade; the clock tower I was sitting under was modern, but what did it matter? "You have the American dream, we have the Shenzhen dream," said my host.[1]

Lanciel Cui is the manager in this region of China for a large Israeli shipping firm. Unlike many Chinese, she has already traveled the world. She regaled me with her experiences of the Faroe Islands and of the

41

northern English town of Grimsby ("Why," she wondered, "are the school kids roaming around the shopping mall in the daytime?" and "Why does everyone look so pasty?"). Her parents typify the modern Chinese success story. Both came from peasant farming stock; her father rose to become a university dean, while her mother served as a military doctor. Neither would now recognize their country. Lanciel is the quintessential Western-style career woman in her forties, a single mother juggling to maintain a work-life balance. She flies regularly to Beijing and Shanghai for meetings, knows the airline schedules by heart, and catches the last flight home whenever she can. Lanciel, like everyone else in Shenzhen, is an "immigrant." While Hong Kong, just across the harbor, was still in British hands, this place was a sleepy fishing village. Its population has soared to a staggering 13 million. The economy increased at an average of 28 percent per year for more than two decades. In the early 1990s, Chinese planners believed their country's main economic centers—Shanghai, Shenzhen, and others—would take fifty years to overtake Singapore. That has already happened. As for Hong Kong, plans are already being discussed to merge the "backwater" that was once considered a global financial hub with Shenzhen.

Shenzhen was therefore as good a place as any for me to look at the Chinese version of the pact. The first free economic zone, it was the test bed for Deng Xiaoping's economic reforms, the laboratory for the post-Maoist embrace of capitalism. It was a tour of Southeast Asia that alerted Deng in the late 1970s to the urgent need for change. He was shocked by the modernity of cities such as Bangkok, Kuala Lumpur, and Singapore. On his return to China, he said: "Singapore enjoys good social order and is well managed. We should tap their experience and learn how to manage things better than they do."[2]

From the moment Deng launched his "Open Door" policy and his "four modernizations" program—focusing on agriculture, industry, science and technology, and the military—China has sought to find a way of reconciling open markets with closed politics. The last major Marxist-Leninist dictatorship stayed in power, but only by embracing capitalism.

Lanciel has taken the day off to show me around. Keen to start my tour of the city, I decline the offer of cheesecake or other delights from the Austrian-style *konditorei* and jump into her 4x4. We drive down manicured, tree-lined streets, with bright red bicycle lanes that would not be out of place in a provincial German town, past a gated community and plush condominiums. In front of me is Window of the World, a replica theme park with its own Eiffel Tower, Leaning Tower of Pisa, and Egyptian Pyramids, plus a 4,000-square-meter indoor ski resort. It takes us the best part of an hour to drive from one end of the city, the modern center of Futian, to the old heart. Lanciel points out a small quaint building on our left. The Skylight Hotel was once one of the city's tallest buildings. Now it would barely make it into the top one hundred. It also once marked the edge of the city; now millions live beyond it. Nearby are two more firsts that Shenzhen can boast—the first stock exchange in China (there are now two) and the first McDonald's (there are now more than a thousand). We drive past a giant picture of a smiling Deng, with the city's modern skyline super-imposed behind him. Lanciel points out that a few years ago the memorial was moved back several meters to allow the highway, Shennan Boulevard, to be widened. "Even after his death he didn't stand in the way of progress," she says with a smile.

On each day of my trip, newspapers across China and in Hong Kong carry articles extolling the marvels of the great leap into capitalism, marking its thirtieth anniversary. Many of the pieces are strangely gripping, a mix of bombast and self-effacement, of personal anecdote and national endeavor. As he sought to reassert his control in 1991 after the Tiananmen crisis, the ailing Deng famously said (or was supposed to have said), "To get rich is glorious." He urged China to "create more Hong Kongs." At least 2,000 Special Economic Zones opened up in the early 1990s; they were concentrated in the Pearl River Delta of Guangdong province in the south, with Shenzhen at its heart. Eventually there were many more experimental cities, motors for the most extensive and ambitious program of profit-driven economics yet produced. "Some must get rich first," Deng proclaimed, arguing that the different regions should "eat in separate kitchens" rather than putting their resources in a "common pot."[3]

We stop at Coastal City, a shopping mall less than a year old, the latest of thousands of palaces of consumerism scattered across China. I walk past a succession of shopfronts and cannot find a single person buying anything. The global economic downturn has already hit the city, but store owners are trying not to show it. They are keen not to lose face. At lunch, in a Taiwanese restaurant overlooking the mall's indoor skating rink, Lanciel introduces me to her friend Peter. His company exports household goods around the world. My hosts say that several thousand factories have closed in Guangdong province, more than has been officially acknowledged. Peter says he can now reach the nearby city of Guangzhou in little over an hour. Before, the 150-kilometer journey would have taken him at least twice as long.

Peter points out that real-estate prices in Shenzhen have fallen by at least 40 percent. A downturn in the market, he says, was inevitable. Prices had been based on speculation and propped up by local government officials, many of whom had made a fast buck. Wealth creation has relied on several multipliers: commercial bank lending, privatization of the entire housing stock, and, more recently, the limited privatization of land. Peter says the central government had been worried for some time about the cavalier approach in regions such as Guangdong, and had been trying, with limited effect, to bring local officials into line. "Beijing saw the problems well before the hierarchies in Shenzhen and Shanghai," he says. The central government officials "wanted far greater controls on property prices, but the politicians are in bed with the developers." The figures bear out their concern. Corruption among "red barons" in the regions is said to cost around 15 percent of China's GDP every year. Some 90 percent of China's richest 3,000 businessmen are related to party figures, and fewer than half of the high court's judgments on corruption are enforced.

I am struck by the candor of my two hosts ("Everyone knows what goes on with corruption and local officials, but there's no point in going public with it," says Peter) and their knowledge of the world. They talk about shopping trends at Walmart and Tesco, about the collapse in the U.S. and European housing sectors, and about the effect on specific factories in Shenzhen that have supplied them. We talk about interest rates and about inflation ("Our government puts our inflation rate at 5 percent, but as soon as you look around you realize those figures must be made up," Peter adds). There is no sense of isolation here; rather the opposite. And yet, no matter how much they criticize the practices of the Communist Party, particularly the local party, they see little reason to change the political status quo. How could anyone possibly give the vote to nearly 800 million uneducated peasants, I am told time and again on travels, and expect China to remain peaceful and stable?

Resuming our tour, Lanciel points out some of Shenzhen's striking modern buildings. As town halls go, I have never seen anything like Citizens' Plaza, a glass structure occupying an entire block that has a roof undulating like a wave. The Boaon and Longgang districts on the northern outskirts contain no such delights—only vast concrete warehouses and factories belching out thick smoke.

What remains of the countryside has been destroyed. The ground seems a mixture of mud, sand, and scrub. A number of the hills surrounding these industrial behemoths have had their peaks chopped off, in order to provide the sand for land to be reclaimed. Throughout this period, people were told the same thing: Shenzhen must not stop growing. Wealth or clean air: In the headlong rush to modernization, the people were told they could not have both. The government chose for them. The economic crisis now has its compensations. The skies are much clearer than normal, Lanciel tells me, because output has fallen. She says that until a few days ago, she has not seen the sun for months. The cost of China's headlong growth has long been evident. The World Bank estimates that over the past decade around 750,000 people in China have died prematurely each year from pollution, and that the health costs of environmental damage account for about 5 percent of GDP annually. The World Bank, in successive assessments of carbon emitters around the world, estimated that sixteen of the twenty most polluted cities across the globe were in China.[4]

We stop at a traffic light in the middle of this industrial jungle. On the other side of the road, a dozen or so young female workers, all in identical red overalls, emerge from one industrial monstrosity, darting across a dangerous four-lane highway to get to their bus stop. Here is the epicenter of the "Walmart miracle"—the low-margin, high-production revolution that supplied China with unparalleled wealth and the West with goods at unparalleled low prices. At the peak of the cheap output boom in the early and mid-2000s, half the world's jeans, air-conditioning units, furniture, textiles, and shoes were made here. The relaxation of the long-standing *hukou* system of residency permits was a key factor. More than 100 million people, officially deemed to be rural dwellers, flooded into urban areas. Shenzhen alone was said, at the peak, to have 8 million temporary migrant workers. By the middle of this decade, some had begun to organize, seeking to form nonofficial trade unions, and to protest at living conditions. Partly as a result of local agitation, and partly to counter international consumer concerns about "sweat shop" labor, a new employment law introduced in January 2008 raised the minimum wage.

Then came the collapse in consumer demand in the West and the ensuing sharp fall in exports on which China—and this region—especially depend. Locals insist that the most cavalier managers in Shenzhen are not from the region itself, but from Hong Kong and Taiwan. Several cases have been recorded of factory owners suddenly locking out their workforce and then disappearing, going somewhere outside of China's legal jurisdiction to avoid censure over breaking employment or other laws. With no job and no compensation, the workers have no choice but to return to the countryside. By the start of 2009, some 600,000 migrant workers from Guangdong province had been forced to leave, according to official figures. The Chinese Academy of Social Sciences has put the rising urban jobless rate at nearly 10 percent—more than double the government's published rate. Given the propensity to understate problems, the actual totals could be appreciably higher.[5]

The most recent figure for "mass incidents," the official euphemism for protests, puts the number of participants at 87,000 per year.[6] With a small number of exceptions, most protests were linked to specific grievances, such as job losses or concerns about corruption or exploitation. They were not overtly political in tone. Officials are nervous, but they point out that, although protests did take place in the mid-1990s, during the rapid liberalization of the economy introduced by then prime minister Zhu Rongji, when some 50 million workers in state-owned enterprises were laid off, they eventually fizzled out.

Publicly, a number of different messages are being put out by the party. The government's information strategy is dogged but also subtle and sophisticated. The state-run central media seem to do little to play down the protest movement. Some experts, Chinese and Western, with whom I spoke suggested that the experiment with greater openness about economic issues has less to do with the principle of free expression and more to do with expediency. The experts argue that the national media have been publicizing specific cases of popular unrest over factory closures and other problems to show the perfidy of local administrators—and thereby demonstrate the need for the central government to keep corrupt officials in the hinterland in check. But there is a further message, and it goes to the heart of the pact between the Chinese Communist Party and the middle class. If you value your new comforts, do not encourage the mob. Your lifestyles will be guaranteed only through central control, which should not be challenged, particularly in a time of adversity. For years, annual growth averaged more than 9 percent. It began to be taken for granted on both sides, so the sudden fall in 2008–2009 was bound to leave people nervous. But insecurity can be as strong a social adhesive as optimism once was.

When the *Hurun Report*, a lifestyle magazine-cum-research institute, began its first annual Chinese "Rich List" in 1999, a personal fortune of just $6 million could get someone into the top fifty. By 2007, the list included five hundred individuals, and even those at the bottom of the list had at least $100 million. Even more remarkable has been the dramatic rise in the number of billionaires: According to *Hurun*, the number of billionaires (in dollars) jumped from 7 in 2004 to 106 in 2007. Below this level emerged a rapidly expanding class of millionaires. In 2008, at the height of the boom, China had 415,000 people with $1 million in disposable assets. This made the country home to more millionaires in real terms than any other country in the world.[7] With China's level of inequality also among the highest in the world, the social ramifications were not lost on the party top brass. Already in 2005, the priority, as set out in the eleventh five-year plan, had shifted to "scientific development." Two ideas had taken hold: that the quality of growth was as important as the amount of growth, and that inequalities within regions and between regions needed to be tackled. The exhortation by Jiang Zemin to build the "well-off society," *xiaokang shehui*, was followed by the move toward the "harmonious society," *hexie shehui*. Members of the new generation of the Chinese super-rich adopted a lower public profile than their Russian counterparts, keeping their luxuries out of view of the rest of the population. Their acquisitiveness is no less pronounced than it was before, but they were told to be careful not to flaunt their riches; they should be seen as contributing more to the broader society and taking less personal advantage of their position.

The earthquake in Sichuan province provided them with an opportunity to prove themselves. Within a week of the disaster in May 2008, the top one hundred richest people in the country collectively donated $120 million.[8] As with Russia, Singapore, and many other countries, those who had done well for themselves in China knew what they needed to do to keep on the right side of the authorities. They also made sure that their newly won private freedoms were not endangered by any temptation to interfere in the public arena.

The Chinese trade-off is the easiest of all to understand. I first visited the country in the mid-1980s. Then, most aspects of life were still rigidly controlled. People had little choice about where they could live, what kind of job they would have, even, in some cases, what clothes they could wear or whom they could marry. For the middle classes (although by no means for the rest), all that has long gone by the wayside.

These freedoms are not trivial. They are the ones that are experienced on a day-to-day basis. They have meaning and value, especially if they have not been experienced before. Many Chinese adopted the ubiquitous symbols of luxury that globalization brought them—Armani, Mercedes, and golf. Shenzhen is at the forefront of the Asian infatuation with the sport and would not countenance anything that is second best. The city has at least a dozen exclusive golf clubs, attracting players from across Asia on tailor-made weekends or holidays. The Mission Hills Golf Club is the biggest in the world, including no fewer than twelve courses designed by some of the world's top professional players, eight restaurants, a hotel, private residences, and two swimming pools.

I have little interest in the sport, so when Lanciel drives up to the Noble Merchant Golf Club, explaining that this is where I will have my last meeting of the day, I respond with a wry smile. Lanciel tells me that her brother-in-law, a lawyer, has assembled some friends and business contacts for a dinner in my honor. We are led to a banqueting room that overlooks the course. I pick up a brochure from the receptionist on my way: "NM-Golf's another superiority [sic] is the complete lighting system for the 18 holes. The system makes night daytime so that the busy members can enjoy playing golf comfortablly [sic] and conveniently whenever they have spare time," it says. "It is good to know that the State Guest House of NM-Golf is the first luxurious clubhouse in Shenzhen, providing state banquet series dishes only."

I am greeted by Wang Heping of the Shenzhen Lawyers Association. A kindly, animated man, he introduces me to the assembled guests on the veranda of our private dining suite. The group includes several local journalists, two industrialists, an asset manager, an architect, a philosophy professor from Nanjing University who has flown down especially for this occasion, and two senior figures from the Shenzhen Municipal Bureau of Culture. The event does not begin auspiciously. I make a rather limp attempt at a joke about soccer being the international language, at which the other guests try valiantly to laugh. Mr. Wang gets straight down to business and asks me for my assessment of the current state of China. I reply that I would not presume an opinion as I am there to learn. This is deemed not to be good enough, and so I proffer my thoughts about the "pact." Just how far were they all prepared to sacrifice their freedoms in return for prosperity and security? From that point, aided by good red wine, the evening takes off.

The conversation is a mix of the impassioned, the philosophical, and the quizzical. We discuss the importance of family, the election of Barack Obama, and the global downturn and the possible remedies for it. One guest takes a pessimistic view of China's economic prospects. "Everyone is blindly waiting for a recovery. They think the ship has a small leak. But it's going to take in a lot of water before this is done," says one. Naval metaphors are apparently in vogue, and another is used about political reform: "This is like a long boat journey on the ocean. There is no destination. We must listen to the passengers," another of my interviewees comments. I interpret that as a call for more democracy, but I am not absolutely sure, so I press them on the West's approach to civil liberties and its application in China. "This is a dilemma for people like us," someone says. "We know the value of democracy and freedom, but how do we achieve this?" Another man counters that China will embrace "universal values of human rights, democracy and that sort of thing in ten years from now," before adding, "We don't believe in fundamentalism. We are more opportunistic and pragmatic."

Only occasionally is nationalism allowed to intrude. The dinner coincides with an emergency summit in Washington of the G-20 to discuss the financial crisis. We all agree that this marks the first, belated, official recognition of China's place at the economic top table. At this point the architect produces a sheaf of papers and proceeds to read out a prepared speech. The others guffaw at his earnestness, but he is not to be denied his moment. He talks of China's humiliation at the hands of foreign powers and how "we couldn't have dared dream about this life ten years ago." China's economic prosperity has not been due to political reform, he says, but can be attributed to the entrepreneurialism and industriousness of the Chinese people. It was unfair of other countries to dictate any particular course of action for China, particularly environmental restrictions that would curb its growth. "The world is small; its resources are limited," the architect says. "You [the West] have already eaten most of the good food." This, I thought to myself, was a variation on another line I had heard that night: "America eats tomorrow's lunch today. China eats the lunch it failed to eat 150 years ago."

As for my own eating, during the architect's discourse I am making a hash of extracting anything I can from an extremely expensive crab. My embarrassment is alleviated somewhat as one guest chips in: "Chinese reform is just like that. It's delicate, difficult, and messy." Everyone descends into laughter. The mood darkens again when the subject moves to the identity of modern China. "We don't know who we are," suggests one of the journalists. "People are trying to believe in something." The Chinese people, he says, are "trapped in transition." He is citing the title of a book written by a Chinese American academic, Minxin Pei, in 2006, which has galvanized the debate about the political and economic trade-off. Pei argued that strong economic growth has diminished the chance of political reform in China. Through a process of "illiberal adaptation," he said, the ruling elites have entrenched their power, and will continue to do so. Another of the guests turns to me and adds: "We are different from you. We are a flock of sheep; we follow the deep grass, and the whip of our rulers." Finally, one of the assembled, who until this point has not spoken, offers a brief thought: "The only thing we have left is our traditions, and our only tradition left is the family." During the dinner, each point is made forcefully and rebutted equally forcefully by someone else. Even the men from the local culture bureau lose their reserve and weigh in. The subject turns to the Olympics, overwhelmingly regarded by those seated around me as a great display of Chinese professionalism and pride. One guest disagrees: "The opening ceremony might not have been Communist, but it was collectivist. We were embarrassed, humiliated. It was too regimented."

We talk late into the night. We leave with handshakes and bear hugs. As he walks me to our car, Mr. Wang asks me for my impressions. I tell him I found the evening remarkable for its candor. I suggest that I will not quote any of the attendees by name, just to make sure. He says he hadn't thought of that, but does not protest. I ask him how he organized the gathering. He says he invited three or four of the men and asked them to bring people they knew. In other words, everyone was speaking without knowing whether they could trust others around the table. "We talk openly in our close circles, but never at formal gatherings such as these," he says, expressing surprise at the extent of the openness of his colleagues. I sense that he is both excited by what has happened and just a little worried. For him and his friends, such displays of free expression mark a venture into the unknown, a break with the convention that has made them feel contented and safe.

In Beijing, for all the superficial attempts at cosmopolitanism, political discussions remain more guarded. That is no particular surprise, as it is the seat of power, and many of those I spoke to there had ambitions that would not be enhanced by an excess of criticism.

I am sitting in the Zi Guang café, near the east gate of Tsing Hua University, with a collection of half a dozen scholars. Some are students, and some are professors.[9] One of them, a teacher in literature and a translator for the Communist Party, has brought her laptop for the conversation, which unnerves me a little. Is she blogging our conversation (in which case, fine)? Or is she noting it for official use (in which case my interlocutors are hardly going to open up)? Either way, she makes no secret of what she is doing, and is affable throughout. When it comes to the economy, the discussion is candid. The scholars talk about friends who have lost money on the Shanghai stock market (which by this point has shed two-thirds of its value). One person speaks of a friend who sold his home several years ago in order to invest in shares of stock. It was a calculated gamble for this individual.

For others stocks became a social security fund, and they are now without a nest egg for retirement.

For years, China's global advance was watched with trepidation in the West. By the middle of this decade, Chinese money, through its Sovereign Wealth Funds, was being invested in parts of America that the indebted and cash-strapped U.S. government could no longer reach. By 2007, China had accumulated a staggering $1.2 trillion of foreign exchange reserves to invest, much of which had been placed in U.S. Treasuries or government bonds. Some of that was done in conjunction with Singapore funds, as the links between the governments of China and Singapore increased. In 2006 and 2007 alone, Chinese stakeholdings in corporations and banks in the United States, the West, and the developing world increased inexorably. The total holdings of the Sovereign Wealth Funds, by the end of 2007, amounted to $150 billion. In the minds of some U.S. politicians, China's rise was at least as threatening as Japan's had been in the 1970s and 1980s. Congress jumped on a popular bandwagon, setting tariffs for Chinese goods at prohibitively high rates and opposing a number of takeover bids. In 2005, Congress ensured that the proposed takeover of the energy giant Unocal by the China National Offshore Oil Corporation (CNOOC) would be abandoned by imposing a number of legislative restrictions that led Unocal to opt for a lower but less controversial rival bid from America's Chevron. In 2008, a Chinese firm and its American partner withdrew an attempt to buy the U.S. telecommunications firm 3Com after the Pentagon publicly expressed a number of national security concerns at the idea of Beijing gaining access to what it said was sensitive U.S. military technology. The Pentagon's fears may have been valid, but underlying them was the almost greater fear that China's economic prosperity was allowing it to go too far in gobbling up U.S. firms. It was all just a little too embarrassing for U.S. politicians to bear.

Initially, Chinese inroads into Western economies were popular in China. But when the expected payoffs did not occur, or worse, the investments showed dramatic losses, there was a backlash there.

Chinese citizens did not like the level of risk. In May 2007, China invested $3 billion in the New York–based private equity firm Blackstone. The symbolism of the Communist state buying into one of Wall Street's rising stars, in the expectation of a more professional handling of its investments, was strong. Within weeks, however, Blackstone's shares plummeted. Chinese bloggers piled in to criticize, and the authorities did nothing to stop them, suggesting a certain tolerance for open discussion expressed in patriotic terms. "The foreign reserves are the product of the sweat and blood of the people of China, please invest them with more care," proclaimed one comment on sina.com, a popular site.[10] Overall, the media debate about the economy has been relatively open in China.

In the Zi Guang café, I try to switch the focus of attention from finance to politics, and my university group becomes more circumspect. A young man who has just returned from a year at Cornell insists that China can continue to "combine the collectivist social and economic model with a high degree of consumerism" (a variation on the established Leninism-plus-market-economy idea). I tell them that I have just been browsing at a nearby bookshop, where I found on the counter the assembled works of Milton Friedman alongside Chairman Mao. They see this as unsurprising. So I ask whether they detect any link between material comfort and a demand for more freedom. "Definitely," says one woman. "Affluence leads to demands for more personal autonomy." She quickly adds that such demands could and would be accommodated through debate within the Communist Party.

The students admit that they exchange information with their friends about technical wizardry that allows them to bypass the latest Internet firewalls. Yet they insist that certain checks should remain in place for the sake of social stability, adding that the main goal of a relaxation in censorship should be greater efficiency and probity. "We need transparency of reporting to improve our accountability system and anticorruption drive and identify mistakes in decision making," says a recent grad. Some of them develop the argument by means of proverbs: "How does a patient cure himself?" one asks, suggesting that

a certain amount of outside scrutiny makes for greater professionalism. And another one, tackling the one-party system, says, "How will
a horse run fast if it is the only one in the race?"

Their solution, it seems to me, is based around pragmatic statecraft,
a variation on Singapore's view of elections as a form of referendum, or
a simple performance indicator for government. Democracy is thus defined purely in terms of technocratic accountability. The forum for such
assessments, they imply, lies within officially sanctioned structures—
public consultations, expert meetings, surveys, and, most of all, intra-
party discussions that can accommodate different viewpoints. All these
fall into the term, so fashionable in Chinese intellectual circles, of "deliberative democracy."

Can these things be achieved through a single party? The Communist leadership has yet to embrace the "soft" institutional infrastructure that, to a greater or lesser extent, has featured in Western
systems: independent courts, clear property rights, a free press, independent trade unions, effective corporate governance, transparent
antimonopoly rules, free intellectual inquiry, and even a properly functioning welfare system. My student interlocutors are convinced that
China will eventually adopt such mechanisms, but they think it can be
done without changing the existing system in its fundamentals. They
use as a reference point the Sichuan earthquake. "We could not have
reacted as quickly as we did to Sichuan if we had had multiparty
democracy," one of them tells me. "This natural disaster rekindled our
confidence in the necessity of consistency, which only the collectivist
model can provide." They contrast Sichuan with Hurricane Katrina.
Later on they might have added the Indian response to the Mumbai
terrorist attacks.

The Sichuan tragedy marked an important moment. It reflected
the various contradictions at work, as the Chinese authorities struggled
to keep pace with both the opening up of society and the demands of
digital technology. They began in time-honored fashion, trying to play
down the extent of the damage and prevent on-the-spot reporting.
With the Olympics only three months away, the government was

particularly eager to control the message. However, when reports and video began to emerge around the world via the Internet, before there was any opportunity to censor the information, the strategy started to collapse. The authorities quickly relented. They were surprised to see that the immediate consequences were the opposite of their fears. Footage of Prime Minister Wen Jiabao in his scuffed shoes and drab suit, clambering over debris to meet victims and to exhort the emergency services to greater efforts, proved an instant hit. "Grandpa Wen" became the global face of China's grief. For a brief moment it became distasteful to criticize China, as the actress Sharon Stone found out when she suggested the disaster had been due to the bad "karma" caused by its government's human rights record. Wen made several more visits to the area. He even acquired his own Facebook site, which became one of the most popular of its kind.

The carefully news-managed images of the quake helped to reinforce a sense of national solidarity throughout 2008, one of the most important years in China's modern history. Across Beijing and other cities, on signs posted on the sides of buses or in underground stations, pictures of either a panda or a pretty girl appeared with the slogan: "All because of you, Chengdu will be better," a reference to the earthquake-stricken capital of Sichuan province. However, as criticism grew of the long-term measures being taken, reporting restrictions were tightened again. The Propaganda Ministry issued directives to state-run news outlets setting out forbidden topics. These included questions about whether the schools had been constructed to adequate standards, whether government rescue efforts were too slow, and whether Beijing officials knew in advance that the quake would happen, but failed to warn the inhabitants of the area (as the rumor mill was alleging). Several groups of bereaved parents, made up of couples who had lost their only children in a collapsed school, were prevented from traveling to Beijing to lobby the government. Journalists who asked too many questions were told to "emphasise positive propaganda" and "uphold unity, stability and encouragement."[11]

Almost nobody I spoke to was content with the large amount of censorship of the media, although suggested alternatives varied considerably. The thousands of newspapers, magazines, and television and radio stations across China's provinces are all, to a greater or lesser extent, under the watchful eye of the party. (Business journalism has, in recent years, been the most dynamic and outspoken.) According to the International Committee to Protect Journalists, as of December 2008 China had twenty-eight of its own journalists in jail. The number of journalists in prison in China is consistently the highest such number in the world, followed by the number jailed in Cuba. The most common convictions are for divulging state secrets, subversion, and defamation—charges that are regularly used to silence the most outspoken critics.

The party's greatest concern now is the Internet. In 2008, China passed the United States to become home to the biggest population of users—up to 200 million regulars at the latest count. The authorities have tried to block sensitive discussions, using keyword filters and an army of "net nannies" employed by portals and service providers. This "great firewall of China" is manned by 100,000 monitors, also sometimes called "cyber cops" or "chat room mamas." Foreign sites, ranging from the BBC to Wikipedia, are regularly blocked. The government has developed some of the most sophisticated technology in the world for spotting dangerous sites, developing algorithms to weed out postings that include words like "democracy," "Dalai Lama," or "Tiananmen massacre." Both sides play an elaborate game of cat and mouse, with savvy users quickly finding ways of circumventing government blocks. One clever technique has been to use online software to render Chinese-language script vertically instead of horizontally. This, for a while, baffled the keyword detectors. One of the tricks employed by the state is to use thousands of paid commentators who pose as ordinary web users to counter criticism of the government. They are known by independent bloggers as "50 Cent Party members" because of the small sum, fifty Chinese cents, they are said to be paid for every posting.

Sometimes the central government encourages bloggers to vent their spleen. This gives many in the general public a sense of "people power," but the feeling is an illusion; the venting is only allowed when it is about something the government wants to allow people to vent about, such as when vigilantes are permitted to rail against wrongdoing among local officials. The public airing of complaints strengthens the credibility of the federal authorities, who then move quickly to punish the miscreants. In one case, an ostensibly harmless photograph of a Nanjing housing official found its way onto the Web. Sharp-eyed bloggers could not help noticing the $15,000 Swiss watch on his wrist. Two weeks later, he was fired after investigators determined that he had led an improbably lavish lifestyle for a civil servant with a modest salary.

The border between private and public space is the fault line in defining and determining freedom in China. This line is constantly changing and defies easy labels. Many of the students I spoke to were frustrated by the authorities' censorship efforts, which they saw as both aggressive and desperate. Yet they often pointed out that the torrent of information now accessible online has given many young urban Chinese a sense of freedom that their parents could only have dreamed of. They resent suggestions that they are brainwashed, or that their access to information is any less complete than in the West.

The political scientist Anne-Marie Brady suggests that China's central propagandists have studied the theories of "manufacturing consent" by Edward Bernays, regarded as the originator of modern public relations, and Walter Lippmann. In his seminal 1922 book, *Public Opinion*, Lippmann said democracy and the media operated in an environment of low attention spans; the "bewildered herd," he argued, unable to come to intelligent conclusions without prompting, must be governed by "a specialised class." That class would be composed of experts, otherwise known as elites, who could circumvent the primary defect of democracy, the impossible ideal of the "omni-competent citizen." Brady pointed out how governments decree which subjects are open to discussion and which are rendered impermissible. Those topics are then placed outside the perimeter. The state intervenes at all levels of the media hierarchy through a system of news guidance, post-publication review, and reward and punishment. Its most effective tool is a traditional Chinese invention rather than a Western import, a "you know what we mean" style of regulation that allows experimentation, tolerates ambiguity, and then punishes retroactively and arbitrarily.[12] This is the Singapore model adapted for a larger canvas, with less emphasis on defamation suits (the accused in China would rarely have the money to pay), and more on other forms of sanction, from peer pressure to imprisonment.

Then there are the cultural outlets. In many ways Beijing is more avant-garde than Singapore and other Asian cities. A walk around the area of Sanlitun, a district of the city, attests to lively visual arts and music scenes, crowded bookstores, stylish designer clothing, and more. In the academic world, several professors I interviewed who had worked across Asia said they enjoyed at least as much freedom of intellectual inquiry in the Chinese capital as elsewhere. This is opening up with a distinct purpose, as the longtime China watcher Andrew Nathan observed: "This lightly patrolled free zone is not the antithesis but the twin of the permanent crackdown on the political frontier, where the few who insist on testing the regime are crowded to the cultural margin and generally ignored."[13]

This tap was ostentatiously turned off in the immediate run-up to the Olympics and throughout the Games. Back in 1993, China was embarrassed before the world when its bid to host the event in 2000 was defeated amid international public criticism of its human rights record. When it submitted its application for 2008, the Chinese government promised to be "open in every aspect" and to improve civil liberties, providing a face-saver for all concerned. The international community could claim to be working toward universal human rights, although everyone knew that China's enhanced global status was the real cause of the change of heart.

In many ways, the Chinese system had been ideally suited for such a grand venture. With no budget constraints, no transparency, and a large pool of docile migrant labor, the authorities completed, on time, not only the thirty-one Olympic venues, but also three new subway lines and the largest airport terminal in the world.

With so much to do, the government saw manifestations of dissent during this period as especially inefficient and harmful. Repression was intensified to ensure "order." Human rights groups reported the imprisonment of activists campaigning for causes from land rights to AIDS. Several dissidents were punished by "reeducation through labor," meaning they were sent to prison camps without trial. A number of ordinary citizens who used the traditional and permitted method of petitioning over local grievances were detained. Arrests for "endangering state security" rose to their highest level in eight years. Even some of the lawyers defending activists in court were subjected to detentions, beatings, and threats. "It was hoped that the Games would act as a catalyst for reform but much of the current wave of repression against activists and journalists is occurring not in spite of, but actually because of the Olympics," Amnesty International reported.[14]

The Chinese assumed that with so much global political and corporate investment already committed for the 2000 Games, protests from Western governments would be muted. They were mainly right and a little wrong. A number of incidents took place that proved deeply embarrassing. But in the end the West did what it usually does. It went with the money.

At the start of the year, the film director Steven Spielberg resigned as artistic adviser to the Games in protest at China's role in the humanitarian crisis in Darfur. China had long dismissed international concern over its support for Sudan's tyrannical government, which is accused of fomenting a conflict in which at least 200,000 people have been killed and 2 million forced from their homes. Spielberg declared that he and other Hollywood stars would have no involvement in the "genocide Olympics." That condemnation was by no means misplaced, but human rights groups have been equally frustrated with the West's consistently weak response to the long conflict.

Tibet was another area where China's record has come under sustained scrutiny. In March 2008, five months before the Games, Chinese forces broke up protests by some three hundred Buddhist monks in the capital, Lhasa, that had been called to mark the anniversary of the failed uprising of 1959. More than a thousand Tibetans were detained. The Chinese government said rioters killed at least nineteen people. Tibetan exiles said soldiers killed dozens of civilians. Many Chinese responded furiously to Western coverage, or what they were told of Western coverage. On the MSN message board, "I love China" was a popular posting, alongside "I hate CNN."

What ensued on the streets of European capitals further inflamed such thinking. On April 6, 2008, protesters disrupted the processional Olympic torch as it was taken through the streets of London. The scenes in Paris the following day were even more chaotic. The Chinese government encouraged a mood of wounded patriotic pride. Many Chinese were told that Western television had deliberately doctored coverage of the torch protests, the Tibet uprising, and other events involving China. One young woman, who had spent some time as a Chinese student in the United Kingdom, suggested to me that the coverage of Tibet by the BBC "might as well have been written by the Dalai Lama." Another, who had been studying in London on the day of the torch protest, said she had taken part in a counter-protest by pro-government Chinese students. "There were thousands of us defending our country, but we simply disappeared from your screens." My protestations that she might have been misinformed fell on deaf ears.

This was a defining period for Western governments. Should they take a stand on civil liberties? Or should they try to keep their powder dry in order to avoid damaging their delicate strategic and business relationships with the world's third-largest economy? In the end they did a bit of both, managing to frustrate human rights groups and enrage the Chinese government.

The German chancellor, Angela Merkel, caused fury by meeting with the Dalai Lama in Berlin. Her predecessor, Gerhard Schröder, said of Merkel's decision: "Some recent situations have hurt Chinese people's feelings, and I regret it." He was speaking at a seminar in Beijing on "China's Development and World Harmony."[15] Within a year, relations "returned to normal"; Merkel had followed up her attendance at the Games with another visit to China. Britain's Gordon Brown appeared consistently confused. On his first visit to Beijing, he focused almost exclusively on trade, barely mentioning human rights. As the Tibet riots escalated, he declared that he would not be going to the opening ceremony, but would attend the closing festivities. Nobody quite knew what that denoted. When the battered Olympic torch reached Downing Street on that chaotic day in April, he agreed to receive it, and to be photographed next to it, but would not touch it.

It was the French who suffered the most. Their president, Nicolas Sarkozy, initially decided that he would infuse his country's foreign policy with new concern for human rights. He suggested he might pull out from the opening ceremony unless "progress" was made over Tibet. That threat, and the torch protests in Paris, led to an extraordinary anti-French backlash. China's government successfully mobilized a popular campaign against Western interference. The main target was the French supermarket chain Carrefour, the most successful foreign store in China. For several days in April it was subjected to a series of noisy protests. The Chinese government was quite happy to advertise the wrath of the people on national and international news, and to allow its citizens to use the Internet to exhort each other to join in. The goal was threefold: to play to a swelling patriotism ahead of the Games, to punish France, and to warn off future critics.

The Chinese government is a master in the exercise of implicit power. Unlike Russia, it tries to avoid bellicose language. Its specialty is controlled menace, reinforced in the knowledge of its growing economic strength. On the eve of the Olympics, countries that treated China with "respect" were told that they would benefit as a result. The "skip France" campaign succeeded in all its goals. On departing Beijing after the opening ceremony, Sarkozy sought to ingratiate himself with his hosts, declaring the Games deserved a "gold medal," only to swing back again, meeting the Dalai Lama in December. France's business leaders fumed at the lost opportunities, and their counterparts in other countries were excited at the prospect of snapping up an extra contract or two at the expense of the French. This competitive bidding over human rights was not new; it was done with as much alacrity during the Cold War. The British corporate lobby was given a further boost when David Miliband slipped in a change in relations with Tibet just as human rights advocates had their backs turned. On the eve of the American elections that autumn, the foreign secretary issued a written parliamentary statement formally recognizing Chinese sovereignty over the disputed region. Miliband argued that he was only bringing the United Kingdom into line with the United States and the European Union and removing an anomaly, both of which were true. But the point was made. The Chinese were pleased.

The Olympics produced a huge surge in patriotic ardor, and by extension, an endorsement of the pact. Some Western diplomats pointed out that the more they (or NGOs or journalists) criticized the Chinese leadership, the more it seemed to bolster rather than undermine the regime's popularity at home. In July 2008, the Pew Research Center published a survey that was widely reported back in China. Pew summarized it thus: "As they eagerly await the Beijing Olympics, the Chinese people express extraordinary levels of satisfaction with the way things are going in their country and with their nation's economy. With more than eight in ten having a positive view of both, China ranks number one among 24 countries on both measures in the 2008 survey. These findings represent a dramatic improvement in national contentment from earlier in the decade."[16]

Chinese state media and the blogosphere seized on these findings. They were equally enamored of a book published at the time of the Olympics, *How East Asians View Democracy*, by Columbia University Press.[17] The book compared and contrasted eight East Asian countries and concluded that public satisfaction with government was highest in China. Satisfaction was less pronounced in countries more associated with democracy—including South Korea, Taiwan, the

Philippines, Hong Kong, and Japan, which scored lowest. Few questioned the methodology of these surveys. The results appeared to accurately reflect the mood of the Chinese at the time, duly recording their defiance in the face of criticism and their pride in the wake of success. That pride was reinforced by the fifty-one gold medals the host country won at the Games.

Yet throughout the month of sporting action, much of Beijing resembled a ghost town. Many people who normally received visas were refused entry. Hotels, at least those not close to the Olympic Village, reported lower than usual occupancy. A helpful "legal guide" advised athletes, officials, reporters, and spectators on how to behave. They were told to avoid "subversive activities" or the "display of religious, political or racial banners."[18] Sporadic protests did take place, among followers of Falun Gong, a spiritual practice introduced into China in 1992 and immediately seen as oppositionist, and the "Free Tibet" movement, but, in front of Western camera crews, the demonstrators were summarily hauled away. In the run-up to the Games, the Chinese authorities blocked a number of news and other websites. Some were unblocked again after official representations were made by the International Olympic Committee (IOC). (As soon as the Olympics jamboree had left town, many of those sites were blocked again—and stayed blocked.) Beijing residents reported that a number of eccentric regulations were suddenly applied. Restaurants were prevented from serving dog meat, for fear of upsetting foreigners, and a number of shops were told not to sell gin, as officials feared it could be used in the making of Molotov cocktails.

One of the first things I do on my arrival in Beijing on a cold November day is to take a walk around the Olympic Stadium, the Bird's Nest. I want to get a flavor of what it must have been like. I sense a slight hangover. The building itself, only a few months on, already looks a little tatty. The price of admission hardly justifies a desultory costume exhibition on one corner of the ground. Police warily guard the home straight of the running track, for reasons I cannot fathom. Still, the tourists continue to come, particularly from other regions of China, cameras at the ready to capture a shot of their national stadium.

I wonder whether the Olympics really did mark China's successful arrival on the world stage; perhaps they merely provided a brief fillip before a harsher reality dawned. Nicholas Bequelin, senior China researcher at Human Rights Watch, reminded me that China continues to have more than sixty capital offenses, among them nonviolent crimes such as tax fraud. It executes more people than the rest of the world combined. That practice has also become big business: Up to 95 percent of commercial organ transplants are obtained from executed prisoners. Then there is the one-child policy, the most vivid area where the state continues to intrude into the private realm. The official line is that the policy, introduced thirty years ago, has prevented 400 million births, representing an excess population that would have stymied China's economic growth and damaged social stability. Economists predict a major workforce shortage in the medium term as the present population ages. That part is discussed relatively openly. What is rarely mentioned are the human rights consequences—the infanticides, forced adoptions, and various other abuses arising from the policy.[19]

Bequelin and I discussed the tortuous path trodden by the West in figuring out how to address these human rights issues in China. He suggested that politicians are not exclusively culpable, that they take their lead from major corporations. International law firms, he said, are increasingly loath to criticize China for fear of losing business. The same goes for media conglomerates—indeed, for just about all commercial companies. The underlying problem, he said, is not one of principle—China has signed fourteen international treaties enshrining human rights and continues to insist on "progress"—but China's need to save face when it is criticized. The reason the authorities clamp down so hard on dissidents is that dissidents have a propensity to air their complaints in front of foreigners. The task is to find a new language and new mechanisms with which to address these problems. The old Cold War agenda, with its easy certitudes about one system blazing a trail and the other languishing in moral degradation, has long gone. Issues such as multiparty elections and free expression—and the relationship of the population to them—are far more complex, and less black and white, in contemporary China than they were during the Cold War era. "The human rights industry needs to evolve," Bequelin said. "We need to find a new language which talks to people who have grown used to consumerism and a one-party system."

With the economic crisis, unsavory practices seemed to be on the rise in China. The most damaging scandal was one in which several children died, and thousands became ill, after drinking milk formula adulterated with melamine, an industrial compound used to cheat nutrition tests, in the fall of 2008. The official media, once again, began by trying to play down the affair, until the full extent of the problem was exposed. The affair caused people worldwide to question the safety of Chinese products. Chinese officials warned food and drug makers of the punishments, including the death sentence, if they used the economic crisis to cut corners.

The global downturn is at the top of the agenda when I meet Michael Pettis and his students.[20] Pettis is a professor at Peking University's Guanghua School of Management. Even though it is Saturday evening, he is conducting a seminar on macro-economics with eleven young men in a meeting area of the economics building. Pettis nominates one of his pupils to lead the discussion. The students talk variously about predictions of the depth of the recession, fiscal reform, banking liquidity, and the pitfalls of both inflation and deflation. They discuss the extent to which the crisis is already affecting China and how far the growth rate might fall. Pettis leaves them to it, only occasionally chipping in. He asks his charges if they have seen a recent television interview with the prime minister about the state of the economy. "Wen looked really terrified. They are really afraid of something," he remarks. They nod in agreement. "What is it?" No answer is offered.

After the meeting, Pettis and I walk to a nearby club called D22, entering through a narrow doorway into a large, windowless cavern.

Pettis has had a varied experience of China, combining his two areas of expertise. He helped to found his music club in 2006, and he enjoys combining his interest in financial markets with running one of the capital's most vibrant cultural venues. As he fixes me a gin and tonic, he points out that the current crop of students is the first in a long while that will struggle. Some 80 percent of the students who graduated from universities in China in the summer of 2008 had no job prospects, and many have been unable to find work a year later. So worried have they become about finding jobs in the private sector that up to 1 million students have taken the civil-service exam to try for government jobs, a rise of 25 percent from the previous year. With an average of eighty applications from recent graduates for each civil-service position, the frustrations are great. According to the newspaper of the People's Liberation Army, applications to join the military are the highest for a generation.

Many young people, influenced by their parents' harrowing tales of life during the Cultural Revolution, see the ability to be apolitical as a privilege. They are happy to get good marks and to enjoy what little free time their busy schedules permit. Everything else is considered a distraction, even a danger. With employment prospects contracting, it comes as little surprise that people have become even more circumspect about "causing trouble." A popular saying goes, "No one will smash his own foot with a rock." Pettis talks of the mismatch between a "dramatic cultural liberalization similar to that of the U.S. in the 1960s" alongside "the worst education system for the smartest kids," an education system that remains rooted in the old practice of going to school for very long hours and learning by rote. "They are the world's greatest test takers, but the complaints I hear from financial services managers is that many of the Chinese graduates they hire can't cope with ideas outside the box."

Caution may be one explanation for the reluctance among some Chinese to criticize their government, but there is invariably a more confident justification, too: The model of the West doesn't seem as attractive as it once was, now that the financial bubble has burst. The day after meeting with Pettis I am in a private room in a venerable, hundred-year-old tea shop, Sheng Xi Fu, drinking extraordinary gold tea from Yunnan province. I am with two young entrepreneurs, Chenggen Hu and Kevin Ao.[21] Both are part of a trend of returnees from Silicon Valley, people who have honed their business skills in the United States and are seeking to put them to good use in their home country, investing in semiconductor companies. Although they would not describe themselves as such, they could be considered converts to the "new left" movement in China that even before the economic crisis had become concerned about the unquestioning adoration of free-market theories. "For the past ten to fifteen years we just copied the West. Until recently, I thought China would be a purely capitalist society. But the crisis shows that the U.S. is not a good example," Chenggen says. "Before now, you would have been denounced in academic circles if you advocated economic intervention. I suppose China is lucky that the government was not so pro-market. Now even those professors who graduated in the U.S. are questioning the American model." What of the social system? "The Chinese middle class has always wanted to live the American life—a house, car, kids, dogs, that kind of thing. But it isn't open to all of society."

In spite of the startling demographic shift over the past two decades from the countryside to cities, China's population, at 1.3 billion, still includes, by most estimates, around 750 million peasants, most of them poorly educated. The self-proclaimed middle class may be growing fast, and in sheer numbers it may even have reached 200 million, but it is still a small fraction of the total. "Free elections are good in theory, but not now," says Kevin. "With the vote in the wrong hands, the wrong people get selected who then manipulate the electorate." I protest the rather obvious point that this is the last refuge of the elite that does not wish to share power, that this is just what was said in the West before suffrage became universal. It is, he counters, a matter of education and a sense of responsibility. The issue of ethnicity is also cited. Some fifty-five minorities are represented across China. "It is only a short step to imagining how China would break apart if it became a democracy," says Chenggen. "There are too many examples of political change that bring division. Chinese people want a stable life."

I question them about the specifics of China's human rights record. I start with Tiananmen Square, a subject that until now I have been wary of pushing. Kevin says his brother-in-law was one of the protesters, but left the scene the day before the crackdown. He has a good friend who stayed, and who subsequently spent a year in prison. He is now a successful businessman who lives abroad, even though apparently he has the right to return. "The students were good-hearted but misguided," he says. He recalls a dispute in his family at the time: "My father was against the students. Everyone else was in favor. History will prove him right." Kevin says his brother is a senior party figure who has been responsible for the reconstruction of Chengdu, the capital of Sichuan province, after the quake. Many local people complained about the lack of compensation for the damages they and their families suffered. While their grievances may have been justified, Kevin says, they should not have protested during the Olympics, insulting their country.

He brings up the topic of Singapore. "The Singapore model is best for us. In many ways Singaporeans are more Chinese than we are. They want even more control than we do." I cite three alternative models that China might have adopted. One is the brief liberal experiment in the Russia of the late Gorbachev and early Yeltsin years. Another is the tumultuous democracy of Taiwan. The third is India, the world's most populous democracy. Each produces pained expressions. Just look at the economic performance of these countries and compare them to China, they say. "Western people are not open-minded about political systems," Chenggen says. "They can't accept that other systems might be good."

Chenggen and Kevin may not be as well traveled as my Singapore friends, but they appear to be drawing similar conclusions. Again, I am confronted by the realization that some of the most pro-government elements are those with the strongest Western educations. Perhaps I should not be surprised. I had seen enough evidence of the "MBA

crowd" in London, Europe, and the United States, people of all manner of nationalities who for two decades defined themselves through
the global power of money rather than by any issues of political engagement or protest. Their Chinese counterparts are merely seeking to
emulate them.

The Olympics showed how much China has modernized, just not in
the direction of liberal democracy. The state still tells people how many
children they can have. It still restricts movements for the urban and
rural poor. But otherwise it has largely withdrawn from people's everyday lives, giving Chinese citizens unprecedented freedoms to consume
material goods and to organize their professional and personal development. This increased personal freedom has been matched with ever
more sophisticated control of the public sphere. In the 1980s, many Chinese intellectuals supported multiparty elections. Since Tiananmen
Square, political reform has been redefined. Although there are still
prominent thinkers who believe in the country's incremental embrace of
democracy, many modern intellectuals argue that China would do better to avoid elections altogether and focus rather on making the one-
party state more rules based and more responsive. The party is nothing
if not thorough. It has begun to rely on opinion polls, focus groups, the
Internet and other consultations to keep it in touch with public opinion.
A model of "deliberative authoritarianism" has emerged that, for the
moment, at least, appears to have increased the legitimacy of the one-
party state and lessened calls within the mainstream population for what
it understands to be Western-style democracy.

What of those small offshoots of China that have had more experience
with what we think of as democracy? Hong Kong may not be as
bustling as it once was. Perhaps it no longer feels it can compete with
the economic might of Shanghai and Shenzhen. In certain respects
the "one country, two systems" pledge of the Chinese, as they ushered
the British out in 1997, has been preserved. Although the press has
clipped its own wings, newspaper and television reporters in Hong
Kong are still more inquiring than those on the mainland. The stan-

dard for trouble-making is set by the ever vibrant *Apple Daily*. Its owner, the entrepreneur Jimmy Lai, has resisted all cajoling and threats to tone down his tabloid, including an officially encouraged boycott by advertisers. Talk of Tiananmen Square does not have to take place in hushed tones in Hong Kong; religion is openly practiced. It is remarkable to see followers of the Falun Gong, who are banned and persecuted just a few miles away across the bay, mounting noisy protests. The original Joint Declaration signed in 1984 guaranteed the "Hong Kong way of life." The Chinese authorities regarded the later pro-democracy changes introduced by Chris Patten, the outgoing governor, as contradicting what London had agreed to. Chinese academics like to argue that, even until the early 1980s, the colonial rulers of Hong Kong were less amenable to democratic representation, free expression, and free association than Chinese rule is now.

For activists, journalists, academics, and others who are politically engaged in Hong Kong, the danger lies less in codified law than in self-censorship, in fear of the more subtle consequences of speaking out. Joseph Cheng is one of a dwindling band of Hong Kong–based academics prepared to agitate openly for the pro-democracy movement. "I am an activist, I'll remain an activist, but I cannot be optimistic," says Cheng, a professor of political science at Hong Kong's City University. "Most people, even here, think that there is no obvious alternative. People are afraid of change, particularly in difficult times. They think that if you get of rid of the party you will get chaos."

Deeply rooted in the minds of the rulers, and in the burgeoning middle classes, is this fear of *luan*, chaos. The authorities thoroughly research the potential sources of trouble. "Party officials are assiduous in studying historical comparisons," Cheng tells me in his cramped university office.[22] "For example, they have looked at the Solidarity experience in Poland in dealing with their own trade unions; they compare the worship of the 'Polish Pope' with Falun Gong." The political opening of the past ten years has been heavily circumscribed. The day-to-day administrator of Hong Kong, the chief executive, is appointed, not elected. Parliament consists of ordinary constituencies and "functional constituencies," constructs created to give the business community disproportionate influence. As in mainland China, members of the business elite in Hong Kong have worked closely with the Communist Party. These two forces have seen eye to eye on the dangerous potential of a fully functioning democracy, ever fearful that it could provide the catalyst for unrest. Cheng is writing a book about Tiananmen Square and takes part in rallies and other activities organized by the Hong Kong Alliance in support of human rights. He notes that the annual vigil was smaller and more muted in June 2008 than in the past. Part of that could be explained by the Sichuan earthquake and enthusiasm for the Olympics. But researchers at the rival Hong Kong University detect a slight shift in the public mood. Its survey found that the majority of Hong Kong residents still believe that the Chinese students were right to protest in 1989 and that the government was wrong to crack down so hard. But the proportion of respondents who believed that human rights in China had improved since 1989 had risen steadily, reaching 85 percent. Some 77 percent expected those rights to improve further in the future.

Cheng says everyone is being more careful, even in the comparatively freer environment of Hong Kong. "Covert pressure is now strong. I am the only senior professor who organizes things. Even here you don't become a dean or a president, and you don't receive research funds, if you speak out too much. During 1989 intellectuals had low living standards, so they felt they had less to lose. Since then the party has been very skilful in co-opting the elites, and now many academics here and in China are also doing quite well."

Academics are just one of several groups that have been successfully co-opted by the regime. I recount to Cheng the conversations I have had in China about the uprising of 1989 and the choices made since then. They are, he says, fairly representative of the consensus. People have reconciled themselves to their political defeat because they have succeeded economically, he says. "The post-Tiananmen generation has made peace with the government. The general view now is that the students were right in principle, but got it wrong in practice.

By confronting the regime so directly, they gave it no wriggle room. A lot will say gradual reforms are best." Cheng predicts no major disruptions in a system that "still functions sufficiently well" and does not disparage the "deliberative" approach of the Communist Party. "They are experimenting with political reforms within the party. They are trying to be more responsive. Because the leadership doesn't want to give democracy, as we understand it, it must be more responsive." That is surely, then, another variation on the pact, I suggest. "There is, even in a financial downturn, a chance of improvement in living standards if you don't challenge the authorities. As long as you don't cause trouble, you are quite free," Cheng replies. "If you do cause trouble, you quickly become an outcast. The police come for you, the tax authorities come for you, your friends and colleagues are more wary of returning your calls." It comes down, Cheng says, to a "simple cost-benefit analysis." The costs are high, but the benefits are high, too. But what happens, I wonder, if the benefits start to drop?

My final stop is Taipei, capital of Taiwan, or the Republic of China, or the twenty-third province of the People's Republic of China, depending on your point of view. I had come to look at the pact from the opposite end of the telescope, to see firsthand a country which, from a Western "democratization" agenda, ticks all the boxes.

After forty years of martial law, Taiwanese have for more than a decade enjoyed a period of turbulent freedom. For many foreigners, their only knowledge of Taiwanese politics is television footage of members of parliament embroiled in punch-ups. For many Chinese, Taiwan provides the perfect advertisement for the perils of democracy. Eight years of rule by the Democratic Progressive Party (DPP) have just come to an end. The longtime party of power, the Kuomintang (KMT), is firmly back in charge, having reinvented itself, at least for the purpose of the election, as a force for democracy. Yet, just days before I arrive, the former prime minister Chen Shui-bian, a member of the DPP, was led from his home in handcuffs on embezzlement charges. His party protests that this will be a show trial, arguing that the judges have never come down hard on KMT politicians whenever they put their hands into the till. It was no coincidence, after all, that Taiwan's former leader, Chiang Kai-shek, was known as Cash My Cheque.

I decide that I should first pay homage to the man himself. When I arrive at the Chiang Kai-shek memorial hall I am told its name has been changed. The DPP government tried to remove as many monuments as it could of Chiang. Eventually, it was forced to reinstate the statue of the man who took on Mao in the Chinese Civil War, who lost and fled to Taiwan in 1949, and who ruled a government-in-exile for twenty-five years from this new base of operations. The National Taiwan Democracy Monument, as it is now called, is housed in lavish grounds that also accommodate the National Theatre and National Concert Hall—shades of the Lincoln Memorial and the Mall in Washington, D.C. It is no surprise that so much of modern Taiwan is modeled on America, for years the sponsor and paymaster of a dictatorial regime. What mattered was that Chiang was anti-Communist.

I walk the eighty-nine steps (representing Chiang's age at his death) to reach the gargantuan marble figure of a man seated, smiling and holding a walking stick. The same pose is replicated in other statues around the island. The museum downstairs is equally beguiling. The walls are covered with photographs showing Chiang meeting world leaders (at least of those few nations that still recognized Taiwan after Richard Nixon famously went to mainland China for a spot of ping-pong diplomacy in 1972). Chiang's statesmen friends included Nicaragua's General Anastasio Somoza, Augusto Pinochet of Chile, and other unsavory types. The museum's *pièces de résistance* are the two shining black Cadillac Fleetwoods, one from the 1950s, the other from the 1970s, gleaming three-ton monsters of limousines from which Chiang would survey his island.

Taiwan's fraught history casts an intriguing light on the double standards of the Cold War. As long as a country was pro-Western in its geostrategic loyalties, the West glossed over its approach to democracy and human rights internally. That much applied to Chiang and his declaration of martial law. Then, just as Taiwan introduced real freedoms, it was abandoned by the West as the West threw in its lot with the authoritarian Chinese mainland.

This point is emphasized repeatedly by Dennis Engbarth, an American journalist and longtime resident I meet in the center of Taipei. Engbarth has spent much of his life trying to persuade anyone who will listen that Taiwan's democracy is setting an example for others to follow, and that it should not be abandoned. Few people are listening, as—just as on mainland China—they appear to be too busy trying to make money. Issues such as national sovereignty are now seen as the preserve of only the most politically committed. Engbarth becomes agitated at any suggestion such as this, embarking on an impassioned defense of Taiwan's independence, which he and other supporters of the DPP see as imperiled by the advance of China, China's money, and Western ambivalence. He reminds me that when the Taiwanese held their first fully democratic elections in 1996, the Americans still professed to care. The Chinese government tried to prevent the impending democratic experiment by conducting military exercises just off the coast. President Clinton sent two aircraft carriers to ensure the elections proceeded. In little over a decade, Engbarth says, Taiwan has come a long way, overtaking Hong Kong in the democratic stakes and serving as a beacon for others to follow. Which other country can boast multiparty elections, freedom of speech, a growing human rights culture, and a per capita GDP of $30,000 per year so soon after being ruled by a dictatorship for half a century? "It's a rare case of bottom-up democracy, although some people don't realize it is." None of this, Engbarth says, is thanks to the international community. The more Taiwan democratizes, the less anyone seems to care. The double standards were most acute during the George W. Bush administration. For all the neoconservatives' ardor for "democracy promotion," the White House saw Taiwan, and particularly its more obdurate DPP government, as an impediment to progress with China. "Bush was upset with Taiwan for trying to deepen democracy," Engbarth claims.[23]

Apart from a few Latin American countries—a throwback to the old dictatorships—and one or two others, nobody has an official embassy here anymore. With its gleaming Taipei 101 tower (which has enjoyed the accolade of the tallest building in the world since opening in 2004, but is set to lose it with the imminent completion of the Burj Dubai in Dubai), parts of the city center look modern. But compared to the buildings in major cities of mainland China, most of Taipei's buildings seem older and shabbier. The cars are less polished. Scooters are the preferred mode of transport, giving the streets a chaotic, noisy feel. Much of the place seems like a throwback to the 1950s and 1960s when this really did seem like an exciting bridgehead for the West in a largely hostile region.

Andrew Yang of the Chinese Council of Advanced Policy Studies points me to some statistics. Taiwan's investment in China has just reached a staggering $70 billion, almost catching up America's. In other words, Taiwan and China are already heavily integrated, and that is just the way Taiwan's business community wants it. Yang insists there is no appetite for going back. He points out that according to a recent opinion poll, although fewer than 12 percent of the Taiwanese population is in favor of political unification, only 17 percent now supports independence. Change will come slowly, but it will come, and economic interests will take the lead. "Most people want the status quo, in order to let the next generation determine Taiwan's status," Yang says. "For the moment, people are keen to develop other links with the mainland."[24]

That is the strategy of the new government, which has unashamedly developed warm ties with the Chinese Communists. The main objectives are to secure a military truce and pursue financial ties. Yang insists that neither of the two main parties will barter Taiwan's civil liberties in return for economic gain. "We have ninety-eight political parties here, including our very own Communist Party. I love taking Chinese officials to the Central Administration building, and showing the Falun Gong lot protesting outside. I tell them that when they allow that and religion, then they will make progress," he says. But with so many Taiwanese now traveling to and working on the mainland—more than a million Taiwanese, out of a total Taiwanese population of 23 million, are regular travelers or short-term residents in China—I have my doubts. Such rights will surely prove expendable as the mother country absorbs the tiny island.

Within weeks of the KMT's return to power, a deal was signed establishing charter flights between Taipei and mainland cities. In December 2008 those links were significantly expanded, with more than dozen routes every day to a growing number of destinations. Over time, personal experience will have a more pronounced influence than politics, as people see the economic benefits of assimilation into the mainland, probably sweetened by a promise of autonomy of sorts—not unlike that of Hong Kong. Will Taiwan stay as it is, a strange mixture of 1950s' Americana, ancient Chinese custom, and Japanese tradition, spiced up by the sense of defiance that isolation often brings? I doubt it. Is this a case of Cuba in reverse, a case of catch-it-while-you-can, before China, with its inexorable power, absorbs this island without a shot being fired?

Such was the nervousness during the Olympics that television stations across China were ordered to delay "live" broadcasts by ten seconds, to give them a chance to abandon transmission in case members of Free Tibet or other protesters caused trouble. Half a year later, the authorities in Beijing expected no such embarrassment as they planned their live coverage from Washington of Barack Obama's inauguration speech. The incoming president was only a few minutes into his address when he declared: "Recall that earlier generations faced down fascism and communism not just with missiles and tanks, but with sturdy alliances and enduring convictions." The broadcast abruptly cut away from the lectern, leaving the anchorwoman in Beijing and the Washington correspondent on the studio screen mumbling a conversation together about Obama's economic policy in a desperate attempt to fill the airtime. They made valiant efforts over several minutes to ensure that viewers did not hear the president's thoughts about liberty, particularly this sentence: "Those who cling to power through corruption and deceit and the silencing of dissent, know that you are on the wrong side of history." The time difference—it was 1:00 A.M. in Beijing—ensured that not as many people were watching as might have been. Just to be sure, the official censors deleted these and other offending remarks from the translations that followed later in the day. It did not take long, however, for the Internet to be filled with comment about the ultra-sensitivity of the state. More people than before went to various websites to watch the speech in full.

Any hopes that the clampdown during the Olympics would be relaxed once the foreign guests had all gone home proved illusory. Censorship, particularly on the Internet, only increased. A number of campaigns were launched against what the authorities called dangerous or vulgar websites. In one move, the authorities ordered that nineteen sites be shut down for failing to censor content that was considered inappropriate and harmful to young people's physical and mental health. These included Google and China's own Baidu, the world's largest search engines, which, according to the China Internet Illegal Information Center, provide links to a "huge quantity of pornographic sites."[25] A top official in China's Internet Affairs Bureau, Liu Zhengrong, told a media forum in Beijing that the authorities must be vigilant: "You have to check the channels one by one, the programs one by one, the pages one by one," he said. "You must not miss any step. You must not leave any unchecked corners."[26]

In December 2008, some three hundred intellectuals had caused a stir when they posted an online political manifesto they called Charter 08. It was issued to mark the sixtieth anniversary of the United Nations Declaration on Human Rights. The name was intended to recall that of Charter 77, the human rights manifesto circulated by dissidents in Communist Czechoslovakia in 1997. This new document called for everything from private ownership of land to multiparty democracy; it said social tensions and protests were increasing, "indicating a tendency towards a disastrous loss of control." Democratization, it concluded, could "no longer be delayed."[27]

The Communist Party's success and comparative popularity has rested on four pillars: a military security-blanket presence, control over the media, the co-opting of the most important groups in society (particularly the middle class), and double-digit economic growth. Is the edifice that transformed China's place in the world and sustained the party in power about to founder as the economy falters? Before the financial crisis came along, many intellectuals and members of the middle class—on whom the party depended for its support—had adopted a purely pragmatic view of one-party rule. They had seen it succeed, and they had concluded that it was the best means of ensuring security and prosperity. With the global downturn in the economy, all this has changed. Prosperity is no longer ensured. So is the pact beginning to break? It is certainly facing its most severe test since 1989. The dilemma for the leadership is acute. If the party loosens up too much, it could unleash a repeat of the protests that shook the state at Tiananmen. If the Communist Party does not provide enough safety valves for the discontented, it could break apart under the strain.

The rise in unemployment and the potentially dangerous demographic shifts involved could cause some dissatisfaction with the status quo. With tens of millions of workers no longer required in the cities, what would happen if a large proportion of them refused to go home and stay in their villages? Dissidents are taking advantage of the downturn by attempting to organize. Yet stability will be threatened only if a large enough segment of the population concludes that it cannot afford to sit out the crisis and that political change would be worth the upheaval. For many Chinese, particularly those who remember the old days under Mao, what matters is that they have more freedom to determine the course of their own lives than they had before.

The pact made with the post-Tiananmen generation, and the political and human rights clampdown that accompanied it, has been remarkably successful in delivering Chinese from the chaos they so fear. Yet this pact is not static. It is dynamic and uncertain. Those who have been co-opted into it have yet to determine whether it is temporary— the "China isn't ready for greater public freedoms" school of thought—

or it marks a principled and long-term view that such rights are inimical to China's needs. In other words, are the human rights set out in the UN declaration a Western construct, as ultra-nationalists argue, or will China, in time, begin to adopt them? For the moment, many Chinese believe that it is only by keeping out of the public realm that they have won more liberty in the private realm. They ask if they could have achieved the prosperity and security that they demanded from the pact by any other means, but it is a rhetorical question. Many insist that the answer is no.

In any case, the West's performance has surely not convinced them of another route. When Zhou Xiaochuan, the governor of the People's Bank of China, spoke of "the inherent vulnerabilities and systemic risks" in the dollar-based global economy, political leaders around the world took note, and took fright.[28] They could see that he was talking about more than currencies. They knew that, whatever short-term turbulence lay ahead, he was reflecting China's greater assertiveness about its role in the world, and its greater confidence in the political model it had chosen to adopt.

CHAPTER 3

Russia

Angry Capitalist

> Ordinary people wearied of their unprecedented
> freedom to criticise the government because it had
> brought no improvement.

LILIA SHEVTSOVA,
political analyst

It's a summer Saturday afternoon at the Moscow Beach Club. The sand
has been imported from the Maldives. Champagne and fresh lobsters are
being served, and we're invited outside for the entertainment. Two MCs
are extolling the virtues of a luxury car, while pole dancers are gyrating on
a platform. It is drizzling. I enter into conversation with a young man who
works for the British department store B&Q. He berates me over the
United Kingdom's "aggressive" foreign policy toward Russia, while munch-
ing on and slurping his seafood. I don't much feel like answering him, so I
make my excuses and move on. I run into Russia's top television soccer
commentator, Viktor Gusev, and we engage in a more enjoyable exchange,
about the relative merits of each of our countries' national teams.

My spirits lighten further when the band topping the bill begins its
set. Mumi Troll has been around for years, with its mix of rock and

balladeering. My friend Art Troitsky, Russia's top rock promoter, is invited to the stage to introduce them; as they begin to play, I start to understand why they're so popular. I make out some of the lyrics, from the comprehensible "I left my motherland behind" in one song to the incomprehensible "don't inject yourself with a school of dolphins" in another. Later, Art takes me backstage. This time it's no fancy cocktails—just malt whisky served in plastic cups—and some very good chat with the band and its lead singer, Ilya Lagutenko. Around midnight, they leave. We go to another beach party, this one at Rublyovka beach. Normal-looking young Russians—no swagger, no bling—dance to a Brazilian samba band. Others are swimming in the river. As ever with Russia, I am disheartened and heartened in quick succession.

Russia's embrace of conspicuous consumption was the most pronounced of any emerging market. I first visited the country in the late 1970s and have traveled there regularly ever since, with two stints as a correspondent, one in the mid-1980s and one during the heady years of the early 1990s. Early on, I saw the Soviet Union in stagnation and not-so-blissful isolation. The joke was, "We pretend to work, they pretend to pay us." I returned to witness the turbulent years of *glasnost* (openness) and *perestroika* (restructuring) under Mikhail Gorbachev, and later to see his plans first undermined, then accelerated, by Boris Yeltsin. After the unsuccessful putsch of 1991 and the collapse of the USSR that it precipitated, the new Russia underwent a new revolution. It was as much a revolution of the individual mind as it was of the political world. Millions of Russians lost their fear, began questioning authority, and embraced the free expression that blossomed.

That is, of course, not how this era was subsequently portrayed by Vladimir Putin. Instead, the 1990s were to become known as "the decade of chaos." Such thinking revolves around a narrative of "the Russia we lost" (a term borrowed from the title of a popular and compelling film by Stanislav Govorukhin). Many Russians see this as the era of a gold-digging elite combining with the criminal underworld to divide up the spoils; many in the West berate themselves for losing the opportunity to consolidate Russia's move toward democracy. The greater Western error, which was manifested around the world, was to see free markets and democracy as indistinguishable. The mistake began in the late 1980s under Mikhail Gorbachev with "shock therapy," the monetarist theory that decreed the privatization of almost anything that belonged to the state. It was decreed by Western government and international institutions as the Holy Grail that, bizarrely, was supposed to contain the key to a more democratic political outcome. This approach reached its peak in the first years of the post-Communist era, after the failed coup of 1991 led to Gorbachev's ouster and the arrival of Boris Yeltsin as head of a new post-Communist Russia. I remember attending countless press conferences held by the government's young economics and finance ministers, watching as their Western advisers acted as their puppet masters. These westerners displayed an excess of zeal and a shortage of political foresight. The West's overall approach during the 1990s was a mix of condescension, ingratiation, and insensitivity. Russian liberals responded with a cultural obeisance that would later transform itself into resentment.

An entire country's natural resources, mainly oil and gas, were put up for sale at rock-bottom prices. They were snapped up by those in power, by those close to power, and by anyone who was lucky or smart. The first generation of oligarchs arose in a society almost free of rules. Between 1991 and 1996, the Russian state effectively absented itself from the policing of society. Distinctions between legality and illegality, and between morality and immorality, barely existed. There were no hard and fast definitions of organized crime, money laundering, or extortion; commercial transactions entered a sort of limbo where no one knew whether they were legal or illegal—they seemed to be both at the same time. And those engaging in the transactions worked in tandem with the political and security elite, all of whom shared in the spoils.

The first phase of the embrace of capitalism came to a sudden halt in 1998 as "pyramid" investments and other wealth-siphoning schemes came crashing down. Russia stunned international investors by defaulting on its debts, triggering a run on the ruble. As Yeltsin's authority

collapsed, the oligarchs consolidated their position. The most important of these oligarchs was Boris Berezovsky, the man who had taken
control of Channel One television, called ORT. Berezovsky had open
access to people who counted—especially Yeltsin's daughter and her
husband. Together they orchestrated the government, chopping and
changing prime ministers to their liking (in Yeltsin's eight years as president he appointed five prime ministers). All the while, even as a tiny
minority enriched itself, the nation's infrastructure collapsed. The state
failed to pay tens of millions of its workers—from soldiers, to police officers, doctors, and teachers—for months on end. Life expectancy declined; several contagious diseases that had been eliminated in the USSR
returned; and schools and hospitals became dilapidated as investment
dried up. Of the people I knew, those who had dealt with money did
well. Those with talent in other areas, from science to the arts, including
teachers and doctors, saw not just their living standards collapse, but
their sense of pride and identity wither. They had invested their hopes in
the new order, and it had let them down.

Yet for all the disappointments, Russians enjoyed unprecedented
freedoms. The country opened up dramatically. I visited several previously closed regions, in one trip meeting military top brass at the Arc-
tic nuclear base at Novaya Zemlya; in another hiring a military
helicopter in Kamchatka, close to Alaska, and inviting twenty members of the local community, including the priest, to join us on a tour
of the area. I hunted deer in the snows of Siberia with Mikhail Kalash-
nikov, the inventor of the assault rifle that bears his name, and paid a
visit to one of the leaders of the 1991 coup, former prime minister
Valentin Pavlov, shortly after his release from Lefortovo prison. Everyone felt free to speak out. Newspapers sprang up. A whole new generation of journalists who felt unhindered by libel laws or other concerns
over censorship wrote in dailies such as *Sevodnya* (Today) and *Nezavisimaya Gazeta* (the Independent). I got to know Svetlana Sorokina,
one of Russia's best-known TV anchors, who had made her name in
the late 1980s, at the tail end of the Gorbachev era, by refusing to read
out certain items of propaganda on the evening news. She and others,

such as Yevgeny Kiselyov, with his Sunday night show *Itogi*, broke new ground in television news and analysis. They would talk excitedly about tough interviews they had done or scandals that had been revealed. NTV, a new station funded by Vladimir Gusinsky, one of the most prominent of the first generation of oligarchs, was perhaps the biggest breakthrough. It developed a new style of investigative reporting, political analysis—and satire.

Gusinsky, a man of some political principle who nevertheless could not resist money, epitomized the best and the worst of Russia at that moment in history. Like so many Russians of the period, he defined himself through his rapid accumulation of wealth. I got to know him and his wife quite well, and it was a curious thing to watch an intelligent but unflamboyant theater director succumb to the excesses of bling. In Moscow, he enjoyed entertaining guests to lavish banquets presided over by white-gloved waiters. He considered these not special occasions, but ordinary dinners. In London, he luxuriated in a similar lifestyle. On one occasion he seemed to enjoy sending back the lobster he had ordered in a restaurant, complaining that it was too small. He could not resist showing guests the swimming pool in his Chelsea mansion. At the same time, through NTV and *Sevodnya*, he was determined to play his part in Russia's democratization. Most damagingly, though, he seemed not to fully grasp how the democratic process should work. He and six other oligarchs, including Berezovsky, bankrolled Yeltsin's reelection campaign in 1996, allowing television to once again become a propaganda tool. Russian liberals never mentioned the president's alcoholism and deteriorating health. Nor did Western embassies. They knew exactly what was going on but decided that free expression should not get in the way of electoral success. They insisted that the ends justified the means—that if Yeltsin was forced out, Russia would return to a dark age of repression. Free expression was abused in the apparent cause of liberal democracy.

As the 1990s drew to a close, Yeltsin became a source of derision. The more his bouts of drinking and the weaknesses of the economy were exposed, the louder the clamor became for "stability." Those same oligarchs who had manipulated the process to extend Yeltsin's tenure now saw the need for a quick and orderly succession. They trawled through a list of possible candidates and alighted on Putin, an undistinguished former KGB officer whom they had recently installed as the latest of their prime ministers. He had performed well in that post for them, displaying a tough professionalism. His decision to wage war on rebels in Chechnya was proving popular. Russia was beginning to assert itself again.

On the eve of the millennium, Yeltsin startled his country by announcing that he was handing over the reins of government to his prime minister, effective immediately. Putin's rise met the needs not only of many ordinary Russians, but of corporate interest, too. In any case, democracy had been bankrupted well before he assumed his powers. Three months later, Putin secured the necessary "endorsement" of the people, thanks to an election that had been fixed by the oligarchs. They threw money at the campaign, just as they had done in 1996, and ensured that Putin's opponents were denounced at every turn. His more serious rivals, such as the mayor of Moscow, Yuri Luzhkov, and former prime minister Yevgeny Primakov, had been "encouraged" not to stand. The oligarchs suggested to Putin that he must keep to his side of the bargain, that he must deliver on his promises. Those promises were to restore order but to leave the business empires alone. That was the pact between Putin and the new business tycoons. And it was a pact that was more invidious than the ones operating in China and other states in transition because it was portrayed as being in the interests of democracy.

Putin did not take long to assert his authority, and he altered the terms of engagement with those who had installed him. Within weeks of taking over, and even before his "election," the Kremlin ordered the arrest of a well-known reporter from Radio Liberty. Andrei Babitsky's dispatches from Chechnya posed a direct threat to Putin. One of the pretexts for the Second Chechen War was the assertion that Chechens had been responsible for the bombing of apartment blocks in three Russian cities, in which three hundred people were killed. Babitsky was one of those who investigated claims that the terrorist attacks could have been ordered by the Russian security forces. He was charged with spying, held in an isolation cell, interrogated, and then handed over to the Chechen rebels in exchange for two Russian soldiers, as if he were a terrorist.

Putin's message was clear: The media must see itself as a mechanism for delivery, not as an outlet for criticism, least of all as a plaything for business. He then turned on the oligarchs. Gusinsky was arrested and detained for four days. After his case was publicized in international media, the charges were dropped and he was released. He left for Spain, spent a few months in the United Kingdom, then went to Israel, where he is also a citizen, and back to Spain, all in a self-imposed exile to avoid possible arrest if he were to return to Russia. Berezovsky also fled Russia, hopping on his private jet and heading for Britain, where he was granted asylum after Russia charged him in absentia with fraud and money laundering. Putin could have stopped them both from leaving the country, but he appeared content to see them go, apparently assuming they would trouble him less from afar. Berezovsky did not oblige him. From his mansion outside London, he led a personal campaign against Putin, and as a result he was the object of repeated extradition requests from the Kremlin. But what mattered most to Putin was that Gusinsky and Berezovsky had been forced to give up their media power bases. In their absence, their stations and newspapers became organs of the Kremlin, with Putin calculating that any damage to his reputation from the takeovers would be limited. He was right. In the height of this first purge, in November 2000, one poll found that only 7 percent of Russians thought that the main networks were independent to begin with, against 79 percent who thought they were dependent on the oligarchs. In other words, many wondered whether what they had seen of democracy was worth saving.

Putin had changed the terms of his pact with the first generation of oligarchs. They had put him in power, but within months of taking over, he summoned several of them to a meeting where he made his position plain. He consolidated his power and rewrote the rules. These rules now read: I will leave you alone to make money—so make sure I enjoy my cut, but steer well away from the public realm, unless I tell you otherwise. Those who challenged him would come to regret it.

In 2003, Mikhail Khodorkovsky, an oligarch who had become one of the major players with his oil corporation, Yukos, was seized on charges of fraud and tax evasion. He had riled the Kremlin not with his business expansion, but with his political ambitions: He had made the mistake of advertising his credentials as a potential rival to Putin and financing opposition parties in the lower house of parliament, the Duma. The arrest and subsequent trial sent shock waves through Russia and the international financial community. Putin wanted it known that nobody was above the law, his law. "We have a category of people who have become billionaires, as we say, overnight," he declared. "They got the impression that the gods themselves slept on their heads and that everything is permitted to them." Khodorkovsky was sentenced to nine years in a Siberian labor camp.[1]

Putin knew, and he knew that everyone else knew, that he had chosen a single scapegoat. He could have chosen to make an example of any of several oligarchs, but Khodorkovsky's ambitions had been the most brazen. Putin also knew that nobody with serious business ambitions would complain. The Khodorkovsky case led not just to the silencing of dissenting voices in business, but also to the takeover of private enterprise by the security and intelligence elite, the *siloviki*. In short, it dictated the country's entire economic and political course. The robber baron capitalism of the early Yeltsin years had been brought firmly under the Kremlin's control. Key to that was the consolidation of the lucrative energy sector. Under what came to be known as "velvet reprivatization," the boards of Russia's biggest companies—from the oil and gas giants to airlines and railways—were now dominated by Putin's allies. Everyone did well, politically and financially, out of the arrangement, particularly the president. It was dubbed "Kremlin Inc."

In 2004, I was invited to meet Putin. It was part of the inaugural meeting of the Valdai Club, which aimed to host an annual discussion group of experts from Russia and the West. Our arrival coincided with the start of the Beslan school massacre in the northern Caucasus. It was impossible not to feel revulsion at the ruthlessness of the killers as the event unfolded before our eyes on live TV. But my discussions with politicians, journalists, and academics in those fraught few days were dispiriting. One or two editors showed courage, such as Raf Shakirov of *Izvestiya*, a paper that was once a government mouthpiece but had become a serious and critical voice. Shakirov was sacked after his paper reported that the number of hostages in the school was much greater than officials had said. Others whom I had previously regarded as liberals had morphed into nationalistic xenophobes, blaming outsiders for their country's ills and refusing to consider the context for Beslan (two bloody Russian incursions into Chechnya). Was this a genuine ideological conversion, a case of second their masters, or an attempt to deflect attention from the incompetence of the security forces? The politics of grievance, one of the least attractive facets of Soviet political life, remained as ingrained as ever in capitalist Russia. Someone else was always to blame for the country's woes. It was a gut instinct that seemed to be shared as much by the rich as by the poor, as much by those who knew the West well as by those who did not.

I assumed that, with a national terrorist emergency raging, a social gathering with a group of foreigners might not be at the top of the president's agenda. When word came that our event had not been canceled, I surmised that it would consist of cursory handshakes in the Kremlin. Instead, we were bused to Putin's official suburban residence. As we arrived in Novo-Ogarevo, amid the opulent homes of the new suburban elite, we were taken to an anteroom containing a pool table and a plasma television set. There, we watched the eight o'clock news on Channel 2, which had now become the most loyal of all the loyal Russian channels. Its reporters failed to ask any of the hard questions about how the Beslan rescue attempt had been so botched, about how the authorities could have underestimated the number of people inside the school—it had been the first day of the term, and children and teachers had been accompanied by parents and grandparents. Most important of all, pliant journalists failed to ask why Chechnya had disintegrated to its current state. What we did see was image after image of bodies being buried, of mothers and fathers wailing uncontrollably in the pouring rain, of a boy singing "Ave Maria" to a silent crowd in St. Petersburg.

Eventually we were taken upstairs, with the warning that the president was in no mood for this meeting. With a wave of the hand, he beckoned us to a long, rectangular table covered with a white cloth. We were seated in alphabetical order and, as Putin invited questions, I was one of those who tentatively raised our hands. He pointed across the table at me. By way of introduction, I offered our collective condolences. I did not wish to sound insensitive, I ventured, but surely his policy toward Chechnya had some bearing on the broader problem? For the next thirty minutes, Putin gave an uninterrupted exegesis of Russia's recent history. His eyes were fixed and expressionless; he never hesitated or looked at notes. He conceded that the Chechens had suffered terrible hardship during Stalin's deportations. They had fought more valiantly than anyone else in defense of the Soviet motherland against fascism. He also suggested that he might not have done what Boris Yeltsin did in 1994 when he unleashed the first of the modern Chechen wars. "I don't know how I would have acted; maybe yes, maybe no. But mistakes were made," Putin said.

Putin explained that, after the Russians withdrew, Chechnya received what it wanted: "de facto independence." But local leaders allowed it to become run down, encouraged extremism, and turned it into a launch pad for terrorists across Russia. "The vacuum was filled by radical fundamentalism of the worst kind," he said. Men and women were shot by firing squad and beaten with sticks. In 1999, by which point Putin was prime minister, the Russian government had no choice but to go back in, if only to prevent violence spreading beyond Chechnya's border into neighboring Dagestan. All the while, Russia searched for political leaders to talk to: "We even tried to deal with people who were bearing arms against us. We have done what you asked for," Putin told us. The status of Chechnya was not the issue, he said. The independence question had been subverted by Islamists with a bigger goal.

His arguments, if selective in their use of history, were carefully framed and fluently put. It was only when he referred to Beslan that he allowed his emotions to show. Even at his angriest, however, he appeared always to remain in control. He finished his treatise—we were still on question number one—by inviting me to ask myself a question: "Would you like it if people who shoot children in the back come to power, anywhere on this planet? If you asked yourself that, you wouldn't ask any more questions about Russian policy."

Chechnya, Putin told us, was not Iraq. "It is not a faraway land. It is a crucial part of our territory. This is about Russia's territorial integrity." "Certain foreign" elements were encouraging the violence, he said, just to make problems for Russia: "We've observed incidents. It's a replay of the mentality of the Cold War. There are certain people who want us to be focused purely on our internal problems. They pull strings here so that we don't raise our heads internationally." This was a classic Soviet-era reprise about outsiders, particularly from the West, seeking to destabilize Russia and undermine its interests. Russia, he insisted, no longer had "imperial" pretensions beyond its borders. It was not comfortable with the enlargement of the North Atlantic Treaty Organization (NATO) to include once-Soviet Baltic states. He did not see why so-called "partners"—another euphemism for the West—wanted to fly fighter jets alongside Russian airspace. This, he added, resorting to another Soviet-era word, was nothing but a "provocation." His country did not have the resources to guard its borders properly. A weak and unstable Russia was in nobody's interests. "Has anyone given a thought to what would happen if Russia were eliminated?"

It was hard not to sympathize with much of what he said. Putin's growing hostility stemmed in part from the West's failed analysis of the psychology of modern Russia; it also captured a widely held view among ordinary Russians about what they saw as double standards in the West following 9/11. Moscow had rendered help to Washington to fight terrorism, but what help had the West ever offered Russia to help with the Chechnyan problem? Consider the Russian concessions: They had closed an intelligence-gathering post in Cuba and a naval base in Vietnam, and had given the United States a green light to use airbases in Central Asia to support the invasion of Afghanistan. The Kremlin assumed it would enjoy greater understanding of its concerns in return.

Putin's suspicions had been raised in November 2003 when popular protests in Georgia had forced the Soviet-era president, Eduard Shevardnadze, out of office, ushering in a pro-American administration led by the U.S.-educated Mikheil Saakashvili. The "Rose revolution," in which pro-opposition demonstrators handed soldiers red roses as they forced the government to stand down, was seen in Western capitals, particularly by neoconservatives in Washington, as the ultimate expression of people power; for Moscow it was a flagrant example of American manipulation of public opinion and the duplicity of democratic rhetoric. Putin's concerns would be heightened less than a year later by similar events in Ukraine. The election campaign there of November 2004 was marred by accusations of Moscow's role in the poisoning of the pro-Western Viktor Yushchenko and the disputed victory of the pro-Kremlin candidate, Viktor Yanukovych. Following mass rallies, a run-off was ordered, and the "Orange" forces—supporters of the pro-Western opposition, who adorned the streets with orange ribbons—took control of a deeply divided country. For East and West these two former Soviet republics became the focal point not just of a geostrategic struggle—as NATO membership was dangled in front of Georgia and Ukraine—but an ideological one as well. It became essentially a zero-sum game. Russian resentment would grow even stronger as America developed plans for missile defense and radar systems in Poland and the Czech Republic, and supported Kosovo's declaration of independence.

Still, during our session with him in 2004, Putin was prepared to give Bush the benefit of the doubt. He showed no restraint, however, when it came to critical forces within Russia itself. We asked him his views on freedom of speech. It was, he said, an essential part of a country's development, but journalists, too, had to be "efficient." He likened the relationship between state and media to something he had seen in an Italian film; he wouldn't say which one. Maybe he had learned the phrase from his friend Silvio Berlusconi. "The role of the real man is to make advances," Putin told us. "The role of the real woman is to resist them."

We had got through several cups of black tea and finished our individual fruit sponge cakes. It was beyond midnight. We had been with our host for almost four hours. Which other world leader would have given a bunch of foreigners so much "face time," especially at the height of an emergency? Putin struck me as extraordinarily eager to be understood. Before he released us, he wanted one final word on Chechnya. He was prepared to open a dialogue, but not with "child killers," he said. "I don't advise you to meet [Osama] bin Laden, to invite him to Brussels and NATO or to the White House, to hold talks with him and let him dictate what he wants so that he then leaves you alone." He simply could not understand how people abroad could see things differently. Did we have no conscience? With that he stood up and walked around the room, shaking our hands, his eyes firmly fixed on each and every one of us.

Earlier that day, I had gone to a metro station, Rizhskaya, which I had used to go to work when I first lived in Moscow in the mid-1980s. The station forecourt had become a shrine, the latest of several across Russia to victims of the new terror. Along a wall, people had placed carnations, photographs, and poems to their loved ones. On the evening of August 31, 2004, a "black widow," as Chechen female suicide bombers are now called, blew herself up outside the station, by a row of shops. I took the escalator down to the train, past the advertisements for DVD players and detergents. On the intercom, a recorded message asked travelers to look out for suspicious packages and to inform on suspicious people. But to whom should they report their suspicions? Surely they wouldn't expect anything of the young policemen slouching against a railing? In the carriages, everyone looked at everyone else, wondering what they might be planning, but they all knew that they were powerless to do anything about it. My mind wandered to what Putin had said in his TV address to the nation: "We showed ourselves to be weak, and the weak get beaten." I also considered the term *zhurnalyuga*, journalist-scum, which had become popular with Putin and his entourage.

In that same week, two prominent journalists had been prevented, in suspicious circumstances, from reaching Beslan. One was held by police at Moscow's Vnukovo airport after an altercation with a drunk that seemed to have been planned. That was Radio Liberty's Babitsky, who had continued his fearless work. Another collapsed on a plane heading to the Caucasus after being given a cup of poisoned tea. That was Anna Politkovskaya, Russia's most famous investigative reporter and commentator. What mattered to Putin was that the media did not sully his reputation as the man delivering order—hence the use of the word "efficient."

Since 2003, in its worldwide press-freedom index, the organization Reporters Without Borders has each year ranked Russia between 140th and 147th out of roughly 170 countries in the world. It has usually occupied places similar to Afghanistan, Yemen, Saudi Arabia, and Zimbabwe, although it has ended up marginally ahead of Singapore and China. Unlike the regimes of those countries with worse rankings, the Russian authorities have focused less on preventive legislation and more on punitive thuggery. The International Committee to Protect Journalists says Russia is the third most deadly country for reporters. The Russian Union of Journalists estimates that more than two hundred have been killed in ten years. In not a single case has the mastermind been arrested.

The most famous case was that of Politkovskaya herself, who was gunned down in the lift of her apartment block in October 2006. Her work in the Caucasus broke new ground, infuriating the Kremlin. And yet, while lesser-known writers had been killed or injured, there was a sense that her fame rendered her a little safer. Not so. Roman Shleinov, an investigative journalist at the paper where they both worked, explained why: "Journalism becomes a threat and a serious irritant when it begins to influence social dynamics. Politkovskaya's reports had this effect because they were seen by foreign human rights organisations as an alternative source of information. She had become more than a journalist: she was a social activist. It is not criticism of the Kremlin itself that endangers Russian journalists, but the threat they pose to an old system of relationships which benefits a tiny minority of people. And that will not be permitted."[2]

Politkovskaya's death alarmed journalists and human rights groups around the world. In Russia, the reaction was passionate among the dwindling band of liberals, but most people seemed to take it with equanimity. When pressed to comment, Putin said Politkovskaya's influence on Russian politics had been "negligible."[3] It took many months for an investigation to be launched. Eventually, three hit men were put on trial, but in February 2009 they were acquitted. Few were surprised, as the case against them had proven flimsy. The investigators had simply gone through the motions. The people who had ordered the killing were not to be touched. The involvement of the state in an assassination such as this might have been more of a scandal during the late Gorbachev era, or throughout Yeltsin's years, but not under Putin's regime. When the interests of power structures are threatened by independent reporting, contract killers function as the ultimate censors.

Politkovskaya's murder was just the latest in a long line of killings. Journalists and opposition politicians, notably Galina Starovoitova, a prominent liberal, who was gunned down in her St. Petersburg apartment block in 1998, had been targeted in the Yeltsin era, too. But in Putin's time, the frequency of these killings increased, as did the confidence of those ordering them. In 2003, Yuri Shchekochikhin, deputy editor of *Novaya Gazeta* and deputy chairman of parliament's scrutiny committee, died at the age of fifty-three of a mysterious allergy. Nobody for a moment believed his death was due to natural causes. I had known him in the late 1980s and early 1990s; he had been elected to the Congress of People's Deputies, the first and only semi-free parliament the Soviet Union ever had, in 1990. Its chaotic, freewheeling style gave him a taste for trying to turn campaigning into action. Fearless but also eminently practical, Shchekochikhin was a prominent figure in the Gorbachev and Yeltsin years, joining many Muscovites in defending their fledgling democracy during the coup of 1991. Most of that crowd had since disappeared into their consumerist cocoon. He, and a few with him, kept going. As a public opponent of the Chechen war and as a scourge of the KGB and its successors, he had made many enemies.

In provincial Russia, not just reporters but anyone who gets on the wrong side of the authorities and their business and criminal associates is liable to summary punishment. "Local authorities react to publications far more ruthlessly than federal ones," said Shleinov. "The heads of local administrations have free rein in their dealings with journalists. On their own territory, they are small-time 'tsars,' and they mimic the central authorities in exaggerated form."[4] There is a certain similarity with China, where excess in the regions may be greater than in the center, but where the national leadership sets the overall parameters.

When Putin was asked how he would respond to critics who accuse him of limiting media freedom, he once replied: "Very simply. We have never had freedom of speech in Russia, so I don't really understand what could be stifled. It seems to me that freedom is the ability to express one's opinion, but certain boundaries must exist, as laid out in the law."[5] This is a Russian version of the Singaporean "out-of-bound markers," although usually with a stairwell as the venue and a semi-automatic as the means. Journalists such as these who have been either killed or imprisoned, along with a tiny group of human rights activists and lawyers, had broken what the commentator Masha Lipman has called Russia's equivalent of the "non-participation pact." The public agreed not to meddle in politics in exchange for the chance to take part in the consumer benefits of the Russian energy boom.

The Putin era may now be unraveling as Russia reels from the global financial crisis, but in his eight years as president, from 2000 to 2008, he oversaw the greatest period of economic growth and political stability his country had witnessed for a generation. And how the place boomed: A country that had almost gone bust in 1998 built up the world's third-largest foreign exchange reserves. GDP per capita rose from less than $2,000 in 1998 to $9,000 at the start of 2008. With income tax a flat 13 percent, and with every Russian given their own flat free as the Soviet era ended, disposable income was higher than these figures suggested. Unlike in many Western countries, mortgages and excessive consumer debt were rare. It was all based on skyrocketing prices for commodities on global markets. Every $1 rise in the price of a barrel of oil represented a $1 billion increase in government receipts. The Kremlin was cautious in its budget preparations, assuming a fall in prices, and amassed a $160 billion stabilization fund from surplus revenue. Officials thought that would be enough to protect the country from any sudden shocks.

Not everyone benefited, by any means. Most pensioners struggled to make ends meet; some people had their homes snatched from them by various developers' scams; others had failed to recover from the pyramid schemes of the last economic crash. Vulnerable members of society continued to suffer, as they had done in the 1990s. But what mattered was that *enough* people were doing *sufficiently* well and considered themselves to be *sufficiently* free in their personal lives. Those doing well did extraordinarily well. Sports cars, designer shops, and expensive restaurants had, by the mid-2000s, become the norm for a small but significant portion of the population in the big cities. Moscow was said to have the best sushi outside Japan. It boasted more 6-series BMWs than any other city in the world, and it was predicted that Russia would overtake Germany to become the world's biggest market in luxury cars. This wealth helped foster a revival of national self-confidence—the belief that Russians could once again hold their heads high in international company. That self-confidence continued to be manifested in a mixture of hubris and grievance.

Putin had promised his people a new pact, or, rather, the return to an old one in a modern setting. Return the public realm to those in the know, and in exchange the population would receive the security it had lost. Although prosperity was the preserve of a few, the restoration of basic order meant that public-sector workers and others who had not shared in the wealth would at least enjoy a stable and regular income. The main difference between the Putin years and the Soviet era was in the private realm. Putin had no intention of reimposing a travel ban, or dictating where people lived or worked. Individuals were free to go as they pleased and live life as they desired, as long as they did not cause trouble.

In those terms, Putin had delivered. Wealth, which several generations of Russians had never enjoyed, was the perfect antidote to political involvement. The concentration of authority in Putin's hands and the elimination of alternative sources of power resulted in an overwhelming indifference toward politics and the anesthetization of society through consumer goods.

Some journalists continued to take risks, even well into the Putin era. But many of the people I knew opted for a quiet life. Why rock the boat when you could enjoy the good life, paying little more than 10 percent in tax, taking your holidays in Cap Ferrat, and living inside one of the many gated "villages" that were springing up on the outskirts of Moscow? Such a trade-off was similar to that of my Singapore friends, except that I had seen many of these people in the early 1990s coming out to defend Yeltsin's fledgling democracy and vigorously engaging in the political debate. Now they had decided to withdraw.

They had joined the global pact and enjoying the privileges it afforded. I remember one evening in Moscow in May 2008. A billboard opposite the Bolshoi theater reminded passersby that Russia had just beaten Canada in the final of the World Ice Hockey Championships and that Zenit St. Petersburg had just beaten the Glasgow Rangers in the UEFA Cup Final in Manchester. "We do it better," the advertisement declared. The biggest achievement was still to come: the hosting of the dramatic Champions League showdown between Manchester United and my club, Chelsea. It marked, in the words of one Russian fellow supporter, that "Moscow's coming of age." I had witnessed many dramatic changes in Russia, but I still blinked when I saw Red

Square turned into a carnival, with English fans, who had been allowed to enter the country without visas, knocking soccer balls about outside Lenin's Tomb, and touts selling tickets. For the Kremlin, this important public-relations exercise was about to be trumped by something even better.

That Saturday was the final of the Eurovision Song Contest. My rock-promoter friend, Art Troitsky, had been invited onto the set of Channel 2 along with a carefully picked selection of entertainers and groupies. Live current affairs discussion programs had long since stopped, because the authorities did not want to risk the wrong kinds of comments being aired. But this was pure fun, surely. The outdoor stage was to intersperse reaction in Moscow to the live event, which was taking place in the Serbian capital, Belgrade. I was surprised, and intrigued, to be allowed to join Troitsky, but thought that, given the hapless performance of the British entry, I should stay silent. The Brit came last, and I duly kept my head down. The Russian entry, a solo ballad from one of the country's top stars, Dima Bilan, swept to victory. As Bilan performed his victory rendition of "Believe," draping a Russian flag across the stage, the Russian coverage switched to the Moscow studio. A succession of fur-coated, middle-aged showbiz types grabbed the microphone to proclaim how he deserved to win, how his victory proved Russia's greatness, and even how they all had their prime minister and president to thank for the victory. When it came to Troitsky, he said he thought the song was trash and the voting had been fixed among the Slavs and other countries of the former Soviet Union. Audible gasps all around. "Traitor," shouted one woman. "I thought you were a patriot," declared another. "I used to respect your work," said a third, "but now I see you for what you are."

Russian television has, in many respects, moved on from Soviet times. Its production values are slick. Its game shows and entertainment programs are just as popular as any around the world. It is a past master at dumbing down, producing celebrity pap as well as any Western country. It does not, however, do spontaneous expression of contrary views. Troitsky is not naive. He knew how to play the system

during Soviet times in order to get bands promoted. He had been at
the forefront of the Yeltsin revolution, being invited to present or appear on prominent shows on television and radio. Once Putin was in
power editors became more suspicious of him, but it took Troitsky a
while to find this out. He had been invited to take part in the celebrity
edition of the show *Who Wants to Be a Millionaire?* but the day before
it was due to be filmed one of the producers called to say the list of
contestants had changed. He apologized awkwardly, citing a "change
of circumstances." Other cases followed.

Troitsky's friend, the TV presenter Sorokina, asked the chairman of
the station, Konstantin Ernst, what was going on. Ernst told her: "You
know very well, Sveta. He's uncontrollable."[6] Shortly afterward,
Sorokina herself was taken off air. First, she was told that her evening
chat show would have to be pre-recorded from then on to prevent
"dangerous" opinions by guests and members of the audience from
being aired. Then the show was stopped altogether. In 2008, *Novaya
Gazeta* published an article on blacklists on Russian TV. Troitsky was
one of several people on it. The paper quoted a television source as
saying that one remark he had made on a show in 2004 had caused
particular offense to the Kremlin.[7] This is what he had said: "People
usually either trade freedom for security, or security for freedom; look
at recent Russian history in this respect—under the Communists we
had no freedom, but relative security; under Yeltsin we didn't have security, but there was plenty of freedom; with Putin, we've got neither
of the two."

Even as wily and prominent a figure as Troitsky was taken aback by
the fury directed at him that night on the Eurovision show. This, after
all, was only a question of popular music, hardly an issue of existential
importance to Russia. As we drove home in the early hours, he received a succession of texts, some supportive, from friends, but others
were threatening. He had broken the pact. The issue was not important enough to put him in harm's way, but he had been warned.

His colleagues had not needed to react the way they did. No overt
pressure had been applied. They chose to, however, seeing in their

flamboyant displays of patriotism perhaps more lucrative future contracts. The new business culture was working in harmony with authoritarian thinking.

Self-censorship has become a natural instinct among journalists and others in Russian public life. The human rights community, or what is left of it, is regarded as a bunch of incurable romantics; nongovernmental organizations are seen as agents of hostile foreign forces. Russia's parliament, which throughout Putin's tenure was a rubber-stamping body for the Kremlin, has passed a series of laws clamping down on what it calls "antistate behavior." One piece of legislation grants the security services the right to kill enemies of the state at home and abroad. Another gives law-enforcement agencies the right to view acts of dissent as forms of extremism or treason, crimes punishable by up to twenty years in prison. Treason has been redefined to include damaging Russia's constitutional order. Human rights advocates say this marks a return to Stalin's time. Again, few people complain.

As ever, Western countries displayed characteristic confusion and double standards in their dealings during the Putin era, just as they had done, in differing contexts, in Gorbachev's and Yeltsin's times. One of the ironies is that throughout this period the United Kingdom played host to Russia's economic boom, despite the fact that the two countries had a difficult political relationship. Britain had by 2006 become the second leading investor in Russia. Most of the money, however, was flowing the other way. When Peter Mandelson, one of Prime Minister Tony Blair's closest confidants, declared back in the mid-1990s that New Labour was "intensely relaxed about people getting filthy rich," perhaps even he did not realize quite what would ensue. London, under the Labour government, advertised itself to the new global elite as a less regulated and more tax-efficient place to do business than any of its rivals. The government provided far more attractive ways of avoiding paying tax (legally), and made it far less likely that you would be caught if you evaded paying tax (illegally), than almost any other government in Western Europe. It was no wonder that Russian oligarchs made the British capital their home. The city became known among Russians as Londongrad, where "ultra-high-net-worth individuals," as they were branded by the real-estate agents, could enjoy their luxuries undisturbed. A quarter of a million Russians settled there.

In summer 2007 I confronted Alistair Darling, the chancellor of the exchequer, over the "Londongrad" phenomenon. I asked him if there was anything Britain would not do to prostrate itself to the super-rich. Would the government even consider, as many had been urging, imposing a tax on nondomiciled residents? He looked bemused, confining himself to a smile. I told him many Russians I knew were perplexed at the laxity of the British government in letting in so many people with controversial records. He shrugged his shoulders, said I was "exaggerating" the problem, and murmured something about the British capital being the "world's financial hub." This was Britain's part in the pact.

British intelligence was concerned by this arrival of an entire subculture of fabulously wealthy individuals with dubious records. There was surprise among some at the Foreign Office about the decision to grant asylum to Boris Berezovsky. The security services noted a large rise in Russian Federal Security Service (FSB) activity, pointing to an inextricable link between Russian business and political interests. In April 2006 the U.K. government created the Serious Organised Crime Agency (SOCA), which would function along the lines of the FBI in the United States. Blair promised that the new body would "make life hell" for gangsters, drug barons, and people traffickers. The Russian mafia was one of the most powerful players in a crime industry said to be worth at least £20 billion in the United Kingdom. SOCA and its predecessor organizations had only one significant success: cooperating with the Russian authorities to arrest three small-scale computer hackers who had been blackmailing British and Irish bookmakers. They were sentenced in October 2006 to eight years each in jail. After that, the broader trail against Russian criminality went cold; when it came to the Russians, the British appeared reluctant to investigate all but low-grade crime such as drugs and prostitution. This reinforced a suspicion of an absence of political will in Whitehall to deal with Russian money laundering, as this might undermine the city's reputation as the world's financial capital.

Everyone was getting in on the act. Public relations companies were making their money on spreading Kremlin propaganda; financiers were striking deals. The extent of the camaraderie would later be laid bare in the unlikely setting of Corfu. It transpired that Mandelson, who would later be appointed business secretary in the Labour government, and the conservative shadow chancellor George Osborne had separately been ingratiating themselves with Oleg Deripaska, one of Russia's most controversial, and initially wealthy, oligarchs with close links to the Kremlin. Osborne's soliciting of money for his party became the bigger controversy, but Mandelson's actions might have caused more of a stir. What was the European Union's trade commissioner, as he was then, doing as a regular visitor on a luxury cruise ship owned by a tycoon who at that point had had his entry visa to the United States withdrawn?

In the House of Lords, members queued up to take on "consultancies" for various oligarchs. They earned handsome retainers for their job of providing dubious political respectability. One told me he was advising a financier on how to sue newspapers for delving into his business practices. Journalists showed an increasing reluctance to investigate corruption as the Russians began using British legal firms to threaten them. "We've been told to steer clear of the oligarchs," one national newspaper editor told me. "It's too much trouble."

Alastair Darling's apparent equanimity that day was even more startling given that, six months earlier, in November 2006, Alexander Litvinenko, a KGB operative turned dissident, had been poisoned in the heart of London. With that murder, the Kremlin had put down another marker—of the consequences, anywhere in the world, for any Russian challenging its supremacy. Initially, the British declared that, for all their indulgence on the economic front, they would take a stand on Litvinenko. The man at the center of this approach was Anthony Brenton, the British ambassador to Moscow. Brenton had already riled the Russians by attending opposition rallies. He urged Downing Street, in a number of private memos, to take a harder line on Putin, reporting without equivocation on the increasingly dictatorial tendencies of the Kremlin. A few weeks later, Britain said it had uncovered a plot to assassinate Berezovsky in London and announced that it was expelling four Russian diplomats in response to the Kremlin's refusal to hand over the man suspected of Litvinenko's murder. The Russians responded in kind, with tit-for-tat expulsions, while the vilification campaign against Brenton was intensified. Thugs from the Kremlin youth organization, Nashi, took to jumping in front of his ambassadorial car whenever it left the compound and heckling him at public meetings. The fact that they had apparently obtained copies of the ambassador's daily appointments diary, enabling them to trail him, reinforced suspicions of FSB involvement.

Nashi was not a fringe organization of headstrong young people. Established by Putin's deputy head of administration, Vladimir Surkov, it was central to the Kremlin's attempt to devise an ideology and a visible means of proselytizing it. Surkov, whose nickname was "the grey cardinal," coined the term "sovereign democracy," defining it as "a society's political life where the political powers, their authorities and decisions are decided and controlled by a diverse Russian nation for the purpose of reaching material welfare, freedom and fairness by all citizens, social groups and nationalities, by the people that formed it"—a somewhat convoluted way of saying that Russians could control their own destiny, keeping potentially hostile foreigners at bay.[8] His philosophy rejected the idea that there can be only one type of democracy and argued that each country should have the freedom and sovereignty to develop its own form. Nashi's adherents defined themselves through a combination of nationalism, anti-Western rhetoric, and animosity to "oligarchic capitalism" (although the cleverer oligarchs made sure they offered money to Nashi to keep its people at bay). Nashi argued that Russia was potentially a wealthy country, but that this wealth should not be confined to a small number of super-rich, with their propensity to live abroad and spend much of their money abroad. The organization presented itself as young, modern, and social, combining teenage adventures and frolics at a number of holiday camps with its more serious endeavors. Back in their home cities, followers had the opportunity to rough up their enemies, particularly those who took part in antigovernment demonstrations. Within a year of its creation, it numbered more than 200,000 members, of whom 10,000 were regular activists, or "commissars." Nashi thugs were increasingly used alongside Interior Ministry police to break up demonstrations. Often these took place away from Western cameras, though sometimes they were filmed. On one such occasion, in May 2007, a group of protesters, including members of the European Parliament, tried to draw attention to increasing hostility toward homosexuals in Russia. Several demonstrators, such as British human rights campaigner Peter Tatchell, were knocked to the ground and kicked. They, rather than their assailants, were arrested.

A month later, Brenton took it on himself to fly to London. It was the weekend of June 30 and July 1, just days after Gordon Brown had succeeded Blair in Downing Street. He insisted on briefing the new prime minister, and his young foreign secretary, David Miliband, on the dangers posed by Putin's Russia. Brenton told them that the Litvinenko killing was just the start and urged them to pursue a hard line, linking human rights and the rule of law to economic and political links.

Britain was involved in another, equally important struggle as well—over control of Russia's vast and lucrative energy reserves. Standing in the way of the Kremlin were the Western oil multinationals, particularly BP and Shell, which had secured a number of deals on what the Russians later complained were absurdly generous terms. BP had set up a joint venture, called TNK-BP, with a number of oligarchs, securing a 50 percent share at what the Russians would claim was a preferential rate. The Russian operation drove much of BP's growth during this period. It made a healthy profit, and the

Kremlin wanted to grab it back for its allies. Most foreign oil companies buckled under the pressure. Shell sold a large part of its stake in the $20 billion Sakhalin-2 project to the energy conglomerate Gazprom. BP held out. Its executives were hounded and harassed on the streets of Moscow, their offices were raided, and two young British-educated Russians were charged with spying. But Russia's political and business leaders held all the cards. They knew that eventually BP would fall into line, which is what it did. The British company knew that something was better than nothing. It was not lost on British ministers that, no matter how bad the diplomatic relations, business between the two countries was flourishing. The financial links were simply too close, and too mutually beneficial, for them to be sacrificed on high politics or principle.

British companies had rarely shown scruples when it came to dealing with Russia. Whenever their services were required by Russian energy giants, they were happy to oblige. When part of Yukos, the company seized from the jailed Khodorkovsky, was floated on the London Stock Exchange, the sale attracted a number of competing buyers. The financier George Soros had been a lone voice in urging Western institutions to boycott the offering; Andrei Illarionov, a former economic adviser turned critic, called the listing a "crime against the Russian people."[9] Such complaints fell on deaf ears. By the end of 2007, more than twenty major Russian companies, with a combined market capitalization of around $625 billion, were listed in London. That was far more than on the New York Stock Exchange, where standards of disclosure were comparatively higher. The Americans, whatever their many other failures in regulating their financial markets, were less eager to prostrate themselves before Russian money.

Many Russians I spoke to were bemused by the complaints of unsavory dealings involving the oligarchs. The British, they told me, had brought it on themselves. If they hadn't wanted polonium poisoning, if they hadn't wanted industrial blackmail, they should not have been so eager to welcome Russian money. They had brought it on themselves.

In March 2008 it was announced that Brenton would leave Moscow. The Foreign Office denied that Britain had raised the white flag, saying only that his term had come to its natural end. The Kremlin portrayed the ambassador's departure as a victory, suggesting that London wanted to adopt a more conciliatory approach. British companies operating in Russia, which had quietly expressed misgivings about the ambassador's hard line, breathed a sigh of relief.

The Londongrad phenomenon suggested that frosty political relations need not hinder warm business ties. Most Western European countries took a more indulgent approach, seeing politics and business as inextricably linked and going out of their way not to antagonize the Kremlin and Russia's top industrialists. The states that depended the most on Russia for its oil and gas, Germany and Italy, had been the most reluctant to challenge the Kremlin's clampdown on human rights. Within months of leaving office as German chancellor in 2005, Gerhard Schröder became supervisory board chairman of Russia's dream project, the Nord Stream gas pipeline, the most expensive pipeline ever built. A few weeks before, in one of his last acts in charge of his country, Schröder had signed a $5 billion agreement for Russia to supply natural gas to Germany. When the leader of the opposition Free Democrats, Guido Westerwelle, had pointed out the strange coincidence and attacked Schröder's appointment, the former chancellor won an injunction to try to silence him.[10] Schröder insisted that it was indeed a coincidence that he had received the appointment just after signing the agreement and that he had done nothing wrong. "I cannot understand this criticism," he told a news conference at Gazprom's Moscow headquarters.[11] A similar offer had been made to Romano Prodi just as he was stepping down as Italy's prime minister. The inducement to Prodi was to become chairman of Gazprom's parallel South Stream project. At least Prodi had turned down the job. Another to decline similar overtures was Donald Evans, a former U.S. secretary of commerce and a good friend of George W. Bush's. Evans had been personally courted by Putin to take a senior position at the oil firm Rosneft, just at a time when its sequestering of Yukos assets was being investigated by the European Court of Human Rights.

What was so dispiriting was that many of the examples of authoritarian abuse were not taking place away from prying eyes, in a secret prison in the Siberian wastes. This was not Stalin's Soviet Union, but a country fully integrated into the global economy. Violence was meted out on the doorsteps of the new rich. In December 2008, police raided the small St. Petersburg offices of Memorial, a human rights group and research center that charts the victims of Communist purges. A number of riot police wearing black face masks broke into Memorial's headquarters and took away its files. The raid coincided with an unprecedented public offensive by Kremlin-backed intellectuals who accused Memorial of distorting Russia's history in order to undermine patriotic fervor. One of Putin's favorite political scientists, Gleb Pavlovsky, complained that Russia was vulnerable to "foreign" conceptions of its history. The raid was covered only in passing by the Russian media. Most people appeared unperturbed. In any case, there was little further appetite for dredging up the abuses of the past. Opinion polls had consistently shown that voters welcomed the restoration of the old Soviet national anthem, and that at least 50 percent of them viewed Stalin's role in history as positive. A new, or rather traditional, version of history was now standard fare in school textbooks.

Shortly after the Memorial raid, Anastasia Baburova, a twenty-five-year-old journalist, and Stanislav Markelov, a human rights lawyer, were shot dead in the middle of the day on a busy street in central Moscow. Markelov had represented *Novaya Gazeta* in several court cases. But on the day of his death he had been focused on another issue—he was just leaving a press conference in which he had discussed his attempt to appeal the early release of a Russian army officer, Yuri Budanov, from prison. Budanov had been convicted in the rape and murder of a young Chechen woman. Markelov, who was representing the woman's family, was shot at point-blank range. Baburova, who was walking with Markelov, attempted to intervene, she was shot as well, becoming the fourth of the newspaper's journalists to be murdered in a decade. The two were mourned by the small human rights world, but, as ever, the vast majority of Muscovites were indifferent. "The killers have no fear because they know they will not be punished. But neither are their victims afraid, because when you defend others you cease to fear," wrote Yelena Milashina, another journalist working for *Novaya Gazeta*. "Those today who are fearful are the people who keep out of trouble, trying to survive these bad times, when the bad times (for some reason) never seem to end."[12]

Incidents such as these were designed to instill fear. But the overall clampdown was not comprehensive. Several newspapers, not only *Novaya Gazeta*, continued to criticize the Kremlin, breaking stories that were damaging to its interests. The radio station Ekho Moskvy has for nearly two decades produced strong, independent journalism for its loyal band of listeners in the capital. Ironically, since 2001 its major shareholder has been Gazprom, one of the bases of Kremlin economic and political power. Throughout, market economics have informed Putin's decisions; newspaper circulation and radio audiences are comparatively small. Therefore it has served his interests to leave certain outlets alone. He could then cite these papers and radio stations in his defense whenever Western leaders questioned him about his democratic credentials.

Curiously, in Russia the Internet is less policed than its Chinese equivalent. From time to time, the authorities have told prominent bloggers to stop their work or tone it down, but there has been no concerted attempt to close down sites. One apparent reason for this relatively relaxed approach is demographic. Russia's population is aging, and the online world is still seen as a minority pastime. Internet penetration is still under 25 percent and is concentrated mostly in Moscow and other relatively wealthy urban areas. For the Kremlin, only television counts. As in China, live coverage is rare in Russia, and chat shows are aired with a time delay in case someone says something untoward. The heads of the networks are summoned to regular weekly meetings to set the news agenda; executives are provided with lists of political opponents who are not permitted on air. The loyalty of important anchors, station managers, and star reporters is bought with unheard-of salaries. That, too, is part of the deal.

One-time political opponents have made similar calculations in recent years. In the parliamentary elections of December 2003, candidates from some liberal groups garnered nearly 20 percent of the vote. Over the next five years, only a few sustained their challenge. How did the rest disappear so easily, and what happened to their supporters? For many years the best known figure was Grigory Yavlinsky. I had made a number of trips with him across the country during the 1990s when he was setting up his opposition party, Yabloko. In the Yeltsin era, Yabloko was a force to be reckoned with in parliament. Yavlinsky twice stood for president. But early into the Putin era he complained that opposition politics was becoming impossible.

Many figures stayed silent, went into business, or allied themselves to the ruling camp. One of those was Pyotr Aven, a minister in one of the first post-Soviet liberal governments. He went on to become a wealthy banker, calling on Putin in March 2000 to model himself on Augusto Pinochet and suggesting that only dictatorship was capable of pursuing market reforms.[13] Undeterred, Yavlinsky and others went through the motions, appearing on Western television stations to criticize the Kremlin, lending a veneer of credibility to the claims that Russia was developing a democracy of sorts. In the parliamentary elections of December 2007, none of the liberal parties came close to crossing the threshold required to gain seats in parliament. Shortly after, Yavlinsky decided to quit the scene. The journalist Arkady Ostrovsky commented that Russian liberals had been more active in their opposition to the invasion of Czechoslovakia in 1968 than they were to the war in Georgia.

The problem for many of these liberals is that under Yeltsin they had allowed themselves to be identified with uncaring shock-therapy capitalism. In so doing, they inadvertently undermined their notion of liberal democracy. Lilia Shevtsova, a leading chronicler of the era, sums it up like this: "The Yeltsin period gave Russia quite a few freedoms. Never had Russia been so free," she says. "But freedom in the absence of orderly habits, with a weak legal culture and egotistical elites, led to chaos and illegality, a disregard for all taboos and restrictions. Russians—frightened by the unfamiliar freedoms and not knowing how to deal with them—swung the pendulum back towards order."[14] Sitting in her office on the corner of Tverskaya Street and Pushkin Square, near the old *Moscow News* office where dissidents would once gather, Shevtsova told me: "Ordinary people wearied of their unprecedented freedom to criticize the government because it had brought no improvement."[15]

In her most recent book, *Putin's Russia*, Shevtsova wrote of the period in which he came to power: "Putin received mass support from the main forces in Russian society. The accumulated fears, the disarray, the feeling of being in danger, and the very real Russian 'Weimar syndrome' all pushed people toward a longing for order and a new face in the Kremlin." She recalled something the sociologist Yuri Levada wrote in the last edition of *Moscow News* of 1999, as he assessed the Russia that awaited Putin's leadership: "No researchers had ever seen Russian society in this state. All the fears and passions that had been biding their time came to the surface and the hidden layer of our consciousness was exposed."[16] Shevtsova reminded me of a remark by Sergei Kiryenko, a former prime minister. He spoke of "liberalism of lifestyle," which, he said, had superseded the obsolete "liberalism of outlook."[17] That was April 2000—even before the Putin era had begun to take hold.

Shevtsova likened Russia's new middle class to rentiers, people who have benefited from the state's largesse to a bloated bureaucracy. The members of this middle class were not dissimilar to the business and political elites of some parts of Latin America in the 1970s and 1980s, who enjoyed a good life as long as they did not inquire too hard about the actions of the ruling juntas. Russia's elite had left one civilization, but had not arrived at another. "We are lost in transition. We may be here for some time," Shevtsova said with her usual eloquence.[18] That seemed to me to be a good summary of where many Russians found themselves. They would not have seen themselves as defenders of

Putin's worldview, but nor did they see the need to cause trouble. For years they had done well by him, with the riches that accompanied his rule. What they wanted was less brutalism and a stricter adherence to the rule of law, but they were not prepared to challenge him too hard and risk losing what they had.

In September 2008 I returned to Russia for my first encounter with Putin in four years. This time at the Valdai conference we were given two for the price of one—both Prime Minister Putin and his protégé, the new president, Dmitry Medvedev, spoke with us. We were curious to see how this cohabitation would work. Nobody for a minute, in Russia or abroad, doubted who was really in charge. Before those meetings the members of the Valdai Club had taken part in round-table discussions in Rostov-on-Don. The consumer culture had brought at least three sushi restaurants and a number of designer clothes stores to this pleasant southern town. Yet the discussion inside the conference was all about a return to the Cold War.

A few weeks before, Georgia had launched a military offensive into the region of South Ossetia, which had long been allied to Russia. The Russians have used the date 8/8 to portray themselves as victims of terrorism, using a similar formulation to 9/11 to mark the date the conflict began (August 8, 2008). The Kremlin responded by launching a disproportionate assault on Georgia itself. Victory was quickly achieved, but at the expense of a sharp deterioration in Russia's relations with the West. It did not take long in our discussions before the scale of the anger began to manifest itself. Vyacheslav Nikonov, grandson of Stalin's foreign minister, Vyacheslav Molotov, had become another of Putin's favorite "thinkers." He told our group that Russia had shown through its tough military response in Georgia that it had "never been so strong since the fall of the USSR." He added: "We are all paying the price of ten years of Western contempt for Russia." A slightly milder variation on this theme came from a young television commentator, Sergei Brylov, who told the Valdai discussion: "The West has achieved the consolidation of the Russian political class."

For the main event, we were flown to Sochi, a Black Sea resort town that was already sprucing itself up in preparation for hosting the 2014 Winter Olympics. Putin looked fit and relaxed; he was sarcastic, quick-witted, and at times angry as he entertained us over fine food and wine at a villa, which was said by locals to be owned by his friend, the oligarch Deripaska. Since the Rose and Orange revolutions in 2003 and 2004, respectively, the Russians had watched events unfold in Georgia and Ukraine with mounting concern. Thanks to political in-fighting and corruption, neither country had become the beacons for democracy that the United States had so hoped they would be. But they had, in the view of the Kremlin, become a geostrategic bridgehead for America right in the heart of the former Soviet Union. Putin portrayed Russia as embattled and encircled by an aggressive West, particularly the United States and the United Kingdom. "What did you expect us to do—to defend ourselves with catapults?" he shouted. "If an aggressor comes into your territory you would punch him in the face and be right to do so. Should we have wiped the bloody snot away and bowed our heads?" For three hours he regaled us with his customary mix of threatening and emollient language. He said he had treated Bush "better than some Americans do," but warned America, and the West more broadly, that the time was over for unilateral action. The Romans may have destroyed Carthage, "but the Roman Empire was destroyed by barbarians. We have to look out for the barbarians." He insisted: "Russia is no threat to the U.S. or Europe. We don't have any imperial claims any more."

As I watched, transfixed, I could not help concluding that this quintessentially Russian politics of grievance had found its apogee in this man. He no longer pleaded for understanding, as had been the message of his meeting with us during the Beslan massacre in 2004. Perhaps he felt he no longer needed it, because in the intervening years Russia had forced its way, through money and brute force, back to the top table.

Unlike Putin, who had kept us waiting for an hour and a half, the following day Medvedev breezed in, exactly on time, to meet us in the bizarre setting of a top-floor banqueting room of the Gum department store, opposite the Kremlin. After greeting all of us in turn, he told us that he had wanted to spend the month of August tackling corruption, strengthening the rule of law, and reforming the economy. But war was war. "The protection of the lives and the dignity of Russia's citizens, no matter where they are, is the most important task of the Russian state. The U.S. learned major lessons from 9/11. The events of 8/8 have lessons for us." He made it clear he would be prepared to defend Russians militarily wherever they were in the world, and that any attempt on behalf of Georgia or Ukraine to seek membership in NATO would escalate tensions with the West. The hand of the Bush administration had been evident in goading the Georgians to challenge Russia.

Medvedev said he had tried several times to argue his case with the Americans, but the conversations went nowhere. Bush had asked: "You're a young man with a liberal background. Why are you doing this?" Medvedev had replied: "I really didn't want this. But there are times when image is nothing and action is everything." The Russian president then told us: "I don't want Russia to be a militarized state living inside an iron curtain. I've lived in that country and it was boring and uninteresting." He acknowledged that Russia had failed to convince much of the outside world that it was different from the old Soviet Union: "Some think that not only are we the legal successor to the USSR, but we are also the ideological heirs. This is simply not true. We have a completely different set of values." With that he toasted us with some excellent red wine (French, as Georgian has long been banned in Russia), concluded our two-hour meeting, and posed with us for a group photograph.

The following morning we had our final meeting. The timing (eight o'clock) and the setting (a nondescript Holiday Inn beyond the Moscow beltway where we had been staying) spoke volumes about the state of the Russian opposition. In order to show its adherence to free expression, the Valdai organizers had invited Garry Kasparov, the former world chess champion and Russia's most visible opposition leader, to meet our group. Kasparov said he had found it increasingly difficult to hold meetings in international hotels in the center of the city. The managers, often westerners, had decided it did not make commercial sense to rile the Kremlin. Kasparov told us he had been allowed to see us only after creating a scene at an international media forum a few months earlier.

Every other meeting we'd had that week had been featured on prime-time evening news; it came as no surprise that there was not a camera in sight for our discussion on this occasion. Kasparov spent much of his time analyzing how other opposition figures and organizations had been outwitted by the Kremlin. Most of them, he said, had mistakenly believed they could influence attitudes toward freedom of expression, and human rights and democracy more generally, from within. "All the forces of liberalization and democratization from the top are exhausted," he told us. "It's over." It was time to work "in parallel" with mainstream politics. Yet Kasparov was adamant that, even though the forces of democratization were exhausted at the top, among the elites, the clamor for change was growing from the bottom. The Putin era, he declared grandly, was drawing to a close. He claimed that recent protests over the issue of high fuel prices had assumed a political dimension. "This regime is in a state of agony," he said. Most of the panelists there that day quietly dismissed his analysis as wishful thinking.

In the early months of the global economic crisis, the government appeared confident that, thanks to its large stabilization fund, Russia would emerge relatively unscathed. Some took that argument one step farther. "The United States and its ideas of the superiority of liberal capitalism and the limited role of the state in the economy have been dealt a severe blow," commented Sergei Karaganov, a veteran political scientist. "It turned out that the Old West's model of a mature liberal-democratic capitalism, which seemed to have won for good, was no longer the only ideological benchmark for the rest of the world. States of the new capitalism—naturally more authoritarian, in line with their stage of economic and social development—offered a much more attractive and attainable political development model for lagging countries."[19] Putin delivered a similar message in front of the annual gathering of the world's business and political elite in Davos, Switzerland, in January 2009.[20]

He was quickly proven wrong. Russia's downward spiral became one of the most pronounced of any country around the world. The immediate response from the Kremlin was relatively adept. It staved off a run on the banks, a remarkable achievement given the fragility of that sector, helped by the stockpiling of gold and hard-currency reserves when times were good. Still, the stock market and the ruble plunged. Billions of dollars were wiped off share values; many people lost their savings; and millions became unemployed. As for the oligarchs, they were said to have lost an astounding $250 billion. Many had little choice but to go the Kremlin, cap in hand, and beg for loans to save their empires.

Even during Putin's tenure, sporadic street protests had taken place. The authorities usually did not intervene, because the demonstrations were invariably called to highlight a specific grievance, such as low pensions or high electricity rates. Seldom were they overtly political in nature. That began, gradually, to change. On December 21, 2008, a rally in Vladivostok in the Russian Far East, originally called to complain about customs duties imposed on the import of foreign cars, turned into an anti-Putin rally. So worried was the Kremlin that it sent elite Interior Ministry troops thousands of miles across the country. Undeterred, the protests continued into January 2009. Political opposition began to coalesce under the banner of a new organization, Solidarity, which took its name from the 1980s' Polish trade union that helped precipitate the collapse of communism. In Boris Nemtsov, a former deputy prime minister, it had a charismatic figurehead. Groups such as these were an increasing irritant to the Kremlin, but they were still some way off from posing a direct political threat.

During the 2008 Valdai conference, I was struck by one observation in particular. It had come from Timothy Colton, an American academic and Yeltsin's official biographer. Russia, he said, provided no model for soft power. It possessed "no ideology of global scope and appeal." That much was true, but there was an appeal of sorts domestically, and for a long time it had worked. The Russia of the Putin years had consolidated around wealth, nationalism, and grievance. Putin had not derived his legitimacy from abstract concepts such as the rule of law, probity, and transparency, but from two things: the regime's capacity to deliver political stability, and economic growth. Had he been lucky, or clever? Had he generated all that wealth during the oil boom, or had he merely been its beneficiary and custodian? It did not matter. He had passed the efficiency test, a variant of the same test that was applied in Singapore and China. At least that was what people were led to believe before much of the wealth evaporated. Putin had presided over an economy that was increasingly dependent on oil and gas. He had called for diversification into new areas, but had shown no serious intent. He did not believe he had to.

Putin's problems provided a small opening to Medvedev. He used his own increasing profile around the world to assert his own brand of what he called "rules-based" politics, to smooth over some of the rougher edges of Putin's particular brand of authoritarianism. It was tempting to believe what he had implied to us that day at our meeting, that he was a genuine reformer but had been sidetracked by the war in Georgia. Medvedev gave a similar message whenever he spoke to Western audiences, and he instructed his confidants to do the same on their travels. They encouraged people to read much into the president's renewed commitment to fight corruption, signified, for example, by a meeting he had held with Mikhail Gorbachev to discuss civil liberties, and the reconvening of an obscure human rights body that had actually been created by Putin in 2004. Medvedev and his people bridled whenever comparisons were made with China. The age-old debate about Russia's European or Asian place has long been settled.

Russian opinion polls suggested that citizens were not so sure about Medvedev's rhetoric about democratic reform, retreating into the safety and familiarity of Putin's tougher message. Surveys showed a consistent animosity toward Western political values (as opposed to

Western consumer values) that had pre-dated the Georgia crisis, but had been exacerbated by it. The New Economic School in Moscow published data collated between 2003 and 2008 on attitudes toward democracy. Skepticism or hostility toward the United States was as pronounced among young people as among their grandparents. Among those aged thirty-five to forty-five, there seemed to be a little more enthusiasm for democratic reform, but the difference was small. When asked whether Western society provided a good model for Russia, 60 percent responded negatively, and only 7 percent positively. This attitude, the pollsters said, had hardened each year. Disapproval of the West was as pronounced among the rich as among the poor. The survey concluded that Russians were among the least enthusiastic in the world about the West's political ideals, a good deal less keen even than the people of Belarus, which is known as Europe's last dictatorship.

When all is said and done, what happened in the Putin era, what happened to the people I knew, might have been more dramatic, more brutal than in other countries, but the trade-off was no different from anywhere else. Money was there to be made, by Russians and foreigners alike. The pact came under strain because the anesthetic of wealth had begun to wear off, and Russia's citizens had no other comforts to fall back on.

CHAPTER 4

United Arab Emirates
Easy Money

> Democracy is a system in which to provide the best
> possible life for people. It's not an end in itself.

AYMAN SAFADI,
media executive

They were all there. Hollywood and Bollywood mixed with members of royal houses, National Baseball Hall of Famers, and other assorted celebrities. Dubai was bearing witness to the most garish party it had ever hosted. The Atlantis, a gargantuan, pink monstrosity of a hotel, made its debut in November 2008. Some 2,000 B- and C-list celebrity guests were flown in from around the world for a lobster feast and fireworks show that was heralded as seven times grander than the one that had marked the opening of the Beijing Olympics. A very particular pact was on display. In the deserts of Arabia, a traditional Bedouin state was feting a palace of greed owned by a South African Jew. The highlight of the evening was a special performance by Kylie Minogue, a global gay icon.

A business model had been built on complicity, all in the name of consumption. The United Arab Emirates had become a dream destination for those who wanted to get rich quick, but who remembered not to ask too many questions of the authorities. They could indulge their wildest fantasies behind closed doors. The ruling families could click their fingers, and statesmen, entrepreneurs, and artists would flock to them. Everyone was welcome, irrespective of color or nationality, united in the goal of wealth creation. To that end, everyone would turn a blind eye to whatever everyone else was doing. This was a truly global dream come true, and for a decade or more everyone involved emerged a winner.

Then it crashed. Just as the Atlantis was opening its doors, the economic edifice came tumbling down. The price of oil plummeted to $50 per barrel, a third of its peak value. Property values plunged, as did the stock market. Tens of thousands of foreigners—Britons, Indians, Russians, Americans, and more—panicked. The liquidity crisis made them desperate to recapitalize, and they attempted to offload their properties at any cost. Distressed selling brought prices down even faster; a domino effect was set in motion, and half of the region's construction projects, totaling a staggering $600 billion, were put on hold or canceled, leaving a trail of half-built towers on the outskirts of the city stretching into the sand beyond.

Thousands of foreigners who had gone to Dubai in the hope of making an easy fortune saw themselves fall suddenly into debt. Jobless people lost their work visas and then had to leave the country within a month. Many were anxious to leave anyway. After falling into arrears, which is punishable by jail under UAE law, thousands literally fled the country. Airport parking lots were filled with cars abandoned by their owners, keys left in the ignition and notes of apology taped to windscreens. The Atlantis, like all the hotels that had preceded it, had never imagined that business would dry up. There would be, so the marketing claimed, no shortage of people willing to pay as much as $25,000 a night for a room. Guests would enjoy opulence unmatched by anyplace else in the world. They could, for example, gaze at the many sharks and rays in a vast glass-lined aquarium in the lobby. Within months, the hotel was reduced to taking out advertisements offering cut-price package holidays.

Dubai was the playground of the Emirates, and as such, it was the one that suffered the most when the dream collapsed. Abu Dhabi was the more serious player. It did not need to try, as oil guaranteed its riches. Abu Dhabi has 95 percent of the UAE's oil and is responsible for more than half of its GDP. It has more money than it can possibly spend, and over the years it has sought ever more inventive ways of doling it out. "They have more oil than God has dollars," one businessman told me. Its trade-off was more sophisticated than the ones I had observed in other countries, and in some ways more sinister. Everyone was asked to turn a blind eye to the actions of others.

"If this formula succeeds, this is the new world," said Ashraf Makkar, drinking tea with me in one of Abu Dhabi's many luxury hotels alongside its tree-lined corniche. Once a correspondent with the Reuters news agency, he is now a media adviser to the Mubadala Development Company (MDC), a not insignificant job in a not insignificant company. MDC is the investment arm of the largest and wealthiest of the seven sheikhdoms that make up the UAE. Makkar, a burly, pugnacious man, gently berated me for a piece I'd written that had been brought to his attention. I had wondered out loud whether the Sovereign Wealth Funds established by the Gulf states, China, Singapore, and others, which had been buying large stakes in global corporations, might pose a danger to what is left of liberal democracy by dictating the terms of engagement around the world.[1] Makkar recited whole sentences of a piece I had long forgotten, although I remembered the headline: "Singapore Ticks Off British Writer." My admonishment this time was private, verbal, and very discreet. I had nothing to fear, he told me: "This is the place where globalization works." Everyone was coming to Abu Dhabi and its brasher and younger cousin down the road, Dubai, not just for the wealth but for the message the Emirates were sending about how they had become a global model of multiculturalism. "Look at the lights. Nobody does Christmas better than these guys do," Makkar said, insisting that this Muslim state was a model of religious and ethnic harmony: "This is the only place you'll find Indians and Pakistanis playing cricket together. What transforms things is a sense of ownership. People have a vested interest in seeing this place succeed."[2]

It was the present ruler's father, Sheikh Zayed bin Sultan Al Nahyan, who transformed Abu Dhabi from a few huts scattered in the desert, reliant on pearl fishing and a declining livestock trade, into this gleaming metropolis. Sheikh Zayed came to power in 1966 with the support of the outgoing British colonialists. While Bahrain and Qatar opted for independence, the sheikh enticed others to form a federation, the United Arab Emirates, promising to share his land's copious resources, but granting the other clans considerable autonomy. Having overseen his emirate's acquisition of wealth through oil, Sheikh Zayed decreed in the late 1990s that his city-state should diversify into the ultimate travel destination for business, sports, and arts events—and for European sun worshippers—all at the top end of the scale. He insisted that this be done without offending the indigenous Bedouin culture and without indulging in the unregulated development and louche and flamboyant cosmopolitan society of Dubai. Zayed saw little need to open up society, let alone the royal family, to scrutiny. "Why should we abandon a system that satisfies our people in order to introduce a system that seems to engender dissent and confrontation?" he said. "Our system of government is based upon our religion and that is what our people want. Should they seek alternatives, we are ready to listen to them. We have always said that our people should voice their demands openly. We are all in the same boat, and they are both the captain and the crew."[3]

Succeeding his father in 2004, Sheikh Khalifa bin Zayed Al Nahyan proceeded to open up Abu Dhabi further, but with each step carefully controlled. The sheikh had all the palaces and luxury hotels a monarch could wish for; what he really wanted was for his kingdom to be taken seriously, and he was determined to spend his way to that end. Culture, he discovered, was a commodity to be purchased. He earmarked some £20 billion for an elaborate cultural center, hired the world's best architects, and licensed the most prestigious museum "brands" to establish branches in Abu Dhabi. The site that was chosen, Saadiyat, "the Island of Happiness," was one of several islands constructed on reclaimed land to increase Abu Dhabi's size. Here Frank Gehry, the architect behind the renowned Guggenheim Bilbao, is building the latest—and largest—Guggenheim. The French modernist Jean Nouvel is designing the world's first outpost of the Louvre. Each museum will lend works, and each is being paid hundreds of millions for the use of its name. Alongside these monuments to gargantuan fantasy will be the new Sheikh Zayed National Museum, designed by Norman Foster, and a 6,000-seat performing arts center designed by Zaha Hadid. The cultural "hub" also contains a branch of the Sorbonne and will soon house a campus of New York University, the first American liberal arts school to be established abroad. Discussions have also taken place with the New York Public Library, among other major world libraries, as well as with New York's Metropolitan Opera and Lincoln Center.

There was plenty of resistance, more in France than in America, to the general idea of exporting culture to the desert. The skeptics' view was summed up by the Sorbonne's president, Jean-Robert Pitte: "Can we really bring culture to camel riders and carpet sellers?"[4] Art critics accused the sheikh of "bribing" Western museums to give their seal of approval to what was merely the artistic version of the leisure theme parks being built all over the Gulf. Design critics complained of "architectural megalomania." Gehry himself condemned the decision to build so many high-profile buildings so close to each other on Saadiyat as "a group grope."[5] A number of leading cultural figures in Europe and America complained about the sheer cheek of using money to buy culture—as if that had not originally happened in their own countries. Early in 2008, more than 4,000 French academics, art historians, archaeologists, and others signed a petition opposing the Louvre partnership, insisting that France's cultural patronage was "not for sale."

It took more than eighteen months for the deal with the Louvre to be settled. A former senior French diplomat, Jean d'Haussonville, was put in charge of the project. He saw his mission in terms of France's time-honored *mission civilisatrice*, its mission to civilize others through French culture. French voters and art-goers, he said, would appreciate the idea of helping "to deter [Islamic] fundamentalism through culture." Such ideals—lofty and condescending in equal measure—disguised the real motive: cash. Abu Dhabi paid more than $500 million just to use the name "Louvre." The total package was $1.2 billion.

To appease critics, the French government has created an advisory board for the Louvre to ensure that artistic standards and artistic freedom are not compromised. Critics predict that the museum, when it opens around 2012, will have to accommodate its socially conservative hosts. "Thank goodness Monet painted waterlilies [and not nudes]," said the newspaper *Libération*.[6] D'Haussonville admitted that the final say would rest with the local government, not the advisory board. "At the end of the day, it is their country, and their museum, so they can refuse any pieces."[7]

Those who attack the cultural compromises inherent in projects such as the one at Saadiyat may have a point, but they have chosen the wrong targets. Given the limitless depth of his pockets, Sheikh Khalifa is not to be condemned for seeking to spend some of his money on high art. More at issue are the morals of the Western sellers, but, as I have seen in the dealings between Western institutions and foreign governments, rarely are ethical considerations brought into play when it comes to a deal. The test now is whether these universities and museums will bring intellectual adventure and controversy into a land where freedom of expression is limited and democracy virtually nonexistent.

When George W. Bush chose Abu Dhabi as the destination to deliver a speech on "democracy and advancing freedom" in January 2008, the point was not lost on some that he had picked a nation with one of the least developed set of political institutions in the region. Here was the political branch of the same compromise. Since its formation nearly forty years ago, the UAE has witnessed only one transfer of power and has held just one national election, of sorts. In 2006, an electoral college selected by the UAE's royal families voted for twenty people to join a Federal National Council. The other twenty members were handpicked. That council has only consultative powers. Political parties are banned, and there are restrictions on press freedom.

I discussed the extent and the manner of censorship with Martin Newland, a former editor of the *Daily Telegraph* who was lured to Abu Dhabi to start an intriguing new venture. *The National*, an English-language paper, was launched in April 2008. It was, said its chairman, the Crown Prince, "born out of a vision that recognises the key role that a free, professional, and enlightened press plays in the national development process."[8] The aim, in other words, is to bring international journalistic standards to the Emirates without unduly rocking the boat. This attempt fell far short of the greater risk taken by the Qatari royal family when it established the al-Jazeera television station back in 1996. Although the channel has refrained from airing any form of criticism of its paymasters (entering into a pact of its own), it has blazed a trail in the Middle East in producing independent and robust journalism. Still, *The National* does mark progress of sorts. I put to Newland something that Makkar had said to me: "When you want to say something in the local press, you can say it as long as you say it in the right way." Newland developed the thought. "As a marketing principle you won't sell papers if you attack the country's leaders," he says. "But that doesn't mean you're prevented from doing strong journalism." He points out stories that his paper has broken on the decision to move to nuclear energy as examples. "Maybe they don't like 20 percent of what we do, but they appreciate the fact that we are showing Abu Dhabi as a normal society."[9]

As in Singapore, these arrangements are left deliberately vague in Abu Dhabi. Nobody quite knows when they have overstepped the mark until they have done so. Sheikh Khalifa has long decreed that journalists should not be jailed for excessive criticism, and his government has been reluctant to use defamation laws against journalists. However, as the economic crisis began to grip the nation, so the UAE responded in the classic manner of countries where freedoms are granted instead of enshrined in law. In early 2009, the government introduced new curbs on free expression. Ministers had become alarmed by the media's increasing criticism of its business model and by publicity surrounding a number of major corporate scandals. The law proposes fines of up to $150,000 for "whoever publishes news misleading public opinion in such a way as to harm the national economy." Even larger fines would be imposed on journalists criticizing the royal family. Ministers emphasized that critical news stories would be permitted as long as they were "well-researched" and "balanced."

The new clampdown showed the fragility of the deal. It increased the already large information gap in which reliable data were hard to come by and rumors were bound to flourish. Rules governing other areas of cultural life are similarly ill defined. Films and books are often censored if they are deemed offensive to cultural tastes or excessively critical of the government. In one recent example, publication of a book by Christopher Davidson, a lecturer at Durham University and a specialist in the UAE, was delayed. Davidson accused the authorities of censorship. The National Media Council denied this charge and released the book for sale, but insisted that it contained "a plethora of errors."[10] The authorities pay huge sums to Western public-relations firms to put out press releases or answer difficult questions on their behalf, which can lead to strange situations where reporters in the UAE must phone London to find out about events taking place in Abu Dhabi or Dubai. Western corporate skills can always be called upon to do the bidding of regimes around the world, irrespective of politics or ethics.

Not just on the record, but privately, too, many westerners I spoke to were happy to emphasize the positive aspects of Abu Dhabi society, although often in order to contrast it with the coarseness of neighboring Dubai. Newland stressed that 160 languages are spoken in the tiny country. "We can prove here that the clash-of-civilizations theory doesn't work. Here on the street you can find a Pakistani tribesman alongside a Goldman Sachs banker. People can live happily alongside each other. This is proof positive about globalization," he said.[11] I can't say that I ever saw the said tribesman and the said banker arm in arm, but Newland is right in pointing out a cultural mix of sorts. Western-ers in their shorts and locals in their dishdashas seem at ease with each other in the restaurants and shopping malls. It is the earning and spending of money that brings them together.

Ayman Safadi, head of the media company that runs *The National*, sees Abu Dhabi as a role model for the Middle East. "Look around you, and you will see that the states functioning best in the region are either monarchies [his native Jordan, for example] or emirates. Com-pare this place with Yemen or Egypt or Syria. The big population cen-ters of the Arab world are no longer the power bases. I haven't met one Emirati who is unhappy about the formula here," Safadi told me. How many businessmen in Tehran or Beirut could establish them-selves with so little hassle from the authorities, clans, or religious zealots? "Western judgments on Abu Dhabi are unrealistic. Here we have a different form of accountability." As for relaxing the ruling fam-ily's grip on power, or at least providing counterpoises, he said: "You have to pace democracy. Elections are a vital tool in a democracy, but you cannot reduce democracy to elections. Democracy is a system in which to provide the best possible life for people. It's not an end in it-self." The establishment of *The National*, and the greater, albeit cir-cumscribed, freedom it enjoys, is essential to this process of pacing democracy. Safadi pointed to a recent study on educational standards in the Emiratesthat concluded that the level of critical faculties among indigenous students was too low. It is a problem that has an effect on the jobs market: Local inhabitants are finding it increasingly difficult to secure, and sustain, demanding jobs.[12]

I have been driven for nearly two hours along a freeway as soft as a carpet. Trees line the road, sustained by constant watering in the desert. Behind them the sand dunes gradually shift from golden to red. Al Ain, on the border with Oman, is the second-largest city in the Abu Dhabi emirate. It is also the center for learning. Only three years earlier, on my previous visit, I found few buildings of more than two stories. The town has expanded dramatically; high rises are springing up. But the old character of the place has not yet been completely destroyed. The landscape, the forts, the open markets, and the barren mountain of Jebel Hafeet that bestrides the town are the nearest approximation to Arabian authenticity to be found around here. I meet Donald Baker, a Canadian, who is dean of the College of Humanities at the UAE University. A number of professors and lecturers have been recruited from abroad as part of the sheikh's concerted drive to improve educational standards. The student rolls have long been a cause for concern. Each year an average of 38,000 students graduate from UAE secondary schools, but only 4,000 go on to university in the Emirates, of whom 80 percent are female. It is a remarkable achievement for these young women, but many of them come under family pressure to give up their studies early in order to start a family. At least at the government level, women's education is regarded as vital to the country's development.

The Zayed Center for Heritage and History, a few miles up the road, is a throwback to another age, a life without foreign cultural imports, a life of material simplicity. The corridors are lined with sepia photographs of sand and souks. "If someone had asked any sheikh twenty years ago if this is how he wanted his country to turn out, he would have been shocked," says Hasan Al-Naboodah, reflecting on how earlier generations would have viewed modern life in the UAE. Naboodah teaches medieval Islamic studies at the University of the UAE in Al Ain, specializing in the history of Oman. "Now this development can't stop," he says. "It will have to continue until the end. Everything has gone beyond our leaders' control." He is exercised by the plight of local people, many of whom, he says, do not do nearly as well as one might think because of the sharply uneven distribution of wealth. What alarms him and others most, however, is the erosion of culture. A soft-spoken man who has studied for long periods in the West, he insists he is not averse to the principle of modernization of the UAE, but to the speed and manner of its practice. He knows that criticism can lead to accusations of sympathizing with Islamists, of dragging the UAE back into the dark ages, all of which he emphatically denies wishing to do. Some people are using websites to express their misgivings, anonymously, on issues ranging from the demographic imbalance to the disappearance of the Arabic language, or the buying up of properties by foreigners and competition over jobs. Most stay silent.[13]

Some get away with stark criticism. In April 2008, a warning by the head of police about social instability made headline news. "I'm afraid we are building towers but losing the Emirates," General Dhahi Khalfan Tamim told a "national identity conference" in Abu Dhabi attended by all the top figures. The very survival of the royal family was at stake, he said. While praising Sheikh Khalifa's decision to declare 2008 "national identity year," he said Emiratis had been late in tackling the demographic problem. The "demographic imbalance," as it is politely called, is stark. Less than 15 percent of the population of the UAE consists of indigenous people. The rest are foreigners. Naboodah describes it to me like this: "Local people are hunkering down in their compounds in a state of shock. They feel marginalized. . . . They don't need a bigger population."

Such are the underlying tensions among local people that the ruling family could not afford to introduce greater democracy, even if it wanted to, he says. He points to the contradiction at the heart of the West's emphasis on "democratization." Free elections for the local population in the UAE, he says, would undermine the ruling family and its entire economic project of growth through foreign labor. "Imagine what would be the reaction if you had a functioning parliament here." Such, he suggests, would be the law of unintended consequences if democracy were introduced into the Emirates. The local population would vote against many of the westernizing changes introduced over the past two decades.

In Abu Dhabi I return to visit an old haunt. In March 2005 I had the dubious honor of being one of the first guests ever to stay at the Emirates Palace hotel. To my surprise, the only other person I found in the breakfast room was the German tennis star Boris Becker. I had arrived one day before the start of an organized press trip. I remember describing in my article the sheer scale of the place—it has 6,000 square meters of gold leaf, 7,000 doors, 12,000 signs, and 1,002 chandeliers—made with Swarovski crystals. In the article I wrote about it in 2005, I said: "The centre of the palace is dominated by a grand atrium, the biggest in the world. Its gilded dome outstrips the one in St Paul's Cathedral. The public lounge is the size of two football pitches. It already employs 1,200 people from 50 countries, a veritable tower of Babel in Armani, short skirts and gold braided jackets. Even with full occupancy, that would translate into four staff for every guest." The most elite guests enjoyed their own entrance. "Their limos sweep through the Palace's own Arc de Triomphe (inexplicably, slightly smaller than the Paris original) and up a ramp to the higher floors. That is, if they would rather not use the hotel's own helipad. The rest of us have to make do with a procession past an orgy of fountains to the main entrance."[14]

My reaction to the place was a fairly standard mix of disdain for the excess but also a little awe, best kept to oneself in polite Western society. Who, after all, would admit to finding such a display of bling anything but vulgar? I could imagine people coming here for a laugh, for a weekend of self-mocking self-indulgence, but I could not see a hotel of such grand scale and small taste becoming popular. That was never the point. In the Emirates, projects such as these are individual follies. They do not conform to standard business plans. In 2008 I was relieved to see more people frequenting the hotel than before. It is now the center of Abu Dhabi's business and diplomatic scene, with presidents, kings, chief executives, and sports stars as regular visitors. But I still cannot imagine how the operators make ends meet.

Traveling between Abu Dhabi and Dubai has long ceased to be an exotic experience. A few years ago one might have seen, from the comfort of an air-conditioned car, the odd Bedouin walking on the sand; the vista is now dominated by buildings, cranes, and more buildings. Dubai has been building, out of nothing, 120 kilometers of canal, with houses on either side. This process is now slowing down, and few doubt it will resume in earnest. Once the joint population reaches 10 million, the two cities will have effectively joined together. Locals predict it will be known as Abu Dubai.

Dubai has long made its more grown-up cousin feel distinctly middle-aged. The package it presented around the world—stability, property deals, high-earning potential, and endless shopping and recreational opportunities—proved consistently attractive to hundreds of thousands of foreigners. Dubai was seen as one of the three links in the "great globalization miracle," as the boom-time saying went, along with Shanghai and Mumbai. London, New York, and Tokyo were dismissed as yesterday's cities. Some of the more sensible in the financial community regarded this attitude as another example of the hubris that had turned Dubai into the construction jungle that it had become. But their voices were rarely heard. Why should they be, when people were having so much fun making so much money?

Dubai turned itself into the global hub of greed. Each symbol of luxury had to be outdone by another, and the developers' thirst showed no limit. Other considerations, such as heritage or environment, were ignored. Few seemed to complain when one new entrant, the Palazzo Versace hotel, boasted a frigid 800-square-meter swimming pool and a beach with artificially cooled sand—as well as wind machines—to protect its guests from the excesses of the summer heat. "We will suck the heat out of the sand to keep it cool enough to lie on," said the president of the hotel group. "This is the kind of luxury that top people want."[15] It seemed to matter little that the UAE was the second-largest carbon emitter per capita.

Sheikh Mohammed bin Rashid al-Maktoum, the ruler, affectionately known as "Sheikh Mo," turned his plot of land from a mini-kingdom to a global corporation. A decade ago, as the oil began to run out and revenues dwindled, he charted a different course for Dubai's prosperity. It was based on property, tourism, shipping (through Jebel Ali), and the creation of a new financial center. Halfway between London and Singapore, it offers tax-free opportunities for individuals and many corporations.

The public-relations talk that one inevitably hears in Dubai is laden
with superlatives. When the Burj al Arab opened in December 1999,
it was the world's first self-styled, seven-star hotel. Its design, a sail-
shaped shard of steel and Teflon-coated glass, became Dubai's national
symbol. The rapturous reception it received prompted the authorities
in envious Abu Dhabi to build the Emirates Palace, which declared
itself to the world in 2005. Not to be outdone, Dubai came up with
the Burj Dubai, billed as the tallest building in the world, outgunning
Taipei 101 in Taiwan. As the race for the gaudiest construction gath-
ered pace, so the advertising reflected the hype: "Monument. Jewel.
Icon. Burj Dubai will be known by many names. But only a privileged
group of people will call Burj Dubai home," proclaims the literature.

Sheikh Mo's plans were not hard to fathom. From B-list Western
celebrities to financiers, soccer players, and tourists, everyone was welcome to take a slice of the pie and come and go as they pleased, as
long as they abided by his rules. A sharp intake of breath accompa-
nies the announcement of each construction project. For years the skyline has bristled with cranes—an estimated 20 percent of the world's
total. Dubai has seen the first ski dome built in the desert; it has seen
vast artificial islands rise from the sea, from "the Palm," home to many
of England's soccer stars, to "the World," approximately three hundred artificial private islands that are positioned to look like the continents of the world. Each was to be owned by someone rich and
famous, who would be delivered to and from the mainland by personal
speedboat. Most of the marketing strategies for these places were
based around celebrities, who were invited to take complimentary or
hugely discounted properties in order to lure other interested parties
into making a purchase. Part of the sales pitch for Burj Dubai was to
seek out world statesmen, such as Henry Kissinger, Bill Clinton, and
Tony Blair, and try and convince them that this was the place to relax
and recharge; here, like-minded people could meet each other in the
lift and feel comfortable in their hermetically sealed environment. It
was, as one developer admitted to me, "designed to increase the brain
power, along with the bling."

From on high looking down over the city, Nicholas Maclean pointed out to me all the various projects under construction. The regional head of one of the main international real-estate firms, he took me through the plans for Dubai in meticulous detail. Over the next four years, some 75 million square meters of office and residential space was to be built, more than trebling the total amount of land under use. The new airport site alone would have eight hundred towers. Such was the demand that the local paper, the *Gulf News*, had at one point three pullout sections per day on property, partly to deal with the speculation, but mainly to accommodate the 300,000 new arrivals per year. "Build it and the people will follow" was the abiding principle. That was before the crash. They are less bullish now.

Dubai rivals anywhere in the world for combining the excesses of luxury with the excesses of inequality. At any time, night or day, gangs of "guest workers"—usually from India, Pakistan, or Bangladesh—can be seen pounding away on building sites. As Human Rights Watch puts it, "one of the world's largest construction booms is feeding off workers in Dubai who are treated as less than human." Employers routinely deny construction workers their wages. Officials with the UAE Permanent Committee for Labour and Immigration told Human Rights Watch that last year alone, nearly 20,000 workers filed complaints with the government about the nonpayment of wages and labor-camp conditions.

Most construction workers secure work in the UAE by taking loans from recruiting agencies in their home country. A typical laborer uses a large portion of his monthly wages ($110 a month, on average) toward repayment of that loan, and without wages he falls further into debt. They have no access to health care or other basic rights. The companies that sponsor these workers hold onto their passports—and often a month or two of their wages to make sure they keep working. The result is virtual debt bondage, a system of indentured labor. Industrial accidents are a regular occurrence. Independent research published in local media found that an average of two to three deaths occur every day. These laborers work in shifts and sleep in shifts, sometimes twenty to a room. Yet, according to UN agencies, there have been up to 300,000 illegal workers in the Emirates at any given time. When the going was good, some workers took part in public protests and strikes in an attempt to improve working conditions. One unpalatable truth was that most workers did everything they could to extend their stay, knowing that they were earning up to ten times what they would get back home, even after all the various deductions and humiliations. Another even more unpalatable truth was that everyone who was making money in Dubai—the real-estate companies, hoteliers, tourism chiefs, the financial whiz kids—knew they were doing it off the backs of the exploited workers from South Asia.[16]

When it came to consumer excess, Sheikh Mo led from the front. His shopping list around the world included the *QE2*—complete with Tilbury and Southampton docks; Barneys, the upmarket department store in New York; a share of Standard Chartered Bank; half of the Las Vegas Strip; and Australia's leading thoroughbred stud operation, to add to his stud farms in the UAE, Britain, and Ireland. Not to be outdone, Sheikh Khalifa has invested in Warner Brothers and in an unlikely English Premiership soccer club, Manchester City, with instructions to spend whatever it takes to make it the biggest club in the world. Most of the sheikhs' buying is done by aides who run private equity-style investment houses; but it is they who stump up the cash.

Sovereign Wealth Funds has been stunningly successful. The biggest of the thirty major funds around the world is the Abu Dhabi Investment Authority (ADIA). Throughout the period of global growth, as oil prices soared, the funds looked for institutions to invest in, looking for steady returns. The Kuwait Investment Authority paid $3 billion for a stake in Citigroup and invested $2 billion in Merrill Lynch; ADIA had already bought a 4.9 percent stake in Citigroup for $7.5 billion. Funds from Qatar and Dubai took hold of a third of the London Stock Exchange.

Initially, the concern was expressed only in one direction. Western politicians complained at how funds owned by authoritarian regimes and run as secretively as any hedge fund or private-equity firm were taking over strategic assets. One of Germany's leading politicians, Franz Müntefering, who went on to become vice chancellor, described them as "locusts." That term became widely used as protectionist impulses increased.

The wake-up call for the UAE came in 2006. The British company P&O, which had six U.S. ports in its global portfolio, including New York's, agreed to a takeover by Dubai Ports World. The acquisition was referred to Congress and to the Bush administration, which gave it the nod. The White House was keen to keep Sheikh Khalifa and Sheikh Mo happy; he wanted to show appreciation for the discreet cooperation of past years. When the deal became public, however, popular opposition led to the House Appropriations Committee voting an astonishing 62–2 to stop the takeover. That humiliation hurt in the UAE, amid allegations of dirty dealings on all sides. Bush was furious. Politicians and business leaders on both sides were chastened, and they vowed to prevent a recurrence. Key to that was a public relations campaign extolling not just the financial virtues of the Emirates, but its atmosphere as an easy place to do business and relax. All outward manifestations of "fundamentalism" were played down. Religion, too, played its part in the pact.

Sheikhs Mo and Khalifa have long balanced the competing requirements of Western influence with religious traditions that forbid alcohol, unmarried sex, and homosexuality. Most of the time the authorities turn a blind eye, particularly in Dubai, where alcohol is freely sold in hotels and restaurants, even during the holy month of Ramadan. The sheikhs have sought to assuage increasing indignation at home and in other Muslim countries about Western decadence by announcing regular crackdowns (accompanied by the odd person being made an example of, before business returns to normal) and making exuberant assertions of allegiance to Islam. On the outskirts of Abu Dhabi, they have been building the Sheikh Zayed Mosque, an architectural feat containing a Persian carpet that is said to be the biggest in the world. Inevitably, Sheikh Khalifa wanted it to be the world's largest mosque, in honor of his father, but neighboring Saudi Arabia complained, insisting that it should not usurp Islam's two holiest sites—Mecca's Grand Mosque and the Prophet's Mosque in Medina.

Dubai's hedonistic image was proving increasingly problematical. One Dubai government official described a particular class of westerner to me as the "the tattoo and sunburn brigade." The lowest point was reached in 2008 with the arrest and conviction of two Britons on charges of having sex in a public place. The "bonking on the beach" story became a cause célèbre back in the United Kingdom. Newspapers sent teams of reporters over to write vivid articles about both their antics and the "brutality" of the host country. This was one of those classic cases of a smattering of racism with a hint of colonialism, not a little xenophobia, and a simplistic view about social customs. The couple concerned had done what hundreds of expatriates do on the main day of prayer for Muslims—they'd gone to one of the city's hotels for the now traditional Friday all-you-can-drink champagne brunches. They emerged, inebriated, and were discovered by a police officer on Jumeirah beach having sex on the sand. He let them off with a caution, but ordered the couple to leave. They ignored the warning and were arrested when the officer returned to the scene. According to police sources, the woman launched a tirade at the policeman after being disturbed for a second time. She is alleged to have hurled abuses and apparently tried to hit him with one of her high-heeled shoes (as George Bush was later to find out in Baghdad, this was a particularly insulting act) before being restrained and taken to a cell. In October 2008, the two were found guilty by Dubai's Court of First Instance of unmarried sex and public indecency and given three-month jail terms. That decision was later suspended on appeal, and the two were allowed to leave the country.

Theirs was an egregious breaking of the pact—a combination of booze, rudeness, violence, and religious insult. Rather than being a symbol of repression, it could be argued that the treatment of the couple was lenient. I can imagine many countries, including some described as "democracies," where they would have been treated more harshly. On Dubai's lively expat websites, most foreigners expressed anger at their actions. Westerners had been allowed to get on with whatever they wanted to do, as long as they did not flaunt it in public. For as long as the money was flowing, it seemed an easy compromise for most to make. No one wanted the actions of a few to ruin the fun for everyone else.

The balancing act extends beyond cultural sensitivities into geopolitics. The UAE has been used a number of times in recent years as a discreet venue for sensitive Middle East negotiations, such as over Lebanon, Libya, or Pakistan. The host government can assure the various parties, with confidence, that their cover will not be blown. The unwritten pact ensures that, particularly after a word in an editor's ear, certain subjects will remain off limits. Abu Dhabi and Dubai have been likened to Vienna during the Cold War—a meeting place for East and West. A less flattering comparison could be World War II Switzerland, which played one side off against the other, providing a financial haven for all participants, with no questions asked.

A modern-day version of this deal is made with the Americans, who have much invested in the UAE both militarily and politically. Although the United States does not have a permanent base there, as it does in Singapore, the U.S. Navy puts more sailors ashore for more days a year at Jebel Ali than at any other foreign port. The U.S. Defense Department supplies the Emirates with billions of dollars of the latest sophisticated weaponry, most significantly Patriot missiles. Having a loyal and well-armed ally so close to Iran serves U.S. interests well. At the same time, the Americans turn a blind eye to the UAE sending daily shipments of Western goods to Iran. This trade, on which Iran is utterly dependent, violates sanctions designed by the United States to punish Tehran for its long-standing defiance on the nuclear weapons issue.

Then there is the terrorism pact. It has long been a curiosity as to how the UAE has avoided a bombing spectacular, given the country's geography, its ethnic mix, and the number of signature buildings that would prove tempting for al-Qaeda and affiliated groups. Such a strike would provide a dramatic publicity coup for militant Islamists. It would lead to mayhem, capital flight, and a collapse in confidence. The Americans know that two of the nineteen men who staged the 9/11 attacks were UAE nationals. It was said that half of the attacks' $500,000 budget was wired to the United States from Dubai. Yet when the Americans directed their ire at Afghanistan and later at Pakistan, they left the UAE out of the picture. They saw that relationship as too important to jeopardize.

Local and Western security services keep a close eye on who is doing what in Dubai and Abu Dhabi, however. Residents say that some people who have gotten into trouble for petty crime are quietly offered immunity in return for reporting on colleagues. Other inducements are offered. One businessman told me: "People are given residency in return for spooking. Others who get into trouble are told they won't be thrown out of the country as long as they cooperate. Everyone assumes there are spooks in every office." He added, in an intriguing example of the deal on offer: "I rather like the fact that if I caused trouble here I'd be caught within a couple of days." The pact, it seems, has a variety of uses.

The number of threats monitored by Western embassies has increased steadily in recent years, but until now they have remained only threats. Perhaps the most compelling reason for the absence of terrorism is the role the UAE plays in laundering the money of some of those deemed responsible for 9/11, through local banks and businesses set up in elaborate chains. It is, say some, a "gentleman's agreement"—you can use the territory for rest, recreation, and wealth creation, as long as you keep your military activities offshore. It is not just al-Qaeda that has benefited. The father of Pakistan's nuclear program, A. Q. Khan, admitted heading a clandestine group that, with the help of a Dubai company, supplied Pakistani nuclear technology to Iran, Libya, and North Korea.[17]

The role of the UAE is not dissimilar to the role played by London, which offered militant Islamists a place to make and save their money in the pre-9/11 era (Londonistan), just as it became a haven for oligarchs of dubious repute after that (Londongrad). Members of a lower-grade form of Russian mafia have also made Dubai their home. It is said that at any given time, half of all the rooms in the top hotels in Dubai are occupied by Russians. From time to time, shoot-outs occur, most famously in the luxury Burj al Arab in 2006 when a Syrian diamond seller was shot dead. The industries in precious metals, drugs, and prostitution are controlled largely by the Russian underworld. Most of the escorts and call girls are flown in quietly, through Al Ain airport, and end up in so-called nightclubs. The best known, at one time, was the Cyclone, where girls are said to be valued by the male clientele according to their nationality, with Russians usually commanding the highest prices. Globalization meets market meets demand. Expat websites gossip endlessly about places such as these, but they are not talked about in polite society or in the official media. Occasionally they are raided and shut down. They then reopen after "renovation," or reemerge at a different location. This is the sleazy side of the pact.

"We want to provide moral integrity," says Nicholas Labuschagne. A South African, he is one of a number of foreign consultants who have been brought in to advise the ruling family. Dubai, he says, wants to shed its reputation for low taste and amorality. Education, health care, and efficient governance provide the key. He points to a new Academic City, with thousands of new places in university and technical colleges. His message is similar to that of several other people I met in Abu Dhabi. The UAE is a far cry from Western concepts of liberal democracy, but it is also far removed from other countries in the region. Is this, I ask him, an attempt to provide a cloak of respectability, or does it signify something more? "We are genuinely seeking to develop a positive model of development for the rest of the region to follow," Labuschagne tells me. "This is not just about money."[18]

My last visit to the region took place in September 2008, the week after the collapse of Lehman Brothers in New York. Most of the financiers, real-estate, and tourism bosses I met in Dubai and Abu Dhabi were cautiously confident that they would escape the sudden economic collapse being experienced in the West. One CEO, while acknowledging the potential dangers, told me his biggest problem at that time was dealing with the plaintive requests for a job, any job, from people he knew back home in Britain who had either lost theirs or feared they would at any moment. "I'm getting inundated by e-mails with people offering their CVs," he said. Most people were reasonably confident that Dubai, even with its exposure to property, would get away with a "soft landing." They convinced themselves that the UAE was decoupled from the economies of the West, and that their wealth pact was more durable than that of the "old countries."

The speed and depth of the economic collapse shook the royal family. Sheikhs Khalifa and Mohammed had, in their different ways, seen their city-states as beacons of this new consumerist world, but more than that, too. They saw them as examples for others to follow, particularly those in the Middle East, a melting pot of different cultures brought together by the allure of prosperity. With thousands bailing out of town, the government announced an expansionary budget to stimulate the economy; an extra $50 billion would be pumped in for infrastructure projects, to add to the $200 billion already earmarked. Such measures were easier to perform in a country where the politically powerful had a stake in every major corporation. The source of the money was the older family member, Khalifa, who came to the rescue of the younger profligate, Mo. Desperate and indebted Dubai was helped by oil-rich and demure Abu Dhabi.

There was another bailout story, too, one which the authorities were even more desperate to keep secret. In the autumn of 2008, the United States and other Western nations secretly began to cajole and coerce the UAE to help them out in this time of need. Old favors, such as America's discreet security guarantee to the sheikhs and its preparedness to turn a blind eye to their dealings with some around al-Qaeda, were being called in.

Henry Paulson, Bush's treasury secretary, had several unpublicized meetings with Gulf leaders and ministers, urging them to inject money into the desperate American car industry and other parts of the economy. The Sovereign Wealth Funds had already taken a large hit, thanks to investment in that very same American economy, but there were still tens of billions ready to be invested. President Bush feted several members of the Emirati royal families at Camp David, including a number of figures in senior positions at the ultra-secretive ADIA wealth fund. It seemed at that moment that the only place in the world with spare cash was Abu Dhabi. It was time, he told them, to repay an old friendship. Another intriguing meeting came at the start of November 2008, when Gordon Brown, the British prime minister, made a two-day visit to the UAE. The trip received little attention back home, as it coincided with the dramatic results of the U.S. presidential election. The prime minister urged China and the Gulf to use their wealth funds to boost the coffers of the International Monetary Fund, which had been forced to dig into reserves to provide emergency loans to European countries in danger of going bust, such as Iceland, Hungary, and Ukraine. He framed his appeal in somewhat narrow terms. The problem was considerably broader than Brown and other political leaders were willing to acknowledge. The West was broke. The so-called democratic world was going, cap in hand, to its new paymasters.

All problems were relative in these new dramatic times. Dubai had flaunted itself on easy money and—in the eyes of its Arab neighbor— easy living. It had indulged in the economics of a housing boom, excessive credit, and other irresponsible financial practices. Dubai is in many ways a brand more than a country, dependent on its reputation for money and luxury, and has little else to fall back on if the glitz comes off. It would suffer in the short term. But, thanks to Abu Dhabi, it would not collapse, and should prepare itself to start afresh.

For those who had not been forced to sell up and leave (mostly those who had bought property early, when prices were low), life would remain relatively unchanged. The White Tribe of Arabia could continue to shop in the same shops they had back home; they could continue to work in environments similar to home. They could top up their tans, play tennis, and drink indoors whenever they wanted. Nothing was required of them except to make and spend money. This was the most undemanding of pacts, and for many people it was an attractive one. This was the money pact, in its purest form. Everyone, from the British office worker to the Lebanese entrepreneur, from the Iranian importer to the American government, had made the appropriate compromises to enjoy what it had to offer.

CHAPTER 5

India
Populous Alternative

The myth of tolerance remains strong . . . we must
surely be one of cruellest free societies in the world.

TARUN TEJPAL,
journalist

Two armed guards lurk behind the lowered gate of Teesta Setalvad's
home in Mumbai. They slouch rather than stand alert as I approach.
I have come to see one of India's bravest campaigners for civil liberties,
the granddaughter of a former Indian attorney general, a woman who
decided to step out of the mainstream in order to expose state abuses and
collusion in what is supposed to be the world's largest democracy.

A journalist by trade, Setalvad edits a monthly magazine called *Communalism Combat*. She set it up because she was alarmed that the national media had given up reporting on the more unpleasant side of life,
concerned rather to portray India as being on a shining path to modernity and prosperity. In particular, they had stopped investigating the role
of politicians and security forces in the many incidents of communal
strife that India has endured over the years. "The media are silent on brutality and caste," she tells me, as we sit on a bench in the courtyard that

divides her home from her ramshackle office. "The relationship between reader and papers has been commodified. Today protests and
real politics don't make news," she says.[1]

I ask her why she needs all the protection around her home. She
tells me she receives several threatening telephone calls every week.
The Central Industrial Security Force, one of India's security agencies, has given her round-the-clock protection, particularly in the
Mumbai area and whenever she travels within her native state of Gujarat. That provides some reassurance, but not much. Bodyguards provided by the Indian state are not among the most feared in the world.
Her security men try their hardest but have failed to prevent at least six
attacks on her car so far. Setalvad is regarded by many in power as a
troublemaker. She tells me that a number of newsagents no longer
stock her magazine. It is, they are warned, not worth the consequences.
Those consequences are not spelled out, but even the unspoken threat
of closure, let alone physical violence, is enough, she says, to intimidate
several of them.

Having toured countries that clearly fell into the authoritarian camp,
I wanted to test the pact in a democracy—and not just any democracy.
India's constitutional achievement over sixty years of independence is
remarkable. This country of more than a billion people, with 2,000 ethnic groups and 200 languages, has, for all but one brief period, doggedly
pursued a path of multiparty democracy, with a separation of powers, an
independent judiciary, and free expression. In theory, it ticks just about
every democratic box. But beyond the ritual of the vote, what freedoms
exactly does it deliver, and for whom? Does it deliver real freedom for
people to determine the way they lead their lives?

Setalvad began *Communalism Combat* after becoming alarmed by a
series of religious riots in the early 1990s involving Hindus and Muslims. The journalists she hired looked at issues the traditional media
had not, including the causes of the violence and the response by the
security forces. Setalvad and her team have consistently alleged that
in areas of India run by Hindu nationalist parties and groups, the police targeted Muslims and other minorities. "As India became in-

creasingly communalized, so did politicians and the police," she tells me. "Muslims have been selectively targeted for detention, ill treatment and torture in a number of states since the start of the1990s."

She and her team have spent years investigating one of the most brutal episodes in the history of independent India. In February 2002, just outside the town of Godhra in the western state of Gujarat, fifty-eight Hindus, many of them women and children, were burned alive as mobs set fire to their train. They had been returning from the town of Ayodhya, the center of a dispute between Muslims and Hindus over the building of a temple on the site of a demolished Mughal mosque. Dozens of Muslims were arrested and charged; they pleaded that they had been taunted by the Hindus. The chief minister of Gujarat, Narendra Modi, decreed a day of mourning so that funerals could take place in the state's largest city, Ahmedabad. Crowds of people, many wearing the saffron scarves and khaki shorts that are the uniform of Hindu nationalism and armed with swords, explosives, and gas cylinders, rampaged in search of vengeance. They poured kerosene down the throats of men, women, and children before setting them alight. As many subsequent investigations have shown, police chiefs and politicians from the ruling Bharatiya Janata Party (BJP) either stood by or helped them in their task, providing them with computer printouts of addresses. More than a thousand people, most of them Muslims, were killed. About 230 mosques and shrines were razed to the ground. When asked to condemn the violence, Narendra Modi instead quoted Isaac Newton's third law: "Every action has an equal and opposite reaction."[2] Modi has neither apologized nor expressed regret for what happened.

Setalvad has many enemies, but Modi in particular does not appreciate her endeavors to pursue justice. He is not one of those colorful local warlords of a failed or failing state. He is one of the country's most talked-about politicians, and he is seen—for better or worse—as a face of modern India. Only months after the Gujarat riots, Modi was reelected as chief minister. In 2007, he won again, for an unprecedented third time. A man who dresses modestly, who is seen as a paragon of fiscal rectitude, and who possesses an alluring gift of oratory, he is already a key player on the national scene. Many observers say it is only a matter of time before he becomes India's prime minister. He is feted by the country's corporate elite, the heads of giants such as Tata, Reliance, Airtel, and Infosys. These men, the types that over the years have graced the covers of *Forbes* and *Fortune* magazines, point to Modi's role in fostering Gujarat's consistently high growth rates, fiscal probity, efficiency, and entrepreneurial spirit. Gujarat is known as the pioneer state, the beacon for the rest of the country to follow, India's version of Singapore. Western entrepreneurs queue at Modi's door, and his state has more internal investment than any other. The saying goes that, unlike the rest of India, in Gujarat the trains really do run on time.

Yet, for several years, Modi has been refused a visa to visit the United States on human rights grounds, a decision that the members of India's business elite see as humiliating and undeserved. They have been lobbying Washington to reverse its decision, confident that it will. Money, they insist, will eventually talk. "In the years after independence, the elite had a great sense of responsibility for the development of the country as a whole. Now all it wants to do is make money and live well. I am from the self-same privileged elite. But if we're not able to take on people like Modi, then what's the point of our democracy?" Setalvad asks.[3] Why is this one individual, this one incident of violence among so many in India, and this one state so important? Everyone I talked to has an impassioned view about Modi. He was alternately viewed as a savior or a dictator (in some cases both). Many ordinary voters, not just in Gujarat, and many international and local business leaders, appeared willing to overlook whatever misdeeds had taken place because they identify in him a chance for India to advance. They see him as providing a hospitable business environment, an oasis of entrepreneurship in a country whose long-term aspirations are impeded by a large and mainly poor and uneducated population, insufficient and decaying infrastructure, and a chaotic political system. This was a similar thought process to the one that greeted Vladimir Putin in Russia and has sustained the Communist Party in China. "Chaos," or the Russian equivalent to it, was the word many Russians used to describe the Gorbachev-Yeltsin years; the Chinese used their own equivalent to warn about what would have happened if the Tiananmen protests had been allowed to succeed.

Modi is the latest politician on whom India's business elite have pinned their hopes over the past two decades. The country has moved a long way from the vision of its founding father, Mahatma Gandhi, another Gujarati, the man who made the spinning wheel the symbol of the freedom movement. Gandhi sought an India in which poverty alleviation, religious pluralism, and the protection of minorities against the Hindu majority would be the abiding priorities. The governments of Jawaharlal Nehru and his daughter Indira Gandhi expanded the role of the state, nationalizing the banks and introducing land reform. Although the economy grew, the gap between India and developed countries increased. A series of financial crises led to a sudden about-turn in 1991, including the adoption of economic liberalization under the Congress government of Narasimha Rao and his finance minister, Manmohan Singh. Rao announced to India that out of economic malaise came the opportunity to "sweep the cobwebs of the past and usher in change."[4] Red tape was cut, capital markets were partly deregulated, labor markets were opened up, and credit became the order of the day. In his authoritative study of the economic changes, Gurcharan Das likened financial deregulation in India to Deng Xiaoping's opening up of China. Das argued that Rao's revolution was, if anything, more important than Nehru's political revolution of 1947.[5]

Modern India was born in 1991, or at least that is what the free-market proselytizers subsequently argued. It joined the ranks of globalized states, offering a new and potentially attractive pact to its people, at least those who would be able to join it. Under its terms, tens of millions of people would be left alone to make money. The state would not stand in their way, turning a blind eye to tax avoidance and other excesses. The new wealthy would be free to become involved in politics if they wished—this, after all, was a democracy—but they would be wasting their energies if they did. As it turned out, they disengaged from politics and from state activity, safe in the knowledge that, once elected, politicians at all levels would look after their interests, as long as they looked after the politicians' interests. That meant their wallets.

From that point on, material spending was elevated into a national pastime. Economic growth was seen as a symbol of national virility. Between 1999 and 2008, India's economy trebled in size. In July 2006, the U.S. magazine *Foreign Affairs* declared India a "roaring capitalist success story" throwing off its shackles on a one-way path to prosperity. The Indian dream became an attractive mix of the old "spirituality" coupled with a romanticized view of its democracy—and now the ability for foreigners to find a Starbucks on many a street corner. Back home, the *Times of India* carried daily reports of takeovers and business deals under banner headlines such as "India Poised" and "Global Indian Takeover." The BJP benefited most, with its alluring slogan "India Shining." The "market wallahs," as they were dubbed, the IT whiz-kids, and the new aspiring call center workers in Bangalore and Hyderabad were all part of a single linear narrative—we are making it, we are joining the world club.[6]

The Gandhian ideal of national self-sufficiency gave way to full exposure to global markets and alliance with the West. Many of the global questions of human rights and social justice—from Burma, to Tibet, to Palestine—were no longer treated with the same priority by Indian governments. Nonaligned status was abandoned, and in return the Bush administration succeeded in persuading the U.S. Congress to wave through a deal in July 2005 allowing India to become a nuclear power. India received a special dispensation. Assisting the economic and military rise of a democratic India, Bush believed, would help reinforce the shift of the global balance of power in favor of "freedom." Like Singapore, the UAE, and China, India came to a deal with America: All would march to a similar economic tune in return for cooperation and a willingness on all sides to turn a blind eye to the more unsavory actions of the state.

The enthusiastic portrayal of India in foreign media as the up-and-coming nation, in competition with China, fed a new-found patriotism. It also loosened the intercommunal cohesion that had been a feature of the early years of independence. The BJP was in position to harness both of these trends as well as to convert *Hindutva*, a sense of Hindu belonging, to the abiding national cause.

In the nearly twenty years of liberalization since 1991, the poor, the 75 percent of the population living on less than $2 per day, have lived a parallel existence. Their plight is as acute now as it has ever been, inextricably linked with malnourishment and illiteracy. The grinding routine of India's downtrodden, and the humiliations they endure, has been documented in trenchant critiques by Pankaj Mishra, Arundhati Roy, and others. Books and films have described the deals between the slumlords, the police, and the politicians; the extortion and protection rackets; the beatings; the constant threats of relocation and demolition; the particular misery the monsoons bring. Research academies provide a welter of statistics, charting levels of inequality. For all the economic growth, less than 1 percent of the budget goes toward public health. Child malnutrition levels remain higher in India than in much of sub-Saharan Africa. UNICEF studies have shown that more than half of all women and three-quarters of all children below the age of three in India are anemic. The problem is not a lack of information or transparency, but a lack of will.[7]

Amartya Sen once asked how India could ever thrive being half Californian Silicon Valley and half sub-Saharan Africa. But it has thrived—and with consummate ease. In cities such as Mumbai, the proximity of the haves to the have-nots is an inconvenience for the wealthy, and they do all they can to avoid contact. City slums, from Juhu to Dharavi, are within view of the passengers in their SUVs, nestled close to airports, railway tracks, and main highways. Air-conditioned shopping malls have helped to shut out the people that shoppers might otherwise encounter in the bazaars on the street. One of the more popular malls for Mumbai's middle class is Atria, which opened in the Worli district in 2006, offering India's first Rolls-Royce showroom, Apple computer outlet, and food mall. It is situated just a few yards from corrugated sheds, a sewage treatment plant, and other manifestations of slum dwelling.

There was nothing unusual about the spending patterns of India's wealthy and aspiring wealthy over these years. They fell into the same pattern as their counterparts from Singapore to Moscow to Shanghai, from London to Milan. Consumer tastes were globalized and homogenized. Perhaps the only difference is the Indians' sense of discomfort at having to endure unsavory sights of the poor on the way to their hermetically sealed pleasures.

The author Pavan Varma has studied the development of the middle class in India during the two decades of economic reform. He divides this group into four segments: the Very Rich, comprising around 6 million people, the Consuming Class (the equivalent of the developed country's middle class), the Climbers (with a certain amount of disposable income, but a strong intention to acquire it), and the Aspirants (who do not have very much but think their children one day might). The first two groups are most important politically and economically; the other two reinforce them in their certitudes.

The paradox for India is that all these groups see themselves as hostages to forces beyond their control. In theory they are. They are subject to a democratic process without precedent in the world in which hundreds of millions of illiterate or barely literate people determine the outcome of elections. Which other country boasts a system of universal voting rights for national, regional, and local governments on such a vast scale? Vote-buying and rigging takes place, as before, but even the harshest critics concede that the electoral process tends to reflect the popular will. And that means the will of the hundreds of millions of the poor. Is it any wonder that the middle classes have adopted a siege mentality? Turnout among the wealthier classes has long been lower than among the poorer, so much so that the newspapers have taken to exhorting the middle classes to vote. The subtext was: Wake up, you wealthy; don't put your fate in the hands of others.

Setalvad's mini-fortress is close to the beach in Juhu, the district in northern Mumbai that is synonymous with Bollywood. Set back from the main roads are long lines of whitewashed villas, many with their own security guards. The Marriott Hotel is the favorite place for actors, producers, and financiers to meet to discuss deals. I am there discussing democracy with one of Hollywood's—not Bollywood's—chosen number, the director Shekhar Kapur. His latest project is a film about water shortages, a far cry from his previous more glamorous ventures. "Economic prosperity is the defining power here. Only the wealthy and the powerful have real freedom in India," he says. "Here the systems are subverted. For example, the judicial system works on a high level, but not for the poor." Why does India have such a loquacious intelligentsia and such a poor body politic? I ask him. "The only way to get ahead in politics is to be corrupt," he says. "Politicians think they have a sense of entitlement after investing so much time in getting elected."[8] Coalition building is a lucrative business. At the national level, ministries such as the ones for telecommunications and transportation provide the best opportunities to cream off contracts. A similar system applies at each rung of the ladder.

Sometimes the odd individual breaks the mold. One of the more attractive features of election campaigns in a number of democratic countries is their ability to produce mavericks. Adolf D'Souza, in Ward 63 of the Juhu district in the Bombay Municipality Corporation (the city government of Mumbai), is one. When I call for directions he tells me that his office is next door to a temple in "garage number one." Surrounded by plastic chairs, crates, a water cooler, and mounds of paper, he tells me of his miniature political experiment. An activist in Juhu's Catholic Church since his teens, he set up his own neighborhood group, the Aware Citizens Platform, in 2002. Members would monitor the performance of candidates for Mumbai's council, the Municipal Corporation. But the ratings among voters were so low that they decided to offer their own candidate next time around, which is where he came in. At the 2007 local elections, D'Souza defeated the candidate from the Congress Party by 600 votes to become the representative of Ward 63. His team spent only 57,000 rupees (roughly $1300) on the campaign; he believes his opponents spent massively more.

"I didn't make specific promises on the campaign. I simply told people that if they want to make a difference they had not just to vote but to participate," D'Souza says. His ward committee meets twice a month to make collective decisions that he has to abide by. Most of his time, however, is devoted to the immediate problems of the district—bad roads, garbage that is not cleared, dodgy sewerage, and dirty water. The problem is that, to get anything done, to hurry things along, contractors invariably require bribes, and unless you stick to the code, you are likely to be frustrated. "Here you can pay your way out of anything. There is an unspoken language," he says.

D'Souza lives with his father and travels around the area in rickshaws. He is paid 10,000 rupees per month (around $200), which would be a comfortable sum for most people, but is derisory for politicians. Estimates of the extent of the corruption among India's three layers of politicians vary. The assumption is that the vast majority, no matter what their level of professionalism at the job itself, use their tenure, particularly at the local and state level, to make money. People point to the odd individual—Manmohan Singh is one—whom they would call "clean." On the polite dinner-party circuit, where politics is treated with a mix of intrigue, disdain, and apathy, such questions raise hackles.

For many potential candidates, politics provides a route out of poverty—their own poverty. "Thousands of men have emerged from among the general mass of deprived people and taken positions in parliaments," says the writer Pankaj Mishra. "They have no special training, sometimes not even basic literacy. A large number are criminals."[9] Even if they are not criminals, they enjoy the trappings of their job. Politicians are dubbed "go-to people"; if you want anything done, the local MP or councillor can help fix it, at a price. When politicians see ordinary people outside their offices petitioning them for help, they see confirmation that they have moved above their fellow citizens in terms of social status and access to wealth. They enjoy the legal trappings of power, such as a car and foreign travel, and they know that their income will be supplemented by payments for "favors," whether that is granting planning permission, organizing access to a government minister, or turning a blind eye to a local problem. D'Souza says he refuses to take bribes. "My colleagues in the council think I am naive, but I don't care if I'm the only person swimming upstream." I ask him what he could have made in bribes so far, if he did take them. "Fifty lakhs" is his response, which corresponds to $100,000. "I could have made in these five years what it will otherwise take me in a lifetime. You could look at it as an opportunity lost."

My meetings with Setalvad, Kapur, and D'Souza—all living within a mile of each other, yet all inhabiting different worlds—reminded me of an encounter I had the last time I was in Juhu, two years before. Then the China miracle was running at full pelt. I remember meeting a group of young Indian entrepreneurs, men in their early thirties who were working in Silicon Valley, California, and returning home on a brief visit. They were earning fortunes spearheading India's software revolution. They pointed to Mumbai's decrepit airport and the slums of Juhu and Santa Cruz nearby. Why, oh why, they declared, could India not just adopt the same practices as the Chinese? Why could they not simply remove these eyesores and impediments to progress? Give these locals some compensation, if you have to, relocate them if you really must, but why should India put up with all this grubbiness? The problem was that these slums contained voters, members of parliament keen to get reelected, and change in them was stalled by a planning process that is one of the world's most cumbersome. Democracy as impediment to growth was a fashionable theory. "Can we afford democracy in this highly competitive world?" was a question I frequently heard. I heard the same in China itself, from young entrepreneurs who had been to India and disparaged this same "chaos." More recently, the same argument has been aired by sports fans. Indians marveled at the speed and efficiency of China's Olympics, contrasting China's success with the hapless attempts at building new stadia for the much more low-key Commonwealth Games in Delhi. Some commentators even suggested inviting the Chinese in to help.

So, is the impediment to such progress not so much the existence of democracy as a political mechanism, but the *quality* of that democracy as a vehicle for delivery? Is the failure of past governments to improve infrastructure and public services the result of having the vote, or the fact that the vote did not translate into pressure for action? Pallavi Aiyar, Beijing correspondent for *The Hindu* newspaper, has made a study of the Chinese and Indian systems. She offers this neat comparison: "While in China the Communist Party derived its legitimacy from delivering growth, in India a government derived its legitimacy simply from having been voted in," she wrote. "The legitimacy of democracy in many ways absolved Indian governments from the necessity of performing. The Chinese Communist Party could afford no such luxury."[10] If elections are not seen as the ultimate performance indicator, as they are in Singapore, are they then denuded of purpose?

In India's case, perhaps elections are there simply to provide a single reference point for the whole population, rich and poor, Muslim and Hindu. It is hard to deny the sheer exuberance of election campaigns. As the 2009 general election was called, the media went into overdrive about the runners and riders, the prospects for the two main parties, the Congress Party and the BJP, and the various coalition-building machinations. From Sonia Gandhi, the Italian-born scion of the great dynasty, to Modi, to several other only marginally less controversial chief ministers, Indian politics is not short of characters. Another candidate who excites passions is the leader of Uttar Pradesh. Mayawati, as she is known, invariably raises snorts of derision from the aspirant middle classes. She is a Dalit, a member of what used to be known as the Untouchables. She is openly ambitious, and she appeals to caste allegiance, which remains strong in determining voting patterns. The middle classes see her as unashamedly gauche. In one of those perennial jibes made about her at not-so-polite dinner parties, it is said that Mayawati once complained that one of the many posters of her in the state capital Lucknow did not show the Gucci label on her handbag. They laugh at one of her campaign slogans: "I'm low caste, I'm unmarried; I'm yours." They disparage her promise to her people that when she eventually makes it to the prime minister's residence in Delhi, they will be able to live like her. Her critics may not be wrong in denouncing her penchant for bling, but they are deliberately singling her out for opprobrium. The elite fear her because she is unpredictable. They have not yet managed to co-opt her into the club, but they are confident that they eventually will.

For all the sniping, most professional and amateur punters could not point to major policy differences between the two main parties at the election. And yet, no matter how great the graft, how low the performance—the Lok Sabha, the lower house, met for only forty-six days in 2008—participation on each election day is traditionally high. Historians such as Ramachandra Guha attribute the high turnout to the power of democracy itself. And they go further, arguing that democracy is what holds India together, a feat of wonder in a country of dozens of disparate languages and nationalities, great geographical variety, and a stark wealth divide. Without democracy, why would there be an India at all, Guha asks? Its survival in the face of intercommunal tension, secessionist movements, and hostile neighbors is certainly remarkable. Democracy is, for most Indians, their own version of the American dream, the unifying power of the constitutional settlement of a nation that shook off its colonial past. Just as China, according to many I spoke to, would fall apart if the grip of the Communist Party loosened, so India would lose its raison d'être if democracy was dispensed with.

"The idea of India is stronger than Indians," the commentator M. J. Akbar tells me. He cites three freedoms that hold the country together—democracy, secular rights, and gender equality (this last category is highly debatable). He compares India with the other countries in the region that took up where the British left off, particularly Pakistan, where a tiny and shrinking elite lives alongside increasingly radicalized masses. India's success, Akbar insists, can be put down to more than the fact that Nehru survived long after 1947 and Muhammad Ali Jinnah did not.[11]

Although Pakistan is dubbed a failed state and one of the most dangerous places on earth, India's death toll from terrorist attacks exceeds Pakistan's. This is rarely mentioned in India or in the West because it does not conform to the narrative of a successful democracy. According to figures from the National Counterterrorism Center in Washington, the number of people dying in India from bombings and shootings between 2004 and 2007, 4,000, was three times higher than the number dying in Pakistan from this kind of violence during the same period. And that did not include the figures from Jammu and Kashmir. The total makes India the second most dangerous place in the world, after Iraq. From Bihar and Orissa in the east to Punjab in the west and Karnataka and Tamil Nadu in the south, almost every state has at some point been affected. Most of the time, however, the elite in Delhi and Mumbai have been able to shrug off the violence, safe in the knowledge that, as long as they take precautions, they will remain unaffected. The same way of thinking applied even to a terrorist attack on parliament in 2001, in which nine people were killed. That event was attributed to specific security failings and did not intrude into the national consciousness.

The events of November 26, 2008, changed that equation. That was the night when militant Islamist fighters stormed the Taj and Oberoi hotels, the central railway station, and a Jewish cultural center, killing 172 people in an audaciously coordinated shooting spree. What mattered was not the *number* of people who died—several other terrorist attacks had been larger—but the *kind* of people who died. The Taj Mahal Palace and Tower, on the seafront next to the city's famous monument, the Gateway of India, was not just Mumbai's most opulent hotel, but the place to be seen for dinner or drinks by the courtyard pool. It was where important business meetings were held; it was the perfect marketing tool for India's elite when they wanted to project power and style to the world. That was why India's television stations rushed their outside broadcast vans to that particular site, even though more people, ordinary people, actually died at the railway station.

For three days Indian viewers were glued to their TV sets. The country has five twenty-four-hour English-language news channels. Such is the nature of rolling news that the temptation is to broadcast information before it can be verified. This was done ceaselessly during the frenzy of coverage, and a number of journalists have subsequently been blamed not just for sensationalizing the news that day but also for putting lives at risk, even for causing the deaths of guests by inadvertantly identifying on air where they might be located in the hotel. One of those blamed was Barkha Dutt, the face of NDTV, who flew down from headquarters in Delhi and alternated her reports from the two hotels. "There wasn't a single briefing; there was no coordinated point of information," she told me. During these three days the state collapsed. Journalists ran around looking for anyone with a quote. "Everyone was briefing—the navy, politicians, the police—and yet I got a sense that nobody knew what they were briefing about," says Dutt, who is also a senior editor at the station.[12]

The Indian channels focused on public outrage, not just at the terrorists themselves, but at the incompetence of the authorities' response. It took six hours for the main commando unit to arrive from Delhi because its plane had been sent to the Punjab on a regular mission, and nobody had the presence of mind to call it back. The regular police were woefully unprepared and inadequately armed; they did not carry even basic radios. "We showed that terrorism is a great leveler," Dutt says. "We showed that the country was completely uncontrolled. We wouldn't even know what it would be like to have proper surveillance." She draws a broader conclusion as well: "People are at the end of their tether in terms of sloppiness. But the danger is that people translate this into a rage over the political process as a whole." Only when Dutt returned to her section did she realize that she had become the brunt of bitter criticism. "The Internet venom was startling," she says. "I was made the fall guy for what everyone was doing."

Strange as it may seem, NDTV is more restrained than most. Two other stations, Times Now and Headlines News, which are owned by the media groups of the *Times of India* and *India Today*, respectively, are an assault on the senses. They do not separate news from comment. They are modeled on the Fox News concept of patriotism first, complexity second.

Although the various channels pursued their own, often mistaken, lines of investigation during their coverage of the gripping and terrifying siege, they all alighted immediately on the central conclusion: This must have been the work of a foreign hand, namely Pakistan. Pundits vied to outdo each other in the vehemence of their condemnations of Pakistan and the darkness of their calls for India to strike militarily at its neighbor. Rarely was it put to these armchair generals that both countries are heavily armed with nuclear weapons. The government's response was more measured than most of the media's. Ministers chose their words carefully, aware that inflammatory language could lead to anti-Muslim pogroms. Muslim leaders in India helped calm frayed nerves by condemning the terrorists.

But the siege of Mumbai was a watershed for India's prosperous classes. It prompted many of those who live in their own private Indias, insulated from the country's dysfunction, to demand a vital public service: safety. A public-interest lawsuit was filed in the city's highest court accusing the government of failing to fulfill its constitutional duty to protect citizens' right to life. Such suits have been an important mechanism for defending the rights of the downtrodden. The supporters of this one included investment bankers, corporate lawyers, and the Bombay Chamber of Commerce and Industry. It was the first time the chamber had lent its name to litigation in the public interest.

The night after the carnage in Mumbai, thousands of protesters gathered at the Gateway monument for a candlelit march, where they vented their fury at their elected leaders. Similar protests took place in Delhi, Bangalore, and Hyderabad. All were organized spontaneously, with word spreading via text message, e-mail, and Facebook. I discussed the events of those few days with Kalpana Sharma, a journalist and writer who specializes in the problems of the poor and of other vulnerable groups. We were sitting in the Leopold Bar, just around the corner from the Taj. The Leopold was where the gunmen had begun their operation that November night, calmly finishing up their dinner and paying their bill before opening fire on customers and staff, killing six people. The manager has refused to cover over the bullet holes, in memory of the events. Sharma recalls her surprise at seeing the well-to-do on the streets rather than in their cars during the protests that followed the tragic night. Their chants included a call for a ban on criminals running for political office; their placards bore demands such as "No Security, No Votes," and "No Security, No Taxes." Sharma said that as she approached one man carrying one of these placards, she had said: "You don't pay taxes, and you probably don't vote anyway." Given the rich's previous disengagement from the state, Sharma's observation was probably correct.[13]

When Shobhaa De, a writer of steamy novels—India's version of Jackie Collins—declared on NDTV that "enough is enough," she was reflecting a public yearning, a sense that something had to be done. The trouble was that nobody knew quite what. De was accused by some of inciting violence against Pakistan, or against Muslims in India. She vigorously denied such charges, arguing that she was about no longer tolerating state incompetence. I was intrigued to meet her. "We are in an intellectual, emotional, and moral crisis," she told me in her opulent apartment in Cuffe Parade, overlooking the Arabian Sea, a home befitting one of the star turns on Mumbai's celebrity circuit. "Icons, movie stars, business leaders: None of them spoke out properly against the terror attacks. The first thing they did was to urge their government to ensure the safety of themselves, their projects and their factories." De said that the elite had become "immunized, institutionalized against corruption," adding, "It's too deep-rooted now."[14]

The fury of wealthy Indians at the Mumbai bombings arose from the realization that their pact had been broken. They had enjoyed a comfortable relationship with politicians and the state. They would finance political parties and line the pockets of their elected representatives. They would privately connive in corruption, while berating its existence in public. They would demand little from the state and receive little in return, except the right to avoid taxation. They would not have to rely on lamentable public services. Their air-conditioned 4x4s would glide over the uneven roads; their diesel-fed generators would smooth over the cracks in the energy supply (in some cities, power can go off for up to twelve hours at a time); their private tanks would ensure a constant supply of clean water. The elite had seceded from active politics and had been happy to do so. They never asked questions of the security forces when violence was meted out to the less fortunate. But what they did not expect, or take kindly to, was that their lives would be put at risk by incompetents at the Home Ministry, police department, army, or intelligence services.

Heads did roll, which was quite a break with tradition in a country where officials are rarely forced out for wrongdoing. Security was stepped up in the major cities. Airports, railway and bus stations, hotels, and government buildings were sealed off. Random road blocks were mounted. But the armed officers often looked as if they were simply going through the motions, and people feared that it would not be difficult for terrorists to mount further attacks. The fear among the well-to-do is not about a security clampdown, but the lack of it. They want their cocoon to be restored.

The media reflected those fears, and played on them, too. In the course of the 1990s, as they sought profitability and increased circulation, most of the mainstream English-language newspapers and magazines—the ones catering to the aspiring middle classes—jazzed up and dumbed down. "Negative" stories all but disappeared from the pages. Rural coverage was rare, as the wealthy were concentrated in a dozen or so urban areas. Major scandals, such as the suicides of tens of thousands of indebted farmers, were barely touched, nor were the long-standing conflicts in Kashmir and the northeastern states. What coverage there was often seemed simplified and sensationalized. None of this was the result of direct censorship—least of all from politicians; rather, it had to do with commercial requirements. The *Times of India* went the furthest in blurring the lines in 2003 by introducing a service called "Medianet." This allowed companies to buy space in the paper, not for advertisements but for a certain number of column inches casting them, naturally, in a good light. Readers seemed either not to notice or not to care. The *Times* then came up with the idea of "private treaties," in which it would take stakes in companies in return for advertisements. These agreements have raised eyebrows in sections of the India media, but overall little concern has been expressed about any effect they might have on editorial integrity or independence.[15] Sales of the *Times of India* continued to increase, and others rushed to copy the examples it was setting. The most popular section of the paper was "page three," a constant diet of gossip and glamorous photographs of India's celebrity circuit—a mix of Bollywood stars, beauty queens, cricketers, and industrialists. They provided the right images for the new, confident, assertive India.

Once in a while, the media do pursue stories on injustice, but usually on behalf of a certain type of victim. The sad story of Jessica Lall was one such case. Lall was a model and actress who, one evening in April 1999, agreed to act as a celebrity barmaid at a party. Late that night a young man, Manu Sharma, and his friends approached her and asked for a drink. She refused, saying the drink had run out. They tried slipping her some money; she refused to accept it. Sharma then shot her dead. The men slipped away in the ensuing panic, but Sharma was eventually arrested. The case finally came to court seven years later, when he was acquitted in spite of all the evidence. The reason? He was the son of a wealthy Congress politician. A public campaign for a retrial, Justice for Jessica, was led by NDTV. Ten months later, under a fast-track procedure, Delhi's high court overturned the verdict and sentenced Sharma to life imprisonment. On one level, this was a laudable case of justice being done and being seen to be done, but would any of this have come to pass if Lall had not been well connected and middle class? Such a question in India would be deemed rhetorical. "Everyone was delighted about the outcome," says Meenakshy Ganguly of Human Rights Watch. "But this was a classic case of the one rule for the blessed, another for the teeming masses."[16]

One of the many curiosities of public life in India is that the English-speaking intelligentsia—an impressive array of authors, commentators, and public intellectuals—has rarely been more vocal, and yet it has rarely had so little impact on political and economic outcomes.

Outright censorship does exist, but it is rare and often subject to successful legal challenge. It is most frequently applied by state, rather than federal, authorities, and mostly against the film industry. The Central Board of Film Certification has the power to ban anything it deems offensive—sex or nudity or violence—anything it regards as inflammatory to religious sensitivities, or anything it regards as politically subversive. Its actions are invariably challenged in the courts, and more often than not it is forced either to compromise or to back down completely. One such case involved a 2002 film called *War and Peace*, which referred to nuclear weapons and to 9/11. The director won his appeal in court after the censors had demanded twenty-one cuts to his movie. The highest-profile recent example was the banning of *The Final Solution*, a film by the director Rakesh Sharma on the Gujarat riots of 2002. The courts argued that its showing could trigger communal violence. That decision was overturned in 2004 after a sustained campaign. The film received wide acclaim when it was finally shown.

The biggest challenge to free expression in India comes from the laws, some old, some new, on "hate speech." It is a problem that other multicultural states, including the United Kingdom, have also had to come to grips with. India's constitution guarantees freedom of speech, but it qualifies that right by imposing "reasonable restrictions," notably, a requirement not to harm relations between religious groups. Given the combustibility of communal relations, some form of protection could be seen as understandable. But a number of recent examples suggest that, like courts in other countries, Indian courts are interpreting the notion of "offense" more widely than before. In February 2009, the editor and the publisher of the *Statesman* in Kolkata—one of India's oldest papers, and one with an honorable tradition of standing up for free speech—were arrested after reprinting a comment piece from a British paper, the *Independent*. The article, which praised secularism and denounced religious intolerance, particularly from Islam, led to angry protests from Muslim groups. The newspaper, which over the years had led the way in the pursuit of free expression, issued a swift apology. Many saw the climbdown as a symbol of a wider problem—mob protest influencing government action and instilling in public life a new mood of self-censorship. Why cause trouble?

One person who has seldom, if ever, posed that question is Tarun Tejpal, who left mainstream journalism in 2000 to start an investigative website called Tehelka. Within weeks, he had embroiled himself in controversy and turned himself into a national name. The Tehelka team devised a sting operation, entitled Operation West End, producing tapes that showed several top government ministers and members of the military top brass taking large bribes for approving defense contracts.[17] Many commentators reacted to the scoop by asking what was new. Such was the level of cynicism among the public that it was assumed that this kind of thing went on all the time, so what was the fuss? Those with something to hide were less blasé. Tejpal narrowly escaped assassination in April 2001. Meanwhile, the government mounted a sustained campaign to discredit his investigation. The defense minister resigned after the tapes were made public, only later to be reinstated. In 2004, Tejpal turned his operation into a magazine as well, employing up to forty journalists. Three years later, his team caught a number of politicians, businessmen, and policemen on camera boasting about how they had overseen the murder and rape of Muslims in Gujarat in 2002, the same bloodshed that Teesta Setalvad's magazine had also probed.

Tejpal's security detail is even tighter than Setalvad's. His office in the south of Delhi is guarded around the clock, and he has armed police with him, operating in shifts, day and night. He pays for them himself. In the height of the arms revelations, his office and home were sandbagged. His operation is frequently on the brink of closure. "It's a miracle that we're still around, in more ways than one," he tells me in his small office. Two weeks after he published his Gujarat story, two promised funders pulled out, although he says he never ceases to be pleasantly surprised by the number of wealthy individuals who want to help him. "People know a free press is vital to democracy and they want this information out in the public domain. But they don't really want their lifestyles to be disturbed either. That is a trade-off the middle class is happy to make."[18]

Tejpal points to a gulf between the constitutional functions of India's democracy and the liberties it provides. "The myth of tolerance remains strong. In fact, through our treatment of caste, gender, children, and class we must surely be one of the cruelest free societies in world." The poor, he points out, have been living with the fear of terrorism, crime, intercommunal violence, and state violence for years. "When you are skirting life and death you have less to lose from sudden outbreaks of violence, and so you tend to make less of a fuss when they happen," he tells me.[19]

"Police encounters" is a euphemistic term used both by the mainstream media and India's law enforcement bodies to explain the death of someone at the hands of the police. Each time this occurs, an official version of what happened is put out claiming that the people killed were militants or "subjects of interest" who were gunned down just before they were about to open fire themselves. These encounters are often staged, with weapons planted on the corpse at the scene. Attempts to hold the police to account have achieved little success. In the state of Andra Pradesh, a lower court ruled in 2007 that police killings should be treated as murder. The decision was promptly overturned by the state's Supreme Court. Former police chiefs have explained that the execution squads are necessary to protect the public from criminals who will not be punished in the courts because of their judicial or political connections. In other words, the police believe they are aiding the democratic process. Controversy arises only when a clearly innocent person is killed. For nearly thirty years these shoot-to-kill encounters have been a regular occurrence in the major cities, and, according to public opinion polls, they are highly popular with the public. Journalists and television reporters are regularly invited to the scene to film the aftermath. Or they are sent elaborate press releases describing the drama of the shootout, which the reporters faithfully reproduce, emphasizing the heroic actions of the officers concerned. These cases are almost never investigated.

Shortly after the Mumbai attacks, parliament voted overwhelmingly to toughen antiterrorism legislation. The most controversial of the changes was to endorse the right of the courts to accept evidence extracted by the police from confessions, and the right to hold suspects without charging them with a crime for up to six months. Over the years, human rights groups have highlighted thousands of cases of the death and maltreatment of people held in custody, but few in India have taken any notice. The security forces have acquired almost untrammeled powers to engage in counterinsurgency across the country. The border dispute with Pakistan over Kashmir, and the long-running insurgency campaigns by the Communist-led Naxalite movement in Bihar and other states to the east, have provided the pretext for a wide array of security legislation. Some of the laws date from after independence; others are more recent. They include the Armed Forces Special Powers Act, which allows the armed forces to shoot to kill and to conduct searches without warrants within the country; the National Security Act, which permits the suspension of rights to legal representation and access to courts; and the Terrorist and Disruptive Activities (Prevention) Act, which has led to widespread instances of unrecorded detentions and torture and the arrest of relatives as hostages when a person wanted by the police absconds. Politicians argue that these measures are necessary in order to defend India's democracy from those seeking to destroy it. Their point is undermined by the almost complete lack of transparency and accountability.

Lawyers and human rights activists argue that the security forces have long targeted the poor, the vulnerable, and minorities, with or without legislation as cover. They provide considerable evidence pointing to what is called a "saffron" bias among the police, particularly in cities run by the BJP or its affiliated groups. They mean discrimination on behalf of Hindu nationalists against minorities. The problem goes far beyond demographics. Civil rights groups estimate that up to 80 percent of crimes reported by members of the public are not investigated by the police. The assumption is that the officers, or their commanders, have been paid off by criminal gangs. Conversely, a similar proportion of charges that are made have been trumped up, or achieved under duress. Governments of all parties have shown little interest in tackling the problem, in spite of efforts by nongovernmental organizations and others to persuade them. Meenakshy Ganguly of Human Rights Watch recounts one example of her own about a meeting she had with a senior government minister. "There he was, sitting behind an empty desk," she tells me. "I talk, giving him several specific examples of problems and abuses by the police and security forces. Nothing would be written down by him or his officials. At the end he would stand up and say, 'I will look into it,' and then leave."[20]

John Kenneth Galbraith once called India a "functioning anarchy."[21] The Mumbai bombings showed how apposite his description was. I wonder, given the frustrations about police competence, how far people are now prepared to go to impose greater order. Some columnists have begun to speak the unspeakable: "I am beginning to hear the same kind of middle-class murmurs and whines about the ineffectual nature of democracy and the need for authoritarian government," argued one pundit, Vir Sanghvi. He was referring to a seminal moment in India's postindependence history, the imposition of a state of emergency by Indira Gandhi in June 1975. Some 1,000 dissidents were rounded up and jailed. Two dozen political groups were banned. The media were ordered not to publish any "unauthorised, irresponsible or demoralising news items." This included cartoons and advertisements. The clampdown on virtually all human rights conformed with India's constitution, as Gandhi justified it by claiming that she needed to thwart "a deep-rooted conspiracy" that would have "led to economic chaos and collapse," making India "vulnerable to fissiparous tendencies and external danger." Democracy, she declared, "has given too much freedom to people." The most vivid memory for many Indians of that era was the forced sterilization of millions of people who had already had two children or more—or who were politically troublesome. A birth-control program that had previously been based on cooperation was turned into an instrument of state repression. In a number of villages and towns, demonstrations against the policy were put down violently by the security forces.

And yet the wealthy and the comfortable responded, as ever, with equanimity. The world's most populous democracy had been suspended with consummate ease. L. K. Advani, the minister for information and broadcasting at the time, and now leader of the BJP, recalled how easy it was to corral the media. He told a group of journalists shortly after the emergency that some "resisted these draconian measures to suppress dissent, and paid the price for it." As for the rest, "when you were only asked to bend, many of you chose to crawl."[22]

Most historians and present-day commentators prefer to dwell on the plus side: the fact that the emergency was withdrawn after twenty months, that Gandhi went straight to the electorate, assuming an endorsement for her firm hand, only to lose, surprisingly, and stand down peacefully. No matter how flawed it may be, India's democracy showed its credentials during that extreme situation.

Indira Gandhi has had a significant historical rehabilitation in recent years. Opinion polls regularly rate her as the most popular politician of the modern Indian era. "People remember her as being strong," explained Swapan Dasgupta, a prominent columnist. "She took no nonsense from hostile forces within the country, and she took no nonsense from Pakistan." According to this theory, India has since then been lumbered with a succession of prime ministers lacking the personal drive or the votes in parliament to push through radical agendas. Most have been ejected after one term. Dasgupta and many like him see Narendra Modi as the only member of the current crop of politicians capable of exercising strong leadership and following in Indira's footsteps. I ask Dasgupta if he has any foreign models in mind. He mentions Lee Kuan Yew of Singapore. It is worth recalling that during the emergency Indira's son and close adviser, Sanjay Gandhi, frequently cited Singapore's authoritarianism as the model for India to follow. For many Indians of that period, Singapore was the first foreign country they had visited. They admired Lee's success in keeping a lid on intercommunal tensions, the professionalism of Singapore's civil service, the cleanliness of the streets, and the combination of pro-market economics and strong public services. Dasgupta then dwells on another possible mentor, Russia's Vladimir Putin. "Putin inherited a collapsed superpower and restored its honor and pride. He pulled Russia back up by the bootstraps. Yes, there are distortions, the mafia, for example, and intolerance of dissent. You could call him autocratic, but he is not a dictator and he does have a popular mandate. Most important of all, he has made it a top-notch country again."[23]

"India Shining" and the other slogans of the past two globalized decades were designed with the very aim in mind of portraying India as a top-notch country. Middle-class India is intoxicated by superpower talk. The writer Pankaj Mishra told me that for this ambition to be realized in a country of such woeful poverty and inequality, the elite has to create a parallel universe. This is the world of Bangalore call centers, IT giants, Bollywood, and industrial giants such as Tata with international acquisitive zeal. This world lives alongside the slums, the fetid sewers, and the disease and malnutrition, but it is able to keep these manifestations of the old India at arm's length. Mishra agrees with Sangupta about the comparison with Russia. The business and political elites in both countries have framed their modernization projects in reference to the West. This sets them apart from China. The thirst for globalized wealth also, argued Mishra, provides fertile ground for frustrations to grow. "The fascistic undertones are unsettling," he said. "But this is also what Indira Gandhi helped create: a widely shared mood among the Indian middle class compounded equally by fear, aggressiveness, contempt and apathy; a climate of opinion in which India's various encircling cruelties feel far away."[24]

Yet, for all the dark warnings, nobody I spoke to, from a wide range of political affiliations, saw any serious prospect of a return to the emergency measures applied by Gandhi. The modern, global side of India—the India outside the slums and the poor villages—is proud of its raucous public discourse and its flamboyant democracy. Indeed, some NGOs and individuals working on community projects suggest that there may be cause for cautious optimism. They point to an increasing representation for lower castes and for women in village communes, called *panchyats*, and in urban local councils. They point to an increasing sophistication among voters, including the technically illiterate. They cite as evidence the impossibility of predicting the outcome of elections in the country. Back in 2004, the experts forecast a BJP victory and got it hopelessly wrong. The optimistic observers further suggest that voting habits and motivations are changing. Identity politics through caste or religion, although still very strong, may in some cases be giving way to a different process that bases itself more on accountability. The city of Delhi has twice re-elected the same administration, in recognition of infrastructure improvements. None of this, say the optimists, is coming from the top; it is rising up from below.

The problem in India is not the lack of formal democratic institutions, but a lack of governance, the ability to deliver social and economic freedoms for the vast majority of the people. After an initial period of state-steered socialism during the early years of independence, politicians and businessmen latched on to globalization, using power as a means of enrichment. The comfortable classes, the people who could have used the country's new wealth to engineer improvements over the past twenty years, either turned a blind eye to society's failings or knowingly played a part in them. They could have been active in the public realm. Unlike their counterparts in authoritarian states, they would not have been punished for causing trouble. Still, they chose not to. The level of complicity, therefore, is surely higher.

CHAPTER 6

Italy
One-Man Show

The lowering of the quality of democracy is embodied by a politics that doesn't ask for the mobilization or participation of citizens. It simply needs a good vibration.

EZIO MAURO,
newspaper editor

In April 2008, within days of securing a stunning electoral victory, Silvio Berlusconi invited his best friend in global politics to be the first to celebrate with him. Vladimir Putin was happy to accept. "I haven't seen him for a long time. I missed him," the Russian president declared as he arrived at the Berlusconis' holiday home on Sardinia's Costa Smeralda.[1] The twenty-seven-room "villa," La Certosa, offered VIPs and family friends (one and the same thing) a botanical garden, an artificial lake with remote-controlled waterfalls, a four-hundred-seat Greek amphitheater, and, just in case, a nuclear bunker.

The Putins were regular visitors. One summer a few years earlier their two teenage daughters had been house guests. One of the Berlusconi daughters had flown back from Australia to join them; the girls had enjoyed the sea and the night life at the millionaires' clubs in

Porto Cervo and Porto Rotondo—under the careful watch of their bodyguards.

Vladimir and Silvio had a natural affinity and similar mindsets—they enjoyed money, beautiful women, and faithful wives; they had no time for judges or journalists or anyone else who asked too many questions. The night before they had watched a show featuring scantily clad dancing girls; then the two men stayed up until 4:00 A.M. discussing the woes of the world. So it was with some trepidation and no little courage that Natalia Melikova, a correspondent for the Russian daily *Nezavisimaya Gazeta,* stood up at a press conference held later that morning by the Italian host to ask Putin to comment on three rumors that had been swirling around Moscow. Was it true that one of his daughters had moved to Munich? Was it true that he was on the point of divorcing his wife, Lyudmila? And what of those reports of his close friendship and impending nuptials to Alina Kabayeva, a glamorous twenty-four-year-old former gymnast voted the most desirable woman in Russia by readers of one magazine and now member of parliament for the pro-Kremlin United Russia Party?

As a furious Putin pursed his lips and pondered his response, Berlusconi exclaimed: "Oh! Is that true?" Putin, who had once suggested to a French journalist who had asked a question about Chechnya that he "have himself circumcised," told Melikova: "You have uttered not a single word of truth." He decided to try to make light of it and to reinforce his credentials as a ladies' man. "You mentioned an article in one of the Russian tabloids featuring the Olympic Champion in rhythmic gymnastics, Alina Kabayeva, and your colleague, the anchorwoman, Yekaterina Andreyeva. Other articles sometimes feature other beautiful and successful women. I think that nobody will be surprised if I say that I like them all, just as I like all Russian women." He paused to accept the applause of Italian journalists and a few elderly local residents who had been allowed in to see their idols. "I think that nobody will be offended if I say that I personally believe that our Russian women are the most talented and most beautiful. The only women who can compare with them in this regard are Italian women. *Grazie.*"

Putin then adopted a more serious demeanor: "I have always re-acted negatively to those who, with their snotty noses and erotic fan-tasies, meddle in other people's lives." Berlusconi followed this up by pretending, mockingly, to mow down the offending reporter with a machine gun. He then joked about swapping the Russian press with the Italian. Melikova was visibly upset. Others laughed nervously.[2] Later, a spokesman for Berlusconi tried to play down the incident: "It was just a gesture, a playful gesture; in fact, it was appreciated, as it helped give the technical time needed for a long Russian translation." "I saw Berlusconi's gesture and I know he has a reputation as being a joker," Melikova said. "I hope there are no consequences."[3] There had already been consequences for the tabloid that had published the orig-inal stories about Putin and Kabayeva, *Moskovsky Korrespondent*. Its website was immediately blocked. The paper, which had only been in existence for a few months, specializing in celebrity gossip, was part of the growing media empire of Yevgeny Lebedev, a former KGB oper-ative turned billionaire businessman. (He would later make the spec-tacular purchase of London's evening newspaper, the *Evening Standard*.) The head of Lebedev's publishing house denied any link with the controversy, saying the website had been suspended because it had overspent its budget. But the ramifications were clear when the paper issued a front-page retraction expressing deep regret for the "in-sults." It added: "We apologise to all those who consider that this story has caused them emotional suffering."[4]

Once they had dealt with the annoyance, Berlusconi and Putin pri-vately resumed their business—and business had for some time been booming between the two countries. Italy was Europe's second-largest recipient of Russian gas, and, along with Germany, its main economic champion in the European Union. Italy's oil and gas conglomerate Eni and Russia's Gazprom were closely linked. Aeroflot was in complex discussions with Alitalia about a possible takeover of the struggling Italian airline. In this respect, the two leaders were merely following a pattern established by Boris Yeltsin and a succession of Italian prime ministers. Even during Soviet times, business contacts were strong.

The friendship between Berlusconi and Putin dates back to 2001. Berlusconi had just won his second election victory; Putin was a year into establishing his hegemony over Russia. Berlusconi would see Putin in an average year more frequently than he would various EU counterparts, let alone President Bush. He would consistently defend the Russian president against international concerns about human rights and authoritarianism. Everything is easier when there is "esteem, trust, respect and friendship," Berlusconi declared. "It is a deep friendship, which, as in all things in life, helps better understanding and making decisions for the best—in this case in the interest not only of our countries but of the global community."[5]

Putin's disdain for free expression, and the dangers faced by troublesome Russian journalists, had long been clear. But is the bar not set higher for supposed democracies? It is easy to belittle the assault on Italy's liberties by focusing on Berlusconi's buffoonery. With his penchant for vulgarity (*brutta figura*, as Italians call it), he enjoys playing to the caricature. This is a man so vain that he has had a face lift and hides his hair transplants with a bandanna; a man who seeks to ingratiate himself with anyone rich or powerful, from Putin to his other "best friend," Tony Blair; and, yet, a man who will offend just about anyone, too, from Queen Elizabeth II to German Chancellor Angela Merkel to U.S. President Barack Obama, whom he described as "handsome, young and suntanned."

The Berlusconi story is about more than the rise of a prankster. The son of a Milanese bank official, the young Silvio created his own small construction company in his mid-twenties. His rise from this point to becoming Italy's richest man, with an estimated fortune of $10 billion, is a story of business prowess, dodgy dealings, and no little mystery. Just who or what financed him at different points of his career remains unknown. Berlusconi came to national prominence in the 1970s, building up his empire first through property in Milan and then in the media, taking his Mediaset company, and its holding company Fininvest, from virtually nothing to control of the three largest private television stations in Italy—Canale 5, Retequattro, and Italia 1—thus ensuring a virtual monopoly of the nonstate TV sector. These channels proved hugely popular, offering a diet of low-grade game shows, soap operas, and sexually titillating broadcasts. In both his political and business endeavors, he was assisted by Bettino Craxi, longtime leader of the Socialist Party. Personal allegiances count for far more than political ones in Italy, and each man contributed to the other's success. Berlusconi's TV stations were funded by banks controlled by the socialists. Once he set up his media empire, he used it to fund Craxi's political machine and to promote Craxi's image on the news. Craxi, in turn, fashioned a media law made to measure for Berlusconi's needs. He became godfather to Berlusconi's daughter at a secret baptism (she was born outside of marriage), and was then best man for Berlusconi's subsequent second wedding.

From the end of World War II until shortly after the collapse of the Soviet Union, Italy was ruled by coalitions dominated by the center-right Christian Democrats, who saw their main task as keeping the Communists at bay. Governments collapsed almost as soon as they were formed, but real power stayed in the same hands. A system of state larceny was enshrined. The collapse of the Cold War order broke that sense of invulnerability and impunity. Along with Giulio Andreotti, the head of the Christian Democrats, Craxi had long been associated with Tangentopoli, the network of bribes and corruption characterizing postwar Italian politics. Craxi managed to avoid Italian justice by fleeing to Tunisia, where he died in exile. Andreotti, nicknamed variously the Prince of Darkness or Beelzebub, is an even more dubious figure. In 1993 he was charged with ordering the 1979 murder of Mino Pecorelli, a journalist who had linked Andreotti to the Mafia and to the kidnapping of former prime minister Aldo Moro. A court acquitted Andreotti in 1999, but he was convicted on appeal in November 2002 and sentenced to twenty-four years in jail. He was immediately released, because of his age, eighty-three, pending another appeal, and the following year he was acquitted again.

Craxi and Andreotti personified the First Republic, which was established in 1947 and lasted forty-five years. Berlusconi personifies the Second Republic that was declared in 1992 and continues to this day. The constitutional apparatus around the two could not have been more different, but the end result was the same—a politics denuded of respectability and credibility, and rotted to the core by corruption.

Yet between 1992 and 1994, Italy seemed to be reborn. For a fleeting moment, voters began to wonder whether their state institutions might be worthy of respect. The courts finally began to tackle a web of corruption so ingrained that every party and almost every senior politician was implicated. Dozens of civil servants and businessmen were arrested and imprisoned during the Mani Pulite (Clean Hands) investigation. Others committed suicide. The political landscape was transformed, with the extinction of all the old parties, the creation of new ones, and the establishment of a constitution designed to bring stability—two blocs in a straight left-right split— and end decades of sordid deal-making. Into this void stepped Berlusconi. He established a very different political party from any that had gone before. It was called Forza Italia, which means "Forward Italy" and is a term borrowed from the vernacular of Italy's and Berlusconi's favorite sport, soccer. Forza Italia was run like a corporation, headed by his friends and contacts, and funded largely by his firm Fininvest.

In 1994, a mere three months after it was established, Forza Italia won its first election. It was a spectacular feat of political conjuring and charisma. In politics, as in business, Berlusconi assembled friends with influence who would be beholden to him. The electoral mathematics required him to form a coalition, and he opted for two other parties on the right. First he joined forces with the National Alliance, a neofascist party led by Gianfranco Fini, a polished, witty, but sinister operator who once described Benito Mussolini as "the greatest statesman of the century."[6] Until the mid-1990s Fini's party had been confined to pariah status. Then Berlusconi made a deal with Umberto Bossi's Northern League, a group that campaigned for Italy's richer north to stop subsidizing the poorer, and more left-wing, south, and if necessary, to secede from it.

The paradox of the Mani Pulite campaign was therefore to have inadvertently helped a man such as Berlusconi to reach the pinnacle of the Italian state. Firmly ensconced in power, he decreed that the business of Italian government was his business. His victory in 1994 could have been seen as a one-off, and indeed his first administration did not last long. Many voters in democratic states have opted for a maverick only to regret their decision and reverse it at the first available opportunity. But Berlusconi was different. It did not take long for voters to come back for more.

Just as the Right had regrouped, so had the Left after the discredited years of the Socialist Party. A number of groups joined together under the curious name of the "Olive Tree" coalition. A succession of center-left administrations hobbled along in government between 1996 and 2001, but they rarely enjoyed power or popularity. They expended most of their efforts trying to adapt Italy's ailing economy to the tough conditions for entering the European Union's single currency.

Berlusconi saw his chance and made his second push. He swept back into office in 2001 after offering voters an easier ride and tempting them with tax cuts. In fact, he achieved little of note in his second term, devoting his efforts to protecting himself from prosecution, as a number of corruption cases were grinding through the courts. Three successive laws were speeded through parliament: one to block evidence of illegal transactions abroad, another to decriminalize the falsification of accounts, and a third to enable defendants in a trial to change judges by shifting the case to another jurisdiction. When the first and third were ruled unconstitutional by the courts, Berlusconi responded by proposing an even more drastic law. This was to grant himself immunity from prosecution. He gave his measure a constitutional imprimatur, stipulating that it should apply to the holders of the top five jobs in the land—president, prime minister, the speakers of the two houses of parliament, and the head of the Constitutional

Court. He then went about protecting his media empire. Legislation was rushed through allowing Mediaset to retain its channels, but also granting it a huge subsidy to pursue its digital ambitions.

Berlusconi's dominance of politics was matched by dominance of the media. He combined ownership of the major private stations with increasing control over state broadcasting. He ensured that recalcitrant editors or managers were removed, usually through a word in the ear of board members. He got programs he did not like taken off the air. The most famous example came in November 2003 when the channel Rai Tre was forced to discontinue a late-night political satire show called *Raiot* after it lampooned the prime minister. The director and writer Sabina Guzzanti, who also appeared in the show, was then sued by Mediaset for airing "lies and insinuations." She turned the saga into a film, *Viva Zapatero!*, which became an art house favorite around Europe.

Berlusconi may have long been the object of scorn in liberal intellectual circles, but what is more intriguing is the appeal of this man to vast swathes of the Italian population. In a democracy, how can a leader who has openly set about to destroy an independent media and an independent judiciary, and whose personal finances are murky at best, command such popularity? Which part of the pact does Berlusconi represent? After all, his three terms in office have not brought great macroeconomic success.

"We have lived with him for twenty years. He's not an accident," says Ferruccio de Bortoli, the editor of *Il Sole 24 Ore*, Italy's main business newspaper. We are in de Bortoli's office at his newspaper's Milan headquarters, discussing the state of Italy's democracy. A man who has tracked and tormented Berlusconi throughout his career, de Bortoli points to the ambivalent approach of many Italians to democracy itself. "Berlusconi is the Italian social success model. He personifies what people would like to be. They would love to have made that kind of money without being caught." I ask him to explain. It comes down, he says, to demographics. The small businessman holds an important position in Italian society. There are more than 5 million firms with fewer than ten employees. To these entrepreneurs, Berlusconi is the epitome of success. He thinks like them. He acts like them. He does, almost instinctively, what they do. He has the same tastes, the same sense of humor. And those at the top whom they respect—other entrepreneurs and people who have made money—tend to regard checks and balances as inimical to wealth creation.[7]

"Business and the establishment consider democracy as a cost, not an advantage," de Bortoli tells me. "Many entrepreneurs and managers complain about how they have to talk to journalists, to open themselves up to scrutiny. They say things to me and to my journalists such as, 'Why can't you do something for your country?' or, 'Why do you wish to ruin my relationship with the market?'" These people want the state to protect them, but they also want it to leave them alone to do their business, and—with tax evasion in the country said to be five times higher than the European average—they want to be able to make money and keep it. The Christian Democrats had given them what they wanted, to their general satisfaction. Now they put their faith in Berlusconi, which is why he does so little to reduce red tape and clamp down on restrictive practices or corruption. Free expression is regarded as an impediment if it stands in the way of individuals making money with impunity. Not only do small shopkeepers buy into this theory, but so do large financial concerns. And the media is no exception.

In May 2003 de Bortoli was sacked as editor of *Corriere della Serra*. His offense was to have riled Berlusconi by publishing a series of derogatory commentaries and cartoons.[8] Founded in 1876, *Corriere* is the giant of Italian newspapers, with daily sales of more than 700,000—a highbrow, liberal, somewhat fusty daily with some of the strongest news values in the country. A paper of the Turin and Milan bourgeoisie, it has long played a central role in national life. De Bortoli ensured that the paper maintained its independence; it opposed Italy's participation in the Iraq War and has consistently tried to uncover political corruption. Its front-page cartoonist, Emilio Giannelli, regularly depicted Berlusconi as a grinning dwarf in a shiny bowler hat and built-up shoes. The board running the newspaper was bombarded with criticism by Berlusconi's friends. The final straw for them was a column that lambasted a line in a speech by the prime minister in which he said: "It will not be permitted for anyone who has been a communist to come to power." One of the newspaper's writers noted: "Mussolini used to say the same words. He [Berlusconi] has no reason to be afraid. But I have."[9] In order to keep on the right side of the authorities, in order to abide by the pact, the board did the necessaries and removed their troublemaker.

Given Berlusconi's hold on television, Italian newspapers form the last redoubt for robust, and trouble-making, journalism. Most of the time the worst sanction they face is the sack, as was the case with de Bortoli.[10] But most newspaper companies also take few chances when it comes to their employees' safety. The security outside *La Repubblica*'s Rome headquarters is elaborate—armed guards, permits, and individual scanning booths. The history of *La Repubblica* is shorter and less illustrious than *Corriere*'s, but under editor Ezio Mauro it has been just as assiduous in highlighting Berlusconi's assault on what is left of his country's democracy.

I knew Mauro during our time together as correspondents in Moscow in the early 1990s. We meet again in his editor's office in Rome and straightaway start to make comparisons between the two countries. We discuss the Russian trade-off that has taken place since then, with many public freedoms subjugated to private ones. Mauro says that Italian society, like many others, has become atomized, with people using the Internet and social networking to vent their opinions but rarely taking part in public demonstrations. "If you want to call it democracy, then it'd be better to call it democratic solitude," he tells me. "The citizen feels alone, feels disconnected from information and thinks he can go it alone. Once there was the possibility of interpreting personal feelings and values within a general framework of common interest. Now the citizen no longer believes in the effectiveness of publicly organized action. The citizen becomes the spectator. Politics is just a big event. The structures of power say to the citizenry: 'You feel alone, you look after your life; you delegate the rest to me. Public affairs are my business.'"[11]

His account of the Italian situation reminds me of the model for this trade-off, Singapore, where public freedoms are traded for the easy material comforts of life. Yet although the trade-off may be similar, Berlusconi is a far less impressive figure than Singapore's longtime leader, Lee Kuan Yew. Whatever one's reservations about the state of free expression and democracy in Singapore—and, as I have described, mine are copious—its founder had a coherent political philosophy and a set of principles upon which to be judged. Yet, one is regarded as an authoritarian; the other belongs to the family of democracies. This is another example of blurred dividing lines, of labels masking a more complicated, and more dangerous, reality.

Mauro argues that Italy is not alone, that much of Europe is following its lead, that the phenomenon is not confined to so-called authoritarian states. He warns off the more direct and simplistic Berlusconi-Mussolini comparisons. The contemporary phenomenon, he says, is more subtle. "People think of Berlusconi as 'old Italian'—quirky, amusing. He's actually very modern and very European. There is little understanding in Europe about this new kind of leadership. Populism offers them a short-term solution; it provides the appearance of a sword-like cut through difficult problems," Mauro says. He calls it "modern populism" or "demagogic democracy."

It is not, he says, represented by leaders of the far right who have captured headlines over the past decade, such as France's Jean-Marie Le Pen or Jorg Haider of Austria. Instead, Mauro points to more mainstream politicians, such as Nicolas Sarkozy, the current French president, and Tony Blair, statesmen who have mastered modern skills of communication. "The lowering of the quality of democracy is embodied by a politics that doesn't ask for the mobilization or participation of citizens. It simply needs a good vibration," Mauro says. "The degradation of democracy has taken place imperceptibly across Europe, and not just in Italy. We are at a tipping point."

I am struck by this point. For politicians to dominate the scene, they need not active support but merely quiescence. I hear that phrase "anesthetic for the brain" once again. Make people wealthy and secure, or at

least allow them to think that they are, and they will cede some of
their public freedoms, even in Western nations.

Having secured his stranglehold in the media, Berlusconi devoted
much of his attention during his various terms of office into shoring
up his position. In order to do so, he needed to move against the judiciary, to ensure that it did not show the same kind of independence of
spirit that it did during the "Clean Hands" era. He set out to trim the
powers of the judges, to get them off his back. One statistic is particularly striking: Berlusconi has escaped conviction in twelve major
cases; he has never been convicted despite being put on trial six times,
accused of embezzlement, tax fraud and false accounting, and attempting to bribe a judge. In some cases he has been acquitted. In others, he has been convicted, but the verdict was overturned on appeal. In
others still, a statute of limitations has expired before a case could reach
its conclusion.

Berlusconi has dressed up his assault on the judiciary as part of a
necessary set of "reforms" to a moribund system. Some reforms are
surely needed, but his record suggests a much narrower motive. An
average trial in Italy can last for up to twelve years. One bankruptcy
case of a small firm in the south started in 1962 and lasted forty-six
years. The longer a case can be drawn out, the more the defense can
claim that the passage of time has weakened the charges. The statute
of limitations has brought up to a fifth of all cases to a premature close,
with the political and business classes being the main beneficiaries. As
in India and other countries that are notional democracies, the legal
system is skewed toward the wealthy and influential. The vast majority of people convicted for white-collar crime are acquitted. Those who
do receive punishment are rarely sent to jail for more than a token period of days or weeks.

The sense of resignation or despair is palpable among the few
members of the judiciary who have sought change. As chief prosecutor in Milan, Gherardo Colombo was one of the key figures in Mani
Pulite, prosecuting officials for corruption. He retired in 2007 and now
spends his time traveling around the country to teach about the rule of

law in educational settings from universities to primary schools. "There is a plaque in every Italian court saying everyone is equal before the law," he tells me. "Now they are trying to affirm the principle that Berlusconi is anointed and untouchable." He says that root-and-branch reform of the judiciary is overdue, but adds that the problem goes deeper, to the heart of the public's priorities: "We have a genuine problem with justice. People see it as ineffective." He traces it back to the 1970s, when hundreds of people died during the period of the Red Brigades' terrorism. Most cases went unresolved, due to fear, bribery, or sheer incompetence. "Many Italians lost confidence in the judiciary then," Colombo says.[12]

The remarkable thing about Berlusconi's popularity is that he cannot even claim to have produced the material wealth that is typically part of the trade-off in such pacts. Italy's economy throughout the past decade has lagged behind that of equivalent Western European nations. He has spent much of his time in office simply looking after his own interests. His second period as prime minister came to an end in April 2006. In office he achieved precious little in terms of economic or social reform. Italy's finances had been in trouble for over a decade, falling down the EU league table for just about every economic indicator. Italy's manufacturing system—the production of machine tools, shoes, handbags, tiles, cheap furniture, ready-made clothes—was gradually being wiped out by more cost-effective goods from developing countries, particularly China. Few serious measures were taken to counter the trend. Between 2001 and 2006, under Berlusconi's leadership, Italy dropped from fourteenth to fifty-third place in the global competitiveness index. Spending on education continued to fall, as it has done for the past twenty years, down to less than 5 percent of GDP. Only half the population has had postmandatory education, which means that only half of the youths above the age of sixteen have stayed in school. This makes the average level of education in Italy one of the worst in Europe. Only a fifth of the nation's young people enter institutions of higher learning, and a majority of those who do go on to study at universities drop out before graduation.

Romano Prodi defeated Berlusconi in 2006 by a margin of only 25,000 votes. Given Berlusconi's poor performance, this was widely seen as a consolation victory. It the two years that followed, Prodi's center-left government abided by many strictures of fiscal orthodoxy set out by the European Central Bank and other economic institutions. Prodi cut the size of Italy's national debt, abolished a host of bureaucratic restrictions, and took decisive measures to counter tax evasion. He earned plaudits from the IMF and the EU but drew dismay from Italy's taxpayers, who suffered for his efforts. Given the priorities of Italy's core voters, this was more of a kamikaze run than an attempt at political longevity.

But the failure of the liberal opposition to propose an alternative to the Berlusconi model goes deeper than this. The political mainstream had reverted to type, spending most of its time looking after itself. Under the guise of clearing the hopelessly overcrowded prisons, Prodi's government declared a sweeping amnesty, which also benefited many in the establishment, including those of Berlusconi's friends who were facing long-term corruption charges. The Left's leading lights presided over another period marked by stagnation and widespread disillusionment. The most vivid symbol of the state's decrepitude was the garbage crisis in Naples, where a strike by mafia-controlled trash collectors in 2008 led to huge piles of rotting refuse spread over a vast area.

The studio of Paolo Flores d'Arcais is crammed with watercolors and oils. Painter, philosopher, journalist, and man of letters, d'Arcais is also one of the best-known critics of the Berlusconi regime. In 2002 he was one of the founders of the *girotondi*, a series of rolling demonstrations named after the Italian equivalent of "Ring Around the Rosie."[13]

He is looking a little tired as he welcomes me into his elegant Rome apartment. He immediately beckons me to his window and points to the vibrant street market below, with a variety of meats, fish, and fruits and vegetables on sale. It strikes me as one of those quintessential scenes of bourgeois Italian contentment. My host explains what really goes on. Early each trading day the same traffic policeman drives up in a van and greets the stallholders. He has an earnest look over their produce and tells them he is checking hygiene standards. Within minutes, the back of his van is miraculously filled with gifts and he goes away. Everyone is content with the outcome. What is needed, d'Arcais says, is zero tolerance for all forms of criminality, from the bottom to the top. But where does one start, particularly when so very many benefit from the status quo?

The evening before, d'Arcais had addressed about 50,000 people in the Piazza Navona. The numbers have fallen sharply since the protests of past years, such as in 2002, when organizers claimed that up to 1 million people had taken part at a single rally. That morning, as I went to see d'Arcais, coverage of the event in a number of newspapers broadly on the liberal-left was instead largely derogatory, pointing out that speakers had spent most of their time attacking each other. D'Arcais is despondent about the state of the opposition. Italy's Left, he says, has had no meaningful purpose or ideology and only a passing interest in democracy. "Has there ever been a center-left administration in Italy that is moral and courageous?" He laughs and answers his own question dismissively. Craxi was no aberration. The socialists had connived in Berlusconi's assault on the media. "That generation of the left grew up in a Stalinist milieu. For them liberal powers and free journalism and the independence of prosecutors is not part of their anthropology. They have helped Berlusconi consistently." D'Arcais points to constitutional reforms introduced in the late 1990s by a socialist-led government designed to produce stronger and more stable government. "At that point Berlusconi was on the ropes, politically, financially, and judicially. These reforms got him off the hook. These politicians are all in it together."

D'Arcais recalls a private dinner he had with Massimo d'Alema, a leading figure of the left. Their meeting took place just as Berlusconi's first term was coming to an end. D'Alema had publicly projected an image of a man keen to break with the past, to help clean up Italian public life, but d'Arcais says he realized then that d'Alema possessed some of the same instincts as Berlusconi. D'Alema "was furious with the judges," d'Arcais says. The Left could not accept the independence of the judiciary any more than the Right could. Two years later, in 1998, d'Alema became prime minister. The new constitution of the Second Republic produced a new type of political rotation, but the old instincts were preserved. That instinct has now become firmly enshrined again. The political class defends its privileges, irrespective of ideological hue.

Such was the failure of the alternatives on offer that Berlusconi's general election victory in April 2008—the third of his career—was as stunning as it was unsurprising. His coalition obtained almost 47 percent of the vote, the highest share of any group for decades. He triumphed throughout Italy, with the exception of a part of the center, encompassing some areas roughly between Rome and Genoa, the Left's last redoubt.

His main concern remained his own fate. With a huge majority in parliament's two chambers, he moved quickly to ensure that the judiciary would never hound him again. He set the tone within weeks of returning to office, devoting most of a speech before the Shopkeepers Association, a constituency close to his heart, to a tirade against the judiciary, calling it a "cancerous growth" on Italian life. Referring to himself in the third person, he insisted that from 1994 to 2006, "789 prosecutors and magistrates took an interest in the politician Berlusconi with the aim of subverting the votes of the Italian people."[14] He quickly introduced a number of legal reforms. The first was aimed at restricting telephone tapping in criminal investigations, a bizarre reversal of what other European countries were trying to do as they sought to expand wiretapping capabilities in an effort to deal with the threat of terrorism. In Berlusconi's case, as ever, the motive was self-preservation. Italian prosecutors had long relied on wire taps instead of the more conventional collection of evidence, particularly in fraud cases. He then sought to reintroduce the plan to grant top officeholders immunity from prosecution, the same one he had proposed in 2003, which had been thrown out by the Constitutional Court. This time he was far more confident of success.

He did not stop there. Also in June 2008, he made a spectacular announcement that 100,000 criminal trials would be frozen for twelve months. The law would delay any cases that had begun before June 2002 and for which conviction would carry a sentence of fewer than ten years in jail. The offenses ranged from manslaughter to theft, kidnapping, grievous bodily harm, extortion, fraud, and corruption. The government said the law would help judges focus on "more serious crimes" and that a suspension of "lesser trials" would help clear the backlog. One of the cases halted was the trial of police officers who had launched a nighttime raid on a school in Genoa during the 2001 G8 summit. The school was being used as sleeping quarters for protesters, doctors, and journalists, and more than sixty people were injured in the raid. Another involved three people who allegedly paid bribes to Iraq in return for more than a million barrels of oil. One of the most publicized cases involved a British lawyer, David Mills, the estranged husband of a British government minister close to Tony Blair. Mills had been sentenced in February 2009 to four years in jail for accepting an $800,000 bribe from Berlusconi in return for giving false evidence in two legal cases against him in the late 1990s. The wheels of justice, it might be argued, had actually turned in this instance, except that Mills was confident all the way through that he would not have to serve any of his term. By the time he had exhausted all his appeals, the statute of limitations would come into effect.

Liberal Italy, that small pocket which continued to attend *girotondi* marches, was in uproar about Berlusconi's latest legal sleights of hand. The twelve-month amnesty was dubbed the "Salva-premier," or "Save the Prime Minister," an interpretation he did little to deny. "My lawyers have informed me that this law may be applied to one of the many fanciful trials that the extreme left-wing judges have targeted me with for political ends," he declared. His justice minister, Angelino Alfano, was even more candid in his defense of the bill. "Having brilliantly won the elections, Silvio Berlusconi deserves to be able to calmly govern this government. And this country needs to be governed," he declared. Much of the country regarded the bill either with resignation or equanimity, or believed it to be his just reward. The pact was in full swing.[15]

Berlusconi believed he could now act with complete impunity to stamp his social model on his country. In one of the first appointments of his new administration, he named a former topless model, Mara Carfagna, as minister for equal opportunities. He suggested that other countries could learn from Italy's approach to women in public life. Berlusconi seemed to define that role as to look beautiful in front of the cameras—and if they did not, then to stay out of the public eye. He chided Spain's prime minister, José Luis Rodríguez Zapatero, for choosing a cabinet that was the first in Europe to have a majority of women. The Spanish government was now "too pink," Berlusconi suggested, adding: "Now he's asked for it. He'll have problems leading them."[16] Such remarks might have played well with much of his constituency. They might have played well with friends such as Vladimir Putin. They seemed to represent part of the prevailing mood.

Most of Berlusconi's personal dalliances with women were regarded with something between envy and amusement by his electorate. Even so, his second wife, Veronica Lario, finally declared in May 2009 that she had had enough of a man "who consorts with minors." She said she was filing for divorce.[17] One would think that in a society in which the Catholic Church has such a major role, people would be appalled. The church, in spite of falling attendance, does still play an important role in Italian society, with around a third of Italy's voters professing to be practicing Catholics. Nevertheless, polls suggest that an overwhelming majority ally themselves with Berlusconi or with his right-wing coalition partners. The Vatican entered into its own pact with Berlusconi, taking a hard line on his personal morality but declining to comment on his politics.

In spite of his entreaties, Berlusconi was not allowed to take Communion after divorcing his first wife in 1985 in favor of a former showgirl. *Famiglia Cristiana*, one of Italy's best-selling Catholic magazines, complained of his "shifting morals." But the Holy See, perhaps expecting Berlusconi to ensure that its doctrinal messages were applied in law, did not complain about his assault on the constitution or democracy—just as it had not done under Mussolini or during the postwar Tangentopoli. This arrangement, dubbed "a clerical dictatorship" by a former parliamentarian, was brought to the fore during the case of a certain Eluana Englaro, a woman who had lived in a persistent vegetative state since a car accident in 1992. Her story became a battleground over euthanasia. When her father finally succeeded in securing support from the Supreme Court for the family's wish to stop feeding her so that she could be allowed to die, Berlusconi, under Vatican pressure, passed an emergency decree forbidding doctors from withholding food. In a rare show of defiance, the president, Giorgio Napolitano, refused to sign the decree, however, calling it unconstitutional. Berlusconi said he would ask parliament to force the president's resignation. Englaro died three days later, but MPs changed the law to ensure there would be no repetition of this case. The church had secured the victory that was required as part of the deal.

Berlusconi took his "demagogic democracy," as the editor Ezio Mauro described it to me, to a new level. He identified, and played on, the resentments felt equally by working-class voters and the millions of small shopkeepers and traders who determine Italy's electoral politics. One of the most alarming sides to Berlusconi's third term was the increasing hostility toward immigrants and others who threatened the "Italian way of life." Such hostility was manifested across society but particularly by those small traders on whom Berlusconi relied for electoral success. Voters expressed considerable fear about the arrival of African asylum seekers, who entered via the island of Lampedusa, and Roma (gypsies), who were using the accession of Romania into the EU in 2007 to use Italy as their point of entry to the West. Berlusconi played to these feelings, describing the various groups coming in as "an army of evil." Several laws were passed in quick succession, packaged as anticrime measures, to address the issue. These speeded up the repatriation of illegal immigrants, imposed far stiffer jail sentences for those breaking immigration law, and required foreigners, including EU citizens, to show they had jobs and adequate living conditions. Citizens' patrols were extended across the country, allowing local groups to keep watch on their neighborhoods. Italian democracy was reinforcing a very particular type of vigilante justice. In one southern town, Foggia, a special bus service was established only for immigrants, to keep them away from working-class districts. This prompted inevitable comparisons with American segregation in the 1950s and apartheid in South Africa. Then, in February 2009, parliament passed a bill compelling medical staff to contact police if they suspected the patient they were treating did not have a valid visa or work permit. Critics pointed out not only the ethical repercussions—doctors turning informers of the kind last seen under Mussolini—but the fear that asylum seekers would avoid seeking medical help, even if they had contagious diseases. These complaints were to no avail. Berlusconi was tapping into the popular mood, making his own personal pact with the people, to keep them safe from "foreigners."

Two days after parliament had approved the latest immunity deal for Berlusconi and his friends, I was walking along the Piazza Venezia in the center of Rome with one of Italy's most prominent writers, Sergio Rizzo. He pointed me in the direction of a small crowd that had gathered outside the driveway of a large building. The group comprised mainly women and older folk, but seemed to be a reasonable cross section of the electorate. These were ordinary voters seeking a glimpse of their hero, Berlusconi, as he emerged from his official residence to go to work. "You have to understand what motivates these people if you want to understand the trade-off here," Rizzo told me.[18]

Rizzo is the author of a book that took Italy by storm in 2007, *The Caste: How Italian Politicians Have Become Untouchable*. It describes how "a greedy and self-reverential political class became a caste and invaded Italian society." That class is "becoming increasingly indifferent to the common good and the notion of sound administration in order to nourish itself," Rizzo wrote. The details are eye-opening; everyone at all levels of society is at it, making the rules, twisting the rules, or breaking the rules in order to give themselves privileges and money. The book shows how towns and villages cook the books in order to maximize subsidies and minimize the tax they must hand back to the center. It lists the number of state organizations that start-up companies must deal with—approximately seventy. That is, seventy sets of individuals to bribe.[19]

"Berlusconi represents the stomach of Italians. Everyone wants to win the lottery," Rizzo tells me, citing two favorite pastimes of Italians—food and playing the weekly "lotto" draw. "He ensures that he gets what he wants by looking after those around him." The president, a figurehead in Italy but notionally in charge, has at his disposal a staff of nine hundred. Rizzo's book lists the privileges of the nearly one thousand members of the two chambers of parliament, of whom an astonishing seven hundred have escort and armed protection. It describes how tiny fringe parties refuse to merge with larger ones because every group in parliament receives copious funding. Italian deputies have raised their salaries almost sixfold since 1948, today earning about double what their U.K., French, and German counterparts do. A governing class of 180,000 elected representatives around the country has at its disposal 574,215 *auto blu* (the Italian term for official cars). Berlusconi has thirteen cars in his cavalcade and eighty-one security agents, which makes him second in the global pecking order to the U.S. president in this regard.

It would be understandable if Italians disowned their political system and withdrew into a cocoon, like the wealthier Indians who are faced with institutional corruption of a similarly unfathomable scale. Rizzo points out, however, that turnout in Italian general elections is around 80 percent, well above the European average. Italians are just as gripped by the drama of election campaigns as other countries, even if, as with India, voters conclude that, once elected, governments are under little pressure to deliver. So if this is not anti-politics, what exactly is it? Many of those I spoke to see a longer-term trend—the yearning for a strong leader, or at least, as in the case of Berlusconi, the perception of one. "Authoritarianism is gradually seeping into many countries, even within the EU. Power is being handed over voluntarily," Rizzo tells me. "Here it simply takes a more obvious form."

The more the global financial crisis took hold in 2008 and 2009, the more relaxed Berlusconi appeared. Perhaps it was the fact that the Italian economy, having grown much more slowly than others in Europe, had less far to fall. Perhaps it was the opportunity presented by the crisis. He exploited the emergency to project himself as the strong man needed for occasions such as this. After a meeting with European leaders on global finances, he danced until dawn at a disco. "If I sleep for three hours, I still have enough energy to make love for another three," *La Repubblica* quoted him as telling the young crowd. "I hope that when you hit seventy, you're in as good shape as I am."[20]

Only the state, he insisted, could be trusted to help the country out of its predicament. In March 2009, he consolidated his power yet further by incorporating Fini's National Alliance into his own party. Berlusconi named the grouping the People of Freedom. He was the star of the show at its founding convention. As he entered the hall, the 6,000 delegates sprang to their feet to give him an ovation, while loudspeakers blared out Beethoven's *Ode to Joy* followed by his campaign song, "Thank Goodness for Silvio." He declared to the jubilant crowd: "We are the party of the Italian people. We are the party of Italians who love freedom and who want to remain free."[21] And in many respects he was right. It depends on one's definition of freedom. In Berlusconi's case it was freedom for individuals to make a living, by whatever means, and away from the prying eyes of the state. As ever, the opposition was no match for Berlusconi and this attractive deal.

With the judiciary and media already tamed, he now had his hands on all the levers of power. His next venture was to change the constitution, granting the president, a post which is at present largely ceremonial, full-fledged executive powers like those given to the top executives in the United States and France. And who would be the perfect fit for a new, more powerful, presidency? It would be tailor-made for Berlusconi's needs. There was only one problem. The term of the present incumbent, Napolitano, is not due to run out until 2013. If Berlusconi proceeded with his plan, he would be sure to encounter resistance. But he had overcome his opponents enough times before to feel confident of success whenever he took up the cudgels.

It would be all too easy to lay the blame for Italy's democratic recession on one man. If democracy is narrowly defined as the will of the majority, expressed in free and fair elections, then Italians might be forgiven for wondering what the problem is all about. If democracy is meant to be about something more, about public participation, scrutiny, and accountability, then Italy could be seen as not so different from the so-called authoritarian states I had visited. The institutions that should be acting as a check on politicians have been equally culpable. "Forget television: That was lost long ago," Rizzo told me. "Even Italian newspapers are very close to power. They cannot be watchdogs. We criticize our politicians, but we want the same privileges." He added: "Systemic corruption is so deep and all pervasive that it no longer matters whether a particular politician takes money on the side, although most of them do." The Mani Pulite period of the early 1990s offered a chance of a break with the past. "Fifteen years ago we had the chance to revitalize our politics," Rizzo said. "We didn't take it."

All electorates, from time to time, take leave of their senses and opt for incompetents or demagogues. A properly functioning system of checks and balances should expose their failings or their excesses. But Italians have voted for Berlusconi three times, with a high turnout and with some enthusiasm. This is a man who has used parliament to debilitate the only other two forces that can stand in the way of his power—the judiciary and the media. The Italian version of the pact is mutual myopia. So low is the voters' view of the state's ability to improve their lives that all they want it to do is to turn a blind eye to what they are up to; in return, they pledge not to trouble their leaders too much. This country at the heart of the European Union, NATO, the G8, and other international institutions is, by most barometers of constitutional and political theory, a failed state. And yet it continues to function quite happily, just as it has always done. The public freedoms have been largely corroded, but at very few times in the country's history had they been held in high esteem in any case. Instead, during both the First and Second Republics—in other words, from the end of World War II to the present day—Italians have been free to enjoy their private freedoms—to stash away as much cash as they could and to enjoy their lives. In so doing, at least during Berlusconi's tenure in office, they were merely following their leader.

CHAPTER 7

Britain

Surveillance State

Britain used to export textiles, iron, steel and pop music; now it exports Orwellian methods for monitoring the masses.

BRENDAN O'NEILL,
journalist

"The British people's commitment to human rights is born from a sense of our history, of rights forged out of shared struggles, and on the belief that free societies offer the best prospects for long-term stability and growth." It was March 2009. David Miliband, Britain's young and intelligent foreign secretary, was delivering his department's annual human rights report. It was hard for the audience to keep a straight face as Miliband declared how the United Kingdom was setting the example for others around the world to follow. Scarcely an hour after Miliband's address, the attorney general announced that she had ordered a police investigation into whether British intelligence agents had been complicit in the Americans' torture of detainees at Guantánamo Bay.

Rewind twelve years. In May 1997, Britain was gearing up for the arrival of Tony Blair and his New Labour Camelot with almost childlike enthusiasm, expectant of a brave, new, and more liberal government.

After all, the human-rights record of the previous Conservative administrations had been appalling, particularly in Northern Ireland, where prisoners had been held without being charged and the words of republican Sinn Fein leaders were not allowed to be broadcast on television (leading to the absurd situation of actors voicing their statements). The governments of Margaret Thatcher and John Major had made frequent use of the Official Secrets Act and other measures to bully journalists and stifle investigation, showing a classically high-handed establishment approach to those whom they regarded as undermining the "British way of life."

Labour vowed to be different. The party came to power promising to restore public faith in democracy. It would do this by rebuilding "trust" and introducing radical constitutional changes that would modernize the House of Parliament and the civil service, making them both more transparent and accountable. Power was devolved in Scotland, Wales, and London. A Freedom of Information Act was passed, albeit after a considerable delay and in a heavily diluted form from the original plans. Most important of all, the European Convention on Human Rights was incorporated into U.K. law, enshrining basic rights into Britain's unwritten constitution.

So how did it happen that the administrations of Blair and his successor, Gordon Brown, would go down as being two of the most illiberal in modern British history?

There is no single answer, but there are many clues. Some are narrowly political. Blair had inherited a package of reform measures from his party machine, but his heart was clearly not in them. Why disperse power when you have suddenly acquired so much of it? The large parliamentary majorities secured in 1997 and 2001 engendered in the prime minister and those around him a hubris that would be their undoing—manifested most famously in the Iraq War, but also in domestic preoccupations. That hubris was accompanied by a less perceptible but equally damaging underconfidence.

Blair believed essentially that Britain was both a Conservative and conservative country and that he would achieve little if he did not acquiesce to the tastes of the majority view as represented to him by poll-sters and selected newspaper magnates and editors. The terrorist at-tacks of September 11, 2001, allowed him to elide his instincts with theirs, but his journey toward an authoritarian mindset had begun be-fore then. Throw in technological advances, such as biometric data collection, and the mix became potent.

By the time Blair left office in 2007, he had bequeathed to his suc-cessor a surveillance state unrivaled anywhere in the democratic world. Parliament passed 45 criminal-justice laws—more than the total for the whole of the previous century—creating more than 3,000 new criminal offenses. That corresponded to two new offenses for each day Parliament sat during Blair's premiership. The scope was extensive: Police and security forces were given greater powers of arrest and de-tention, all institutions of the state were granted increased rights to snoop, and individuals were required to hand over unprecedented forms of data.

Abroad, the government colluded with the transport of terrorist suspects by the U.S. government to secret prisons around the world, granting landing rights at British airports for these so-called "rendi-tion" flights. At home, new crimes were created, such as glorifying ter-rorism or inciting religious hatred. "Control orders" were imposed on people deemed a security threat; this allowed people to be under ef-fective house arrest, even if they had not been charged with a crime, simply because the government claimed that the evidence it had gath-ered, by telephone taps or other means, would not be admissible in a court of law. The government also tried to cut back the scope of trial by jury, suggesting that some cases, such as serious fraud, were too complex for ordinary people to understand.

The more the state intruded into people's lives, the harder it be-came to convince them it was making them safer. Whenever figures registered a rise in crime, particularly violent crime, newspapers in-dulged in a bout of moral panic. Whenever figures suggested crime rates had fallen, newspapers insinuated that ministers had massaged the figures. Yet even though the public doubted the effectiveness of many of these laws, most opinion polls suggested either support or acquiescence for the general idea of being tough—particularly when the specific measures were not explained to the respondents. Civil liberties groups secured one or two notable victories in curbing ministerial zeal, but they felt they were battling against a popular tide.

Perhaps some kind of recalibration of the relationship between state and individual had been necessary. The social responsibility of much of mainland Europe in the 1980s compared well to the more mean-spirited and profits-means-all atmosphere of Britain, in which Margaret Thatcher had famously said there was "no such thing as society." In the mid-1990s, as Labour prepared for office, opinion polls showed the majority of the U.K. population, conservatives and liberals alike, supporting a shift away from that ethos. But a few years of life under Blair, along with a succession of home secretaries with a thirst for authoritarianism, led many to change their views. From the planned introduction of I.D. cards, to the vast extension of closed-circuit television (CCTV), to a universal DNA database, to long periods of detention without charges being filed, to restrictions on protest and publication, the Labour government went about its task with zeal.

One episode alerted me more than any other to the scale of the shift taking place in British society. As editor of the *New Statesman* magazine, the United Kingdom's premier center-left news weekly, I sought to focus on investigative journalism, a dying art in much of Great Britain. In September 2006, I commissioned a piece on the use of CCTV around the country. I asked the journalist assigned to the story, Brendan O'Neill, to try to get into one of the watching stations. It was a subject about which many people speculated, but I had not read a definitive account of how it worked and how widespread the practice was. What O'Neill came up with startled me.

I published the piece as the cover story of the magazine under the headline, "Watching You, Watching Me."[1] In his article, O'Neill describes how he was led "through subterranean concrete corridors, past industrial-sized dustbins emitting odours of rotting food, towards a pristine wooden door that seems out of place in this sewer-like set-ting." He is taken past two sets of secure doors, and then, "I can barely believe what I see next," he wrote. "I am inside what can only be de-scribed as a bunker of spies. Deep beneath the Trocadero—where un-suspecting tourists are poring over maps of the city over coffee at Starbucks and bored teens are playing beat-'em-up arcade games— there is a state-of-the-art CCTV facility where men and women in suits watch the streets of London live on vast tele-screens."

This particular watching station controls 160 cameras, 24 hours a day, 365 days a year. Since becoming operational in 2002, this partic-ular control room has recorded 24,000 "incidents," ranging from "low-level" graffiti, fly-tipping, and public urinating to "high-level" robbery, drug dealing, and prostitution. It has also had 5,000 visitors from more than 30 countries whose governments or police forces are looking to adopt similar systems. The article produced the following statistic: There are an estimated 5 million CCTV cameras in the country; that is one for every twelve citizens, or 20 percent of the CCTV cameras on the whole planet, which, considering that Britain occupies just 0.2 per-cent of the inhabitable global land mass, is quite an achievement. The average Londoner going about his or her business may be monitored by 300 cameras a day. The author concluded: "Britain used to export textiles, iron, steel and pop music; now it exports Orwellian methods for monitoring the masses."

Rereading that piece several years later, I am struck by how dated the tone feels. Perhaps I was a little naive. If so, I no longer am. In the intervening period of time, Britons have become thoroughly recon-ciled to cameras, even dependent on them. Several arguments are put forth by the advocates of surveillance. One says that poor people are more likely to be victims of street crime, so anyone who believes in so-cial justice should have no objection to the cameras. Another is more general and is usually expressed in the form of a question that goes something like this: "You want your daughters to come home safely from school, don't you?" Well, yes, but does that mean we need this? Apparently it does. Time and again, Labour ministers cited opinion polls and private research that showed not just public support for the surveillance but also public impetus for greater surveillance.

Two sets of images show how much things have changed in Britain concerning liberty, surveillance, and security. Recorded at 3:39 P.M. Greenwich Mean Time on February 12, 1993, and later broadcast nationwide, a grainy CCTV picture showed a trusting toddler taking a stranger by the hand and being led out of a Liverpool shopping center. Days later, two-year-old James Bulger was found bludgeoned to death on a railway track. On July 7, 2005, at 07:21, camera number 14 at Luton railway station, just to the north of the nation's capital, captured four young bombers who appeared chillingly calm as they prepared for their mission to blow themselves up, taking fifty Londoners with them.

In the first instance, the camera did not prevent the crime, but its imperfect images helped the police find the two eleven-year-old boys who were later convicted of the child's murder (and who, on their eventual release from custody, had to change their identities for fear of mob revenge). In the second case, the pictures made absolutely no difference to the crime. But their wide dissemination afterward was seen by the government as important for spreading the message that it would stop at nothing in its battle against terrorism. Tony Blair proclaimed after the 7/7 attacks, the United Kingdom's equivalent of 9/11: "Let no-one be in any doubt, the rules of the game are changing." Like George Bush in 2001, he used the terrorist threat to push more draconian laws past a frightened populace. And yet, compared to the United States, Britain has in some areas gone much further. It has become, as the *Washington Post* observed, "the world's premier surveillance society."[2]

How did this come to be? CCTV was first used in retail shops in the United Kingdom, but during the 1970s it gradually moved into public space, particularly the London Underground, trains, and buses. Cameras, fixed and mobile, have long been used to monitor protests and potential trouble spots such as soccer games. The technology has been getting ever smarter. Most cameras now come with automatic car license-plate recognition, facial recognition, and even suspicious behavior recognition. In 2003, software called Intelligence Pedestrian Surveillance was introduced. The program analyzes clusters and movements of pixels in CCTV footage in search of unusual activity. British scientists, backed by the Ministry of Defence and a £500,000 (roughly $800,000) government grant, have been developing cameras with "gait recognition." The aim is to have the software recognize whether people are walking suspiciously or strangely so that a human operator can be alerted.

In September 2006, Middlesbrough, a rundown town in the northeast of England, became the first metropolitan area to use "speaking" CCTV. Cameras were fitted with loudspeakers and monitored round the clock by council officials based in control rooms. The officials barked orders through the loudspeakers if they observed anyone dropping litter or behaving in other antisocial ways. If they obeyed, the operator was supposed to say "thank you." If they did not, the police could be alerted and the evidence used against the offender in court. The government was pleased with the pilot program, which was part of a plan designed to capture and punish miscreants. The plan was called "Respect."

The following year the project was extended to twenty more towns. Not to be outdone, in May 2007 the police in Merseyside, the area that encompasses the city of Liverpool, launched another new invention for combatting antisocial behavior, the Microdrone, a small battery-powered, radio-controlled helicopter that comes with a camera and a loudspeaker. It is so quiet that it can operate from a height of 106 meters without being noticed. According to its manufacturers, it is robust and can return to base even if it loses two of its four rotor blades. One unusual feature is a speaker that allows the police to give instructions to those on the ground. In George Orwell's *Nineteen Eighty-Four*, what so tormented protagonist Winston Smith about the omnipresent telescreen was that it not only watched, but also spoke.

Closed-circuit cameras were only one of many manifestations of the prying state in the United Kingdom. The Regulation of Investigatory

Powers Act, passed in 2000, is another. This snoopers' charter, like
several of the government's assaults on liberty, predated the terrorist
attacks of 9/11. Designed to equip the police and security services for
the fight against crime and terrorism, it was so widely drafted that
hundreds of public entities were brought into its remit and encouraged to avail themselves of the powers. By 2008, more than a thousand interception operations per day were taking place, and more than
six hundred public entities had been given permission to monitor in-
tercepted communications data. Over three-quarters of these were
local councils.

The annual reports of the "interception of communications commissioner" were chillingly matter of fact. In one representative nine-
month period, during 2006, more than 250,000 applications were
made to intercept private communications—and most were approved.
Not only did government departments—such as the Foreign Office,
the Home Office, the Ministry of Defence, and Scotland's First
Minister—enjoy the right to snoop, but so did the tax authorities, the
intelligence agencies, all fifty-two of the United Kingdom's police
forces, and even the fire service. The tone adopted by the communications commissioner, Paul Kennedy, was largely sympathetic to the
prying needs of the state. He hailed the "quality, dedication and enthusiasm" of the army of people listening into telephone calls and tapping into computers, although he noted that more than a thousand of
that year's bugging operations had been flawed. He put this down
mostly to administrative errors. One can only speculate on the kinds of
fascinating conversations some of these council investigators might
have uncovered. Kennedy gave a clue, saying that the suspected criminals tracked included "rogue traders, fly-tippers and fraudsters." The
commissioner was adamant that these powers were also successful in
preventing murders and tackling drugs gangs, people-smuggling, serious violent crime, and "terrorist and extremist organisations." Add to
this the following statistic: More than 10,000 permits were granted
during this period allowing state inspectors to enter people's homes. A
government review found there were 1,043 state powers of entry, in-

cluding the right to check that illegal hypnotism was not taking place or that hedges were not too high.[3]

Not all security officials were so relaxed about the new powers enjoyed and exercised by the state. When he was the government-appointed information commissioner, Richard Thomas warned, in his report for 2008, that "just as terrorism and other threats to our national security remind us that privacy and data protection cannot be absolute rights, so the fight against these evils must not run roughshod over our liberties." "Sometimes the best-intentioned plans bring the most insidious threats, where freedoms are not appreciated until it is too late to turn the clock back," he added. Thomas dismissed out of hand plans to create a government database to hold details of telephone and e-mail communications of the entire population by means of a "live" tap. "Do we really want the police, security services and other organs of the state to have access to more and more aspects of our private lives?" he asked, describing the plan as "a step too far for the British way of life." The project was being masterminded by MI6 and by GCHQ—the government's listening center in Cheltenham—and was called the Interception Modernisation Programme. The budget they were seeking and the scale of the project were staggering. In 2007 alone, 57 billion text messages were sent in the United Kingdom (1,000 per member of the population), up from 1 billion in 1999. The number of broadband Internet connections grew from 330,000 in 2001 to 18 million. Each day some 3 billion e-mails are sent, corresponding to 35,000 per second.[4]

Thomas said he was not aware of such a database in any other country. When in the past police and intelligence agencies have asked telecommunications providers for information on phone calls made, texts sent, or Internet sites visited, the provider has had the right to query the request, which might then go to the interception commissioner and another watchdog. Under the new proposals that right would be removed. "We do have to stand up and say these are our fundamental liberties and our freedoms and lines have to be drawn somewhere, and there should be a full democratic debate about where exactly the lines should be drawn," said Thomas.[5] After more than six years of fighting against the tide, Thomas went into retirement in June 2009.

This was not the only universal database the government sought to create. By stealth—and with little discussion—the United Kingdom amassed the largest-known national DNA database in the world using state-of-the-art technology. By early 2009, this database was said to contain the records of more than 5 million of the United Kingdom's 60 million citizens, including a third of all black men in the country. Records are now kept of everyone who is arrested, meaning that many on the system have never been charged with a crime. New profiles are being added at a rate of one every 45 seconds, for a total of 2,000 per day, or 700,000 per year. Ministers, egged on by the police, suggested the scheme should become universal: Why not maintain records on everyone? Dissatisfied by the rate of increase, they proposed to allow police to take the DNA—usually by means of a saliva swab from the mouth or drops of blood via a finger prick—of anyone stopped, including speeding motorists, litterbugs, and people not wearing seat belts. In December 2008, the European Court of Human Rights ruled that the British government had violated rights to privacy by storing the genetic details of people who were not convicted criminals. Ministers responded by saying they would remove such profiles from the database, but keep the original DNA samples. The inventor of genetic fingerprinting said he had been left "almost speechless" by the government's attitude. "I have significant concerns there," Alec Jeffreys said. "My genome is my property; it is not the state's. I will allow the state access to that genome under very strict circumstances. It is an issue of my personal genetic privacy."[6]

Another government plan was to increase the use of data sharing. Strict rules applied regarding the use of personal information by public entities and law-enforcement agencies; it was only to be used when it clearly applied to an ongoing investigation. In 2008, ministers drew up legislation that, if passed, would have removed all limits, allowing the assembling and aggregating of data among agencies, a potent and dangerous mix. Whenever concerns were raised, ministers countered by saying the public had already proven that it was not bothered. After all, people readily handed all manner of information over to supermarkets, Internet service providers, social-networking sites, airlines, and other businesses, and they seemed quite prepared to have satellite images of their homes accessible on Google. The boundaries between public and private were being redrawn at every turn; the government was merely following a trend that was already under way. Rarely did the government see its role as helping society to navigate a sensible way through the difficult issues of privacy and confidentiality; instead, it used the private sector as a smokescreen for taking violations of privacy to their logical conclusion.

One of the most revealing insights was provided by a state official pivotal to this process. David Omand, Whitehall's former intelligence and security coordinator, wrote in a paper for the Institute for Public Policy Research (IPPR) about the increasing need for the authorities to carry out "data mining." This entails looking at the private and personal data of individuals—including their telephone records, e-mails, shop transactions, and personal movements as tracked on license-plate recognition cameras and CCTV. These are then fed into giant computer banks to be analyzed for suspicious activity. Omand said that the "application of modern data mining and processing techniques does involve examination of the innocent as well as the suspect to identify patterns of interest for further investigation. Finding out other people's secrets is going to involve breaking everyday moral rules."[7] His candor was commendable. For the first time an important government figure had pointed out that, in order to deliver the kind of "preemptive" security needed to minimize risks from terrorism and other threats, the public would have to understand and accept that, as Blair originally warned in 2005, the rules of the game had changed. Everybody's movements, everybody's conversations, almost everybody's thinking patterns (as revealed by Internet searches and other clues), were a legitimate source of inquiry by the authorities.

The ethical issues surrounding these new mega-databases were only part of the problem. What about the professionalism of those running them? A string of embarrassing cases came to light of government departments and agencies losing confidential information. These included the tax authorities, who managed to lose computer sticks containing 25 million child-benefit records, and the Ministry of Defence, which mislaid 600,000 service records. A survey by one respected NGO, the Joseph Rowntree Reform Trust, concluded that of the fifty main government databases, fewer than ten were "effective, proportionate or necessary," while another ten actually broke privacy law.[8]

The government eventually relented on its data-sharing plans. A sustained campaign against the proposal that had brought together groups as diverse as the Licensed Taxi Drivers' Association, the Royal College of Psychiatrists, and the British Medical Association may have had something to do with this. But ministers vowed to reintroduce the plans in due course, as part of other legislation.

Britons had long jealously guarded their sense that, unless they had committed a crime, they should not have to prove their identity, least of all their bona fides, with any figure of authority. They could, in other words, walk the streets unhindered. Over the years, the principle began to erode. The first "stop and search" laws were introduced under Margaret Thatcher's government back in 1984. Since then they have been regularly modified, but never revoked, giving the police the right to stop anyone they wished on the street and then search them based on little more than suspicion. Invariably it was young members of ethnic minorities who were most picked upon. Yet, whatever the threats faced by crime or terrorism, successive governments had shied away from identity cards, a form of documentation practiced in many countries, particularly neighboring European ones. The 9/11 terrorist attacks gave the British government the opportunity to change all of this. Ministers declared, without hint of irony, that they be called "entitlement cards," and that individuals should pay for the privilege of carrying one.

The idea took some time to solidify into policy, but in 2003, amid some fanfare, the government announced plans to introduce an identity-card scheme of perhaps greater sophistication than possessed in any other country. The chip inside the cards would contain up to fifty categories of personal information on each citizen. The legislation gave the home secretary powers to add to that total without seeking a vote in Parliament. In the first few years, public support for I.D. cards appeared to be strong, but opinion polls showed support ebbing away amid growing concern over data losses and estimates of cost increases, which were expected to go from £6 billion ($10 billion) to up to £20 billion ($32 billion). Ministers adapted their arguments to suit the moment. First, they had said the cards would be used to tackle benefit fraud, then it was illegal immigration (which was high) that would be targeted, and finally, terrorism. The home secretary at the time, Charles Clarke, described the bill as a "profoundly civil libertarian measure because it promotes the most fundamental civil liberty in our society, which is the right to live free from crime and fear."[9] In spite of robust opposition in the House of Lords, the upper house of Parliament, the legislation was eventually passed in March 2006, with the intention that by 2010 all citizens residing in the United Kingdom would hold identity cards. Although the timetable began to slip amid the controversy, by November 2008 the U.K. Border Agency began issuing the first identity cards to some foreign nationals from outside the European Union. The Conservatives vowed that they would stop the plans if they took power, although many doubted they actually would.

The I.D.-card debate was a manifestation of a broader problem. I was continually struck by the gulf between politicians' views of Britain's democratic credentials and the reality. Members of Parliament would refer to the United Kingdom as the "mother of parliaments." Rarely would debates go by without references to the Magna Carta, the Glorious Revolution, or other great moments in history. Euroskeptics would marvel at Britain's doughty individualism compared to the herd instincts of those continentals, and most MPs and others in authority would no doubt say that Britain's adherence to

standards of personal liberty is high. Yet it is hard to find a nation in
the self-declared democratic world where more power is concentrated
in the hands of those in power with such a weak mandate.

Many of the most important decisions on criminal justice and civil
liberties were brought about not by primary legislation—which would
have required debates and votes in both chambers of Parliament—
but by ministerial order, which circumvents the MPs. Invariably,
however, when parliamentarians were called upon to vote, they did so
according to party instruction rather than on the merits of the case.
The only time Labour MPs showed their mettle in this area of policy was in November 2005, when they inflicted on Blair the only
parliamentary defeat of his premiership. They refused to endorse
plans to increase pretrial custody to three months—a measure far
more draconian than that existing in any equivalent Western country. In stages, the government had shifted the ancient law of habeas
corpus from twenty-four hours to fourteen days, but it insisted on
the extension because of what it said was the increased danger of terrorist attack after 9/11 and 7/7 and the greater access by terrorists to
new technology.

The liberty shortfall was reinforced by the constitutional shortfall.
The changes that the Blair government had introduced during its
heady first months in 1997 had made some difference, particularly in
establishing new legislatures for Scotland and Wales with specific law-
making powers. But the malaise at the center of political life had barely
been addressed. Parliament at Westminster was a building untouched
by time, where quaint procedures gave members a false sense of their
own importance and led them to overestimate their own ability to affect the life of the nation. The quality of MPs had gradually been deteriorating as the country's best and brightest sought out other
professions. Low turnout and limited mandates are compounded by a
lack of checks and balances. Parliament is seldom able to exercise more
than cursory oversight; as a result, debates are virtually ignored by the
public and the press. Indeed, there is a common saying that if you want
to make sure an announcement will go unnoticed, you should say it

on the floor of the House of Commons. Meanwhile, the select committees of Parliament—unlike Senate and House committees in the United States—are institutionally and intellectually bereft, more of an embarrassment than anything else. Parliament's jurisdiction over other organs of the state, notably the security services, is lamentably weak. Ironically, over the past few decades the two most important guardians of civil liberties in the United Kingdom have been the two least democratic institutions in the country—the judiciary and the unelected House of Lords.

The depth of public disillusionment with mainstream politics and with the state of the United Kingdom's democracy was set out by an independent panel called the Power Inquiry that was established by a group of eminent public figures in 2004. The panel was charged with the task of recommending ways to increase public participation in politics and improve the quality of democracy. When it published its findings two years later, in February 2006, its analysis was stark: The legitimacy of government was being undermined by the voting system, low voter turnout, and much else besides.[10]

The Power Inquiry committee declared that it was time to "save British democracy from meltdown." The most controversial of its thirty recommendations was the suggestion that the minimum voting age be reduced from eighteen to sixteen. Other proposals were for curbs on lobbyists, limits on individual donations to political parties, and enhanced powers for Parliament to hold the executive to account. The committee concluded that descriptions of the British system as an "executive democracy" were inaccurate; a better label, it said, might be "elective dictatorship." Its chairwoman, the lawyer and baroness Helena Kennedy, said the pool from which Britain's political leaders were chosen had shrunk to a puddle. Britain's elected representatives had ceased to be representative. "Politics and government are increasingly in the hands of privileged elites, as if democracy has run out of steam," she lamented. "Too often, citizens are being evicted from decision-making, rarely asked to get involved and rarely listened to." As a result, people were turning away from voting and formal politics in favor of

direct action and single-issue campaigns. The report spurred considerable but brief debate, then was quietly laid to rest.

In truth, there has never been a "golden age" of freedom in the United
Kingdom. Governments of all colors have trodden similar paths, with
prime ministers, in awe of the daily security briefings they receive, led
to believe in a perpetual danger to the state and a constant need for secrecy. Blair and his ministers followed in the footsteps of the Conservatives in setting as their default position a disdain for a liberal
"dinner-party set" that obsessed about human rights. Their pollsters
told them that the British public would put up with just about anything, from CCTV cameras to I.D. cards, preemptive custody, and
stop-and-search laws, in order to feel safer. The pollsters told them
that people bought the line that only those with something to hide
had something to fear. If you kept out of trouble, you would not get
into trouble. Where had I heard that one before?

The problem for the government was that the public was sending out
mixed signals. The problem for the public was that the media was sending out mixed signals. On the one hand, newspapers fed on fear, imply-
ing that Britons had never felt so unsafe; on the other, they warned of a
police state, with authorities forever telling people what to do and punishing them if they did not. The problem for government ministers was
not confusion, but dogma: They reduced the debate on the relationship
between state and individual to a simple matrix, a zero-sum in which
one could either be a naive libertarian who worried only about individual rights or a responsible citizen ever on the alert for threats. Histori-
cally, this has not been a left-right issue, but, after a decade of rule, the
Labour Party had all but abandoned a credible human-rights agenda.
For liberals, this was one of the most dispiriting aspects of the age.

Every country has its pact when it comes to liberty, security, and
prosperity. Most Britons, until recently, have been lulled into a false
sense of optimism about the state of their freedoms and their democracy. Part of the reason for this is historical. They were still wedded to
the memory of World War II, of a small but mighty nation flaying the

dictatorial foe. Part of it was simply a lack of revolutionary moment. The Civil War and Oliver Cromwell besides, the modern history of Britain was one of gradual, even genteel change in which the establishment, after perhaps some initial resistance, learned to adapt, absorb, and take ownership of change—from the suffragette movement for the women's vote to the modernization of the royal family after the death of Princess Diana. Gradualism had imbued in the country a sense of smugness and complacency about the way in which society was being governed.

Blair felt supremely comfortable working within those parameters. He proclaimed the need to "modernize" Britain, but in terms that reinforced the rights of those with power. He expressed his approach with the eminently reasonable notion of "a society with rules but without prejudices." If, looking back at this era, one were asked to identify Blair's most positive effect on society, one might say that it was in the social sphere. Britain became, at least on paper, more tolerant. Laws were passed recognizing civil partnership for gay couples and increasing penalties for discrimination on the basis of race, religion, gender, sexuality, and age. Blair was marking the divide between public freedoms, which were negotiable, and private freedoms, which were sacrosanct. The Singapore model was being adapted, again, to circumstance—a quintessentially British twenty-first-century pact. In the private realm, Britons had never been freer to lead their lives in the way they chose. In the public realm, from their behavior in the local park to their utterances in the media and in demonstrations, Britons were given ever narrower boundaries in which to operate. Overstep them, and the state would be given unbridled powers to hunt you down. Blair summed it up like this: "I believe in live and let live, except where your behaviour harms the freedoms of others."[11] But who and what determines harm? Unfortunately, it was a Parliament denuded of power, a government with scant popular mandate, and security services accountable to almost no one.

After ten years in power, Blair was ousted in a very British coup d'état. The man who had been plotting against him, Gordon Brown, had been his confidant throughout his political life. He was also the man who had presided over an unprecedented economic boom, which would later turn into a recessionary bust. Brown's personality could not have been more different from that of his slick, often superficial predecessor—Brown was serious, brooding, socially awkward, and prone to temper tantrums. In policy terms they had seldom been far apart, in spite of the continuously hostile briefings from both factions during years of in-fighting between what were known as the Blairites and Brownites. Brown privately criticized Blair's decision to go to war in Iraq, but had publicly supported it. He privately chastised Blair for failing to reverse the growing inequality in British society, but as the man in charge of the Treasury he had ensured minimal taxation of the rich or regulation of the banks.

In one area Brown had said precious little. Few knew his thinking on the crucial area of security and how to balance it with individual freedoms. As he angled for Blair's job, Brown hinted that he would take a less cavalier approach to Britain's constitutional norms and civil liberties. He pledged to do away with his predecessor's "sofa" style of government, a clique of officials making decisions out of sight of Parliament and the cabinet. In his first few months, he did change some of the procedures. But in the fundamental relationship between state and individual he continued where Blair had left off. Brown might not have sounded as zealous as his predecessor. Indeed, he laid down a different approach in his first few days in office, dealing with a series of attempted terrorist attacks on London and Glasgow with calm restraint on June 29 and 30, 2007. Yet, as time went on, whenever he was faced with a choice of curbing state excess or demonstrating that he was being "tough" on crime, he opted for the latter.

In October 2007, four months after taking over, Brown set out his approach to human rights in a speech on "liberty." He turned criticisms about Labour's authoritarianism on their head, saying that the new state powers were guarantors of liberty, not threats to it. Brown framed the issue of liberty through a "distinctly British interpretation," one, he said, that "asserts the importance of freedom from prejudice, of rights to privacy, and of limits to the scope of arbitrary state power, but one that also rejects the selfishness of extreme libertarianism and demands that the realm of individual freedom encompasses not just some but all of us." He added: "In my view, the key to making these hard choices in a way that is compatible with our traditions of liberty is to, at all times, apply the liberty test, respecting fundamental rights and freedoms, and wherever action is needed by government, it never subjects the citizen to arbitrary treatment, is transparent and proportionate in its measures and at all times also requires proper scrutiny by, and accountability to, Parliament and the people."[12] That was a classic red herring. Such checks and balances, such scrutiny, might apply if Parliament had shown itself to be a guardian of liberties.

Brown initially seemed uninterested in continuing in Blair's footsteps on civil liberties. But, like his predecessor, he soon became guided by two imperatives—security chiefs warned him incessantly that the situation on the streets of the United Kingdom was very dangerous; meanwhile, pollsters told him incessantly that the support for prime ministers increased whenever they talked tough. He was advised to resume Blair's battle over pretrial custody. The plan was to increase the length of the term, but to portray it as a compromise by making the increase shorter than originally proposed. So, instead of the wished-for ninety days, or the present twenty-eight, forty-two was the number his officials randomly chose. In spite of lobbying for the change, police chiefs could not point to a single instance so far where they had needed the extra time. But that was not the point. They justified it on the basis of the precautionary principle, the argument that they *might*, one day, need it, thereby reinterpreting criminal-justice law according to an undefined possible future threat. This was a variant on the "if only you knew what I know" line that Blair had adopted in reference to the elusive weapons of mass destruction in Iraq—as it later transpired, he used that information deficit to mislead Parliament and the public.

The government was reinterpreting its task of providing security not in order to minimize risk, calibrating security needs against liberty, but in order to set itself up as the guardian of all risk. In so doing, it stood accused of deliberately exaggerating the danger. Figures showed that the number of victims of terrorism among the British public was actually lower than before. In the decade of Labour government, terrorists had killed around 150 people in the United Kingdom (87 in Northern Ireland and almost all the rest on 7/7). This marked a decline of 88 percent from the 1980s. Yet, security experts and ministers countered, that did not take into account the number of attacks that *might* have happened, that were foiled. Some of the cases of foiled attacks, they said, had been reported in the media, such as when terrorist cells were broken and suspects convicted. But in many other cases, the information was not brought to light for fear of jeopardizing future intelligence operations. Ultimately the debate came down to the public being asked to trust the politicians and the security services when they warned of dangers, and asked for extra measures to counter them. After Iraq, that commodity, however, was in dangerously short supply.

A succession of senior figures in criminal justice, including the former head of M15 (the domestic spy agency) and the director of public prosecutions, lined up to oppose the forty-two-day plan and to dismiss the thinking behind it, arguing that the existing twenty-eight-day period was quite sufficient. Theirs was a dogged campaign, marking perhaps the first clear sign that the mood among the public might be changing. Eventually, in October 2008, the ministers reluctantly dropped their proposal. The successful derailing of the legislation sent out a strong signal that law should not be made on the basis of undisclosed fears about an uncertain future. One single line in the sand had been drawn.

The government may be cavalier about others' privacy, but it is zealous in protecting its own. In the last months of my term as magazine editor, I came face to face with one such incident. The Official Secrets Act is the most draconian of all the various laws circumscribing legitimate inquiry. The issue is not the existence of such a law—few would disagree that one is necessary to protect vital national security interests—but the way it has been framed, used, and abused over decades. The law was created a century ago, but in 1989 under Thatcher it was tightened, making it harder to cite a public-interest defense. This is a law that governments of all hues have exploited in order to save themselves from political embarrassment as much as to preserve security.

In early 2006, a Foreign Office official provided me with a series of leaks of information about the government's approach to militant Islam. I was convinced that the debate he was opening up was in the public interest. I had no hesitation in publishing the information. He was charged with breaking state secrets and was harassed and interrogated for a year. I refused a polite but menacing letter from the Foreign Office to provide them with documents. Throughout the case I had the impression that the government had become so arrogant and vengeful against anyone trying to coax out the truth that ministers would invoke all arms of the law to do their bidding. Faced with bullying, we tried a spot of it ourselves. I went for a one-to-one meeting with David Miliband and warned him that when the trial began, we would bring forward evidence that would embarrass senior figures in and around government. This was no idle threat. We had that information. On the first day of the trial, at the Old Bailey in January 2008, the case was abandoned.

State security formed one side of the state's attempt to have a "chilling effect" on legitimate journalism. In that area the United Kingdom is not much different from many other states. However, in comparison with the United States, which through the First Amendment bestows constitutional protection to free expression, and has enforced that protection through the courts, the British government has been steadily introducing legislation to erode it. Some of this legislation could be argued to be well intentioned, such as laws seeking to outlaw racial and religious hate speech. But when a succession of laws were passed that were designed to clamp down on exhortations to terrorist violence, they tightened the notion of speech crime and created the notion of thought crime. Specifically, they made it an offense under U.K. law to advocate any form of violent activity, even in another country, and even if it was an effort to change an illegal or undemocratic regime. While the first two laws were designed to deal with Islamic extremism, the third was aimed at soothing the frayed nerves of the Muslim community by providing Islam (and Christianity) the same defense in law as had long been enjoyed by mono-ethnic groups such as Jews and Sikhs. In so doing, the government entered a minefield, promoting itself, the police, and the courts as the arbiters of taste and offense on everything from newspaper cartoons to theatrical performances and parliamentary speeches.

In February 2009, a Dutch MP, Geert Wilders, was refused entry to the United Kingdom. He had intended to show his anti-Islamic film, *Fitna*, at the invitation of a member of the House of Lords. Wilders was declared a "threat to public policy, public security and public health." The government's decision was widely derided as providing the leader of the small far-right Freedom Party with more publicity than he could have dreamed of. It transpired that a visit he had made to London only a few weeks earlier had passed virtually unnoticed. Shortly after, ministers published a list of sixteen "undesirables" who would be prevented from entering the country, including an American right-wing "shock jock." Again, he could not have hoped for a better marketing boost for his show.

The British public was also encouraged to complain whenever it felt offended. In February 2009, a senior official at the Foreign Office was arrested after he was heard shouting expletives about Israel as he watched a television news report while running on the treadmill at the London Business School gym. He had been asked by other members of the gym to stop his tirade and, when he did not, they alerted the police, who charged him with inciting religious hatred. In an earlier era his behavior might have been regarded as a lack of taste and sensibility rather than a crime.

The state is not responsible for all the erosions of free expression. Much of the silence on controversial issues was voluntary. Self-censorship had taken grip of parts of public life, not just in the media, but also more broadly in cultural life. Public entities and other organizations across the land were tiptoeing away from areas of contention. When chairing a round-table discussion organized by the United Kingdom's main arts funding organization, the Arts Council, I was startled to hear theater directors and art gallery curators admitting that they were trying not to tackle issues of race or religion. Some cited police advice about potential unrest; others cited concern from funders or local authorities. Others took a more fundamental view, accepting the right of communities to be protected from offense. This right appears in the minds of some cultural figures to have taken precedence over the right to free speech. And yet nobody could identify the point at which they, or others, would be overstepping the mark. The context and circumstances might be quite difficult, but as with Singapore, in the United Kingdom the line is drawn so as to be deliberately vague, leaving journalists and cultural figures in a limbo where they must rely on natural human impulses to keep out of trouble. This is a very British expression of the pact.

In one area, the line is drawn very clearly. It is the most pernicious of the current restrictions on free expression—a set of libel laws drawn up centuries ago, successively hardened, and now exploited by the super rich, who are coaxed and coached by voracious British legal companies. These laws are among the most restrictive in the world. English libel law (as opposed to Scotland's, which are marginally different) is founded on an archaic premise: the assumption of a gentleman's good reputation. The burden of proof rests on the defendant in a libel case (in a reversal of the usual presumption of innocence). This rule, along with the very high costs of libel actions, have made British libel laws singularly attractive to claimants and singularly pernicious to journalists and writers. The rich and powerful look for any mention of them in publications in the United Kingdom, either online or in hard copy. They then sue for libel in British courts, knowing that they have every likelihood of winning by default. The cost of litigation is so high that few are able to defend themselves. The plaintiffs string the case along for as many months as possible, ensuring that the defendants run out of money and then attempt to settle out of court, even when they know that theirs is a cast-iron case. The United Kingdom has become the global center of what has come to be called "libel tourism." One senior editor of a national newspaper has said that he has been advised by his management board to avoid upsetting Russian oligarchs or anyone else with the power to disrupt the newspaper's finances.

The increased use of libel has had a chilling effect, and not just on investigative journalism; it has also hindered the work of international NGOs, which have long relied on confidential informants in reporting on tyrannical regimes around the world. They now spend large portions of their budget trying to shield themselves from litigation. English libel law was singled out for particular criticism in a United Nations Human Rights Committee report, which noted that it served to discourage critical media reporting on matters of serious public interest and adversely affected the ability of scholars and journalists to publish their work. Following a libel action brought by a Saudi businessman, Khalid bin Mahfouz, in the United Kingdom against the American writer Rachel Ehrenfeld for allegations she made in her book *Funding Evil*, the issue began to be seen within the United States as a threat to the First Amendment, which guarantees free expression. Ehrenfeld's book was not published in the United Kingdom; the suit was made possible when U.K. residents purchased the book online. She lost the suit but countersued in the United States.[13] In response to the controversy, New York state passed the Libel Terrorism Protection Act (known as "Rachel's Law") to defend its citizens from any future suits in the United Kingdom. Illinois did the same, while other states considered similar legislation. In Washington in 2009, following a sustained campaign by a group of congressmen, the House of Representatives approved the Free Speech Protection Act, seeking to provide similar protection in federal courts. The idea that Britain's professed closest ally requires its own legislation to protect itself from British laws on free speech is deeply humiliating to Britons.

Slowly and belatedly, the British Parliament appears to be waking up to the problem. Three backbench MPs, each from one of the three main parties, joined a group of eminent lawyers to take up the battle against libel tourism. One declared in a debate that lawyers and courts were "conspiring to shut down the cold light of independent thinking and writing about what some of the richest and most powerful people in the world are up to."[14] He cited, among others, cases heard in London, where a Tunisian had sued a Dubai-based television channel, and an Icelandic bank had sued a Danish newspaper. But the prospect of significant change is slim. Parliament appears far more exercised by the many incidents of press intrusion into people's private lives, confusing, deliberately or otherwise, the crucial role of investigative reporting with salacious, low-grade celebrity journalism.

With such weak parliamentary scrutiny, much of the burden of holding the government to account has fallen to Britain's media. The results have been mixed. In my time covering British politics, I was struck by the herd mentality of parliamentary journalists to follow each other and to think only of the next day's headline. Issues such as the state of democracy were derided by reporters just as much as they were by politicians. Around the turn of the millennium, I had a chat with a colleague who had just quit working for a newspaper to become a government information officer. It was one of those periods when Fleet Street was taking potshots at Blair, and I asked him how it felt to be part of an embattled government. He laughed: He had been shocked to discover how little reporters—never mind the public—knew what was going on in Whitehall. "I reckon on any given day you'll be lucky to find out 1 percent," he told me.

In one of his last speeches as premier, Blair described the media as a "feral beast," arguing that newspapers, whether so-called tabloids or broadsheets, and broadcasters hunted in packs, "just tearing people and reputations to bits."[15] He and his advisers took the view that the problem was an excess of criticism and a lack of accuracy and accountability. He had a strong argument for the last two points, but the first was off the mark. British journalism was adept at shouting and screaming, but, whenever tested, such as in the run-up to the Iraq War, print and broadcast media all too often fell for the government line. The New

Labour "spin" was born out of fear and loathing of the media. It succeeded in the short term, producing more pliant coverage, but in the
long term it caused untold damage to free expression in the United
Kingdom. Yet I always had more sympathy with government officials
than I did with journalists complaining about being bullied or hoodwinked. Spin doctors could only succeed in manipulating information
if they were allowed to get away with it. The problem was that editors
and their underlings enjoyed the access to top figures in government
that came only when they did their work for them. That was another
manifestation of the unseemly trade-off in British public life.

The BBC is also a shadow of its former self. Its reputation suffered
considerable harm shortly after the Iraq War. A prominent and controversial journalist, Andrew Gilligan, claimed the government had
"sexed up" the dossier on Saddam Hussein's supposed possession of
weapons of mass destruction. So far so accurate. He went on to say
that ministers and officials did so knowing that the information was
not true. The government identified a hole in Gilligan's otherwise robust argument and mounted a vicious campaign against the BBC,
which led to the resignation of the corporation's director general and
chairman. More importantly, the controversy produced a new atmosphere of timidity in the BBC's journalism. In 2005, I wrote a piece
describing how the BBC had lost its nerve and was beginning to
buckle in the face of authority. For the headline, which appeared on
the magazine's front cover, I played on the organization's acronym,
calling it "Broken, Beaten, Cowed."[16] So enraged was the BBC's new
director general that he sent an e-mail to the company's tens of thousands of staff members denouncing the piece. He produced no evidence to counter it, though, and I received dozens of messages of
support from BBC managers and other employees. In the years that
followed, this genuflecting in the face of authority only intensified. I
felt more saddened than vindicated, as the BBC had been one of the
great symbols of a robust public life.

The crisis in the British media is now acute. The Internet has
produced a new outlet for instant opinion, and the occasional piece

of instant reporting. It has democratized the dissemination of information, but without necessarily improving its quality. Twenty-four-hour instant communication requires politicians and others in public life to produce instant responses to breaking stories, rendering them accountable in the short term for a pithy response; but soon the agenda moves on, the attention span of the inquisitors wavering. Investigative journalism takes time and money, and, as a result of the financial crisis and the changing priorities of the media, it has suffered. One can count on the fingers of perhaps two hands the serious practitioners of investigative work, many of whom rely on whistleblowers.

The threat to robust inquiry is perhaps greater now than ever before in the British system. Newspapers vent their spleen, but they uncover little of what is being done. Much of British journalism has become supine in the face of intimidation from state organs and from libel and other laws. For some time reporters have complained that editors and proprietors are shying away from difficult stories for fear of "getting into trouble": In so doing, Britain's once fearless press is merely following a global trend.

What is most curious in the current British debate is that those who espouse the cause of civil liberties are now routinely branded as being "right wing." They are denounced as being obsessed with the rights of comfortable individuals rather than concerned about the rights and responsibilities of society as a whole. The absence of "liberal" voices espousing "liberal" causes is a cruel paradox. It wasn't always this way. The inability—perhaps even refusal—to take up the cause of individual rights epitomizes the current crisis of liberalism in the British left. In 1997, Blair's first cabinet included several prominent individuals who cared about these issues. Their views were quickly sidelined, and eventually they were replaced by machine politicians who saw the "delivery" of outcomes as the most important marker of success. Civil liberties became a cause to be advocated instead of a core part of the political project.

Labour ministers saw only benefits in the role of the intervention-ist state in changing behavior for the common good. The philosophi-cal underpinnings for increased state power lie in the ideas of the social reformer Jeremy Bentham. His utilitarian notion of the greatest hap-piness for the greatest number was recast by the British government as the greatest security for the greatest number—the "do whatever it takes" line of thinking. The Right took hold of the argument and re-framed it in patriotic, libertarian tones, claiming as one of its own John Stuart Mill, who wrote: "The only purpose for which power can be rightfully exercised over any member of a civilised community, against his will, is to prevent harm to others. His own good, either physical or moral, is not a sufficient warrant."[17] In other words, the role of the state should be limited to protecting individuals from major threats, such as terrorism; its remit did not extend to improving behavior as a means of changing society.

Some prominent center-left commentators did not mind being outspoken supporters of the Labour government's interpretation of the role of the state and individual. Polly Toynbee, the doyenne of this group, put it like this: "There is a moral blindness in pouring out so much righteous indignation over potential minor infractions against liberty while largely ignoring gross inequality. This is a middle-class obsession by those who are least likely to be surveyed. Liberty is tak-ing priority over equality, because it can arouse pleasing middle-class angst. There are real threats to some civil liberties—imprisonment without trial, acceptance of torture—but CCTV and ID cards are not among them." Conor Gearty, a professor of law at the London School of Economics, who has a long history of espousing center-left legal causes, warned that critics of the government were overusing the term "police state." Gearty wrote: "The Left, or at least those parts of it that believe in the progressive power of the state, need to be more careful about defining exactly where they stand when they join in this chorus of dissent."[18]

I disagree passionately with these analyses of the benign nature of the Labour government's surveillance practices. Yet I, too, felt a certain discomfort in seeing the arguments being ceded to ultra-libertarians, the kind of people who in the heyday of Margaret Thatcher celebrated the notion of getting the state "off our backs." Conservatives in the United Kingdom have now hijacked the civil liberties cause, repackaging it as the rights of freeborn Englishmen. What about immigrants and asylum seekers? Former U.S. president Franklin D. Roosevelt's freedom from want is surely at least as important as freedom from intrusion. In any case, this is not a zero-sum game. The Labour government could have been more courageous not just on civil liberties, but also on social justice and fiscal redistribution. These concepts are not in any way mutually exclusive.

These issues go beyond party politics and beyond one country. They go to the heart of the pact. Before the financial crisis, many Britons—at least the floating voters required for electoral victory—had enjoyed increasing prosperity for a decade, indulging in their favorite hobby of borrowing and spending money. The people who really mattered, the top 1 percent, were indulged as never before. Blair and Brown resisted all attempts to tax or to regulate them. Criticism about the efficacy, let alone the morality, of this approach was wafted away. Freedom from intrusion by the tax office was elevated to a sacrosanct right. Meanwhile, ministers vowed that they would stop at nothing—literally nothing—to keep them safe. This was an arrangement that suited all sides, as the polls showed. My remark about Singapore, that the state was "providing a modicum of a good life, and a quiet life, the ultimate anaesthetic for the brain,"[19] could just as easily, albeit in a somewhat different context, have applied to this decade in the United Kingdom.

So in the British case, is it the desire for prosperity or the need for security that has guided the erosion of liberties? It is both, but it is surely history, too, an absence of revolutionary ardor, a belief that change can be brought about gradually and can be absorbed by the system. Blair, in particular, was a strong advocate of private freedoms. Britons could express their social individuality as never before when it came to sexuality, for example. The quid pro quo was an unspoken deal not to meddle with the state—or to protest too vigorously.

Only once in a while did Britons appear angry enough to mobilize. Over this period the police had steadily become more heavy-handed in seeking to ban demonstrations. They began to bribe activists for information and to use cameras to monitor people during the demonstrations themselves. This use of technology was turned on its head in April 2009 during protests of the G20 summit in London on the economic crisis. When one man died at the hands of officers, the initial reaction of the police was to distort the story to exonerate itself from blame. A different version emerged when footage taken from bystanders' cell phones was posted on websites and then reported by the mainstream media. The footage showed the police thuggery in progress. More importantly, it suggested that citizens were beginning to understand that technology could be used against the state just as it had been used by the state against them.

This was an important moment, but the Blair era is perhaps even better defined by some of the other confrontations that took place. One of the most powerful was the arrest of peace protesters for reading out the names of British soldiers killed in Iraq at the Cenotaph in Whitehall, violating regulations restricting demonstrations around the Houses of Parliament. Then there was the arrest of a fifteen-year-old boy for using the word "cult" to describe the Church of Scientology in a demonstration outside the church's London headquarters. The police subsequently issued a public warning that "insulting" Scientology would now be treated as a crime. The most excruciating example, which I remember watching open-mouthed, came during the 2005 Labour Party conference when an eighty-two-year-old man, Walter Wolfgang, was manhandled and bundled out of the hall for shouting "nonsense" during a speech by the then foreign secretary, Jack Straw. Police justified their actions under a notorious clause in the Terrorism Act that gives them power to search any individual in an area designated as being vulnerable to terrorist attack. The opprobrium heaped on Labour Party organizers was intense, particularly when the media discovered that Wolfgang had escaped Nazi Germany in 1937.

The tragedy for Britain is that over the past decade it has had an extraordinary opportunity to combine an emphasis on social justice with civil liberties. In one of the most effective assessments, the former chief prosecutor, Ken Macdonald, juxtaposed the state's indulgent attitude toward the bankers who had brought global finance to its knees with its attitude toward the rest of the population. "If you mug someone in the street and you are caught, the chances are that you will go to prison. In recent years mugging someone out of their savings or their pension would probably earn you a yacht," he wrote. "So no one likes terrorists? Let's bring in lots of terror laws, the tougher the better. Let's lock up nasty people longer, and for longer before they are charged. Let's pretend that outlawing offensiveness makes the world less offensive. This frequently made useful headlines. But it didn't make our country or any other country a better or safer place to live. It didn't respect our way of life. It brought us the War on Terror and it didn't make it any easier for us to progress into the future with comfort and security."[20]

By the end of the New Labour period, not only were civil liberties in jeopardy but democracy had rarely been held in lower repute. The public was both appalled and mesmerized by newspaper revelations in May 2009 about the extent to which MPs had for years been fiddling the expenses they could claim from the parliamentary authorities. Some of the claims, for items such as fictitious mortgages, were plain criminal; others, such as assuming the taxpayer should be responsible for honorable MPs' floating duck islands and moats, were as quaint as they were arrogant. The scandal led to a number of parliamentarians being forced to repay their ill-gotten gains. Some were forced to announce that they would stand down at the general elections. Others did so voluntarily. For the first time in a long time, the public appeared to be genuinely furious with the behavior of their politicians. But how would that anger be manifested? Certainly not on the streets. Amid the handwringing, Brown declared not only that Parliament would change its ways, but that he would be at the forefront of a new "democratic renewal." Given his track record and his desperately low opinion-poll ratings, most people regarded his new-found passion for reform with a mix of disbelief and disdain.

The overall score sheet was bleak. Yet much of the rage was synthetic. Britain had throughout this period signed up to a pact. It is hard to make the case that people were duped. Blair, Brown, and their ministers had been fairly frank about their priorities. Democracy and civil liberties were flexible commodities. The role of government was to create the environment for wealth creation—and to stop in their tracks those who threatened that good.

CHAPTER 8

U.S.A.
Tainted Dream

There is a difference between two lost freedoms: those people know they have given up, and those they don't know they've given up.

MICHAEL KAZIN,
university professor and author

It is easy, particularly for outsiders, to lampoon the eight years of George W. Bush's presidency. It is easy to condemn his administration for its assault on civil liberties, both within the United States and far beyond its borders. It is more important, though, to understand why so many Americans, and not just Republican core supporters, acquiesced to this assault.

The history of the United States after 9/11 offers perhaps the purest example in the world of a citizenry knowingly trading its civil liberties for the promise of security. The pact was made at a time when the country was reeling from shock, but it was nonetheless entered into voluntarily. Bush had a simple message: In order to preserve the way of life in the "land of the free," freedom had to be curtailed. It reminded me of the phrase used by Chua Beng Huat of Singapore's National University: "Understanding the limits to freedom is what makes freedom possible."[1] The dividing lines between countries deemed to be authoritarian and countries deemed to be democracies are not as clear as people in the West believe them to be.

Many American politicians, journalists, and members of the public now insist they were hoodwinked by Bush, that they were not aware of the extent of the deceit on the road to war with Iraq or the many strategic mistakes that followed during the long occupation. They claim they only realized that corners were being cut, in the name of democratization, when they saw the pictures of Iraqis being chained like animals in Abu Ghraib prison. But these claims simply do not stand up under scrutiny. Until very late in the day—and with the exception of some dogged individuals and organizations usually on the periphery of politics—few in the mainstream of public life wanted to challenge the decisions that were being made in their name. By pinning all the blame on Bush and his coterie of neoconservatives, such as Secretary of Defense Donald Rumsfeld and Vice President Dick Cheney, America's broader political class has sought to absolve itself of its responsibilities. The three institutions that should have held the executive to account—Congress, the judiciary, and the media—abrogated their responsibilities, particularly during Bush's first term in the White House. The separation of powers and the rights of individuals, enshrined with such distinction and clarity by America's founding fathers, were cast aside with barely a murmur. How did this happen?

To understand the trade-offs Americans made in the wake of the 9/11 attacks, one must first understand the preceding decade. There were no trade-offs in the 1990s; there was no need for any. Americans— or at least the electorally enfranchised middle class—enjoyed years of material comfort and security. The collapse of communism had reinforced the link between the righteousness of Western liberal democracy and Western free markets, both of which found their apogee in the United States. The steady economic growth of the Clinton years provided not so much an anesthetic—there was no pain to dull—but a daily dose of feel-good factor, a prelapsarian state of blithe indifference. The "culture of contentment" identified by John Kenneth Galbraith had set in early in that decade.[2]

Complacency was the overarching motif of the Clinton era. Perhaps that was inevitable, even excusable. After all, the various conflicts taking place around the world did not directly affect American life or the values underpinning it. The Democratic administration came under little domestic pressure to intervene in the Balkans and stood aside during the genocide in Rwanda. Only during the latter part of Bill Clinton's term, when the true horrors of these and other conflicts had become impossible to avoid, did America summon the enthusiasm for global interventionism. Out of these episodes a new priority emerged in promoting human rights as a tool of foreign policy. It united forces on the American right, the neoconservatives, with elements on the center-left in other parts of the world, notably Tony Blair in Britain. The theory was laudable: The United Nations Declaration on Human Rights was universal and immutable, taking precedence over state sovereignty. Governments were under an international obligation to subject their actions—on a free press, an independent judiciary, multiparty democracy, individual civil liberties, and treatment of minorities—to outside scrutiny. Pressure would be applied to violators, and *in extremis* military action would be used to enforce these norms—all under the banner of humanitarian intervention. The term "responsibility to protect" came into being after Rwanda. It referred not only to the responsibility of sovereign states to protect their own people from abuse, but also the responsibility of the international community to respond, militarily if necessary, when such abuses were not rectified by sovereign states. This doctrine would have great consequences for the Bush years.

It is worth recalling that when Bush took office in January 2001, the concern in foreign governments was not that he would show an excess of zeal in his foreign policy, but that the United States would revert to isolationism. Bush appeared to have promised this result during his election campaign, and Americans appeared to feel comfortable with the idea. Bush had not at any point advocated a proactive policy of "democratization." In his early months as president, he served notice that the United States had no interest in intervening globally unless its primacy was threatened. Bush quickly tore up a number of treaty obligations, such as arms reduction agreements, chemical and biological weapons conventions, and even efforts to reduce small arms. The United States boycotted some of the most important initiatives toward improvements in global governance—from the Kyoto Agreement on climate change to reform of the United Nations. Apart from Somalia, the United States was the only nation that did not ratify the United Nations Convention on the Rights of the Child. Bush made clear that the United States had no interest in subjecting its actions to outside scrutiny. In this regard he was only following the lead set by Clinton, who on one of his last days in office had signed an order recognizing the International Criminal Court at The Hague, but with a recommendation to Congress that it not be ratified. Bush was therefore building on a double standard—the right of America to judge others on their freedom credentials, but the refusal to be judged by them.

The events of September 11, 2001, changed this entire agenda, even if it took some time for it to coalesce into a strategy. Foreigners sometimes fail to comprehend the extent of the shock that befell Americans that day. Unlike Britons, who were used to decades of Irish republican terrorism, or the French, who have suffered intermittent attacks from the Maghreb, or Germany and Italy, where violent left-wing guerrilla groups operated in the 1970s and 1980s, Americans had not suffered terrorist attacks on the streets of their major cities. It is also easy to forget how long that sense of vulnerability and fear lasted. A week after 9/11 a series of letters containing anthrax was sent to the U.S. Congress and to several media outlets, killing five people. It would take some time for the culprit and motive to be identified. The sense that "anything could happen" increased in November when an American Airlines jet plunged into the Jamaica Bay neighborhood of Queens, New York. All 260 passengers and crew, and 5 people on the ground, were killed. Even though the authorities issued statements making clear that they had found no evidence of terrorist involvement, the crash intensified an already heightened sense of panic.

The audacity and theatricality of 9/11 exacerbated the initial shock. A nation had been reduced to panic and tumult by a determined cell of Islamists. America, its president, and its institutions had been shown to be weak, and out of weakness came humiliation; out of humiliation would come defiance from a president who was initially found wanting and a people clamoring for reassurance and action.

Bush's talk of the United States being at war and his promise to do whatever it took resonated with the nation and around the world. As he found his feet and gained confidence, Bush changed the rules of engagement. At each step of the way, Americans either acquiesced or supported him. The president enjoyed high approval ratings in opinion polls, and radio talk shows vocally endorsed this more pugilistic approach. Indeed, Bush encountered no meaningful resistance. He redefined the theater of war, declaring it to be taking place within the heart of the nation, not just in foreign fields. The new War on Terror would require the full mobilization of the country's resources and the active support of its citizenry. Limiting freedom could be justified as a legitimate act of national defense.

On October 26, 2001, the two houses of Congress passed a piece of legislation that would dramatically alter the balance between liberty and security in the United States. The Patriot Act was passed, virtually without debate. Most legislators claimed afterward that they didn't have the time to read the 342-page document. They almost certainly would not have changed their minds even if they had read it. Such was the clamor to be seen to be tough on terrorism that the vast majority supported it with barely a murmur.

The scope of the act was extensive. It gave the authorities the right to unilateral and indefinite administrative detention of noncitizens. It gave the Treasury greater powers to investigate bank dealings in an attempt to stifle money laundering for terrorist purposes. It expanded the definition of dissent, suggesting that opponents of the War on Terror were not just helping terrorists but might be terrorists themselves. Overall it deliberately blurred the lines between intelligence gathering, political surveillance, and law enforcement. Many of the provisions had "sunset clauses" requiring them to be reassessed four years later.

Bush used the moment—as most politicians in his position would have done—to force through his agenda. Such was the public anxiety that he faced few impediments in enshrining his terrorist clampdown in law. However, he heeded the advice of his inner circle to go further. His order regarding covert surveillance on U.S. citizens, going beyond parts of the Patriot Act, was so secret that many in the CIA and FBI were left unaware. The provisions allowed all security agencies to demand personal customer records from Internet service providers and financial institutions without having to justify the intrusions or have them approved by the courts, either ahead of time or by judicial oversight afterward. The order was shrouded in secrecy: A gag order prevented anyone from revealing that such instructions had ever been issued. It took the *New York Times* three years to get the story; once it obtained the information, the paper's editors were so worried about accusations of being anti-American that they refrained from publishing the story for another year.[3]

Journalists appeared reluctant to investigate both the details and the implementation of the Patriot Act. In the months immediately after 9/11, some 80,000 people were rounded up in dragnets across the country. Most were of Middle Eastern origin; many were "illegals," working at gas stations, truck companies, or corner shops. Local inhabitants were told to report anything suspicious to law-enforcement agencies—and they did, providing nearly 100,000 tip-offs, via the phone or websites. Notions about being innocent until proven guilty were often discarded. The overriding priority was to prevent, at all costs, any suspected terrorist from getting away. If the wrong people were locked up as a consequence, so be it. The notion of preemptive justice had been created, without going through any democratic or political checks and balances. The dragnet led to not a single terrorism conviction.

Throughout the country, editors and producers made the choice to suppress stories on issues such as these. One experienced radio producer told me the story of a documentary she had made for a prominent station about the difficulties Arabs and Palestinians were facing in large U.S. cities in late 2001. She disclosed that several people were being held by the authorities without having been charged with a crime, and that their families had not been told where they were. When she took the program to her editors, they were deeply skeptical. Such things were not taking place, they told her. When she provided the evidence, they asked her to tone it down. The program was broadcast locally, but not nationally, for fear of causing offense.

The American Civil Liberties Union (ACLU) compiled a list of foreign academics denied entry to the United States on ideological grounds, particularly from the Middle East, particularly during Bush's first term. "The grounds are broad for inadmissibility. It is possible to exclude anyone for anything. You do not enjoy constitutional rights if you are a foreigner and outside the country," said Jameel Jaffer, director of the ACLU's National Security Project.[4]

One of the most celebrated cases of "ideological exclusion" was that of Tariq Ramadan. The Swiss-born philosopher has long been an influential voice in Europe on matters relating to Islam. That status had if anything been enhanced after 9/11. In 2003, he debated French president Nicolas Sarkozy on television one-on-one. Shortly after London suffered its own bombings, on July 7, 2005, Blair appointed Ramadan to a U.K. government commission on extremism. In February 2004, Ramadan was given a tenured appointment as professor of religion at the University of Notre Dame in Indiana. He had already rented a house, shipped his furniture there, and enrolled his children in local schools when, five months later, the State Department, acting on secret information from the Department of Homeland Security, revoked the visa that it had granted him. It took two years of repeated applications and inquiries, as well as a lawsuit by U.S. civil liberties and academic organizations, for Ramadan to receive an official explanation. Initially they were told he had violated Section 411 of the Patriot Act, which excludes foreigners who "endorse or espouse terrorist activity." Finally, the authorities provided the details. Apparently, between 1998 and 2002, Ramadan had donated $800 to a pro-Palestinian French charity that was suspected of channeling money to Hamas. The charity had not even appeared on the State Department's blacklist until 2003.

The authorities have interpreted the language of the Patriot Act so loosely that, according to official documents released under the Freedom of Information Act, anyone who is guilty of "irresponsible expressions of opinion" can be refused entry to the United States. The ACLU filed a suit challenging the constitutionality of the ban in January 2008. It also took up the case of Adam Habib, whose visa was suddenly revoked in 2006 even though he had already spent considerable time in the United States. Habib, a vice chancellor at the University of Johannesburg, had strongly criticized the war in Iraq and other U.S. foreign policy decisions. The *Christian Science Monitor*, in a report in 2006, produced a roll call of academics and public figures who had been denied visas or had them revoked or delayed until it was too late. The list included a group of seventy-four South Korean farmers and trade unionists who were opposed to a free trade agreement; a Marxist Greek academic, Yoannis Milios; M.I.A., a Sri Lankan hip-hop singer, whose lyrics were deemed to be sympathetic to the Tamil Tigers and the Palestine Liberation Organization; a Bolivian professor of Latin American history and specialist in the Aymara culture, Waskar Ari, who had been offered a position at the University of Nebraska; a Basque historian, Inaki Egana; and Dora Maria Tellez, a former Sandinista minister of health. These exclusions merely built on episodes in U.S. history when the country was under threat, or perceived itself to be so. Those who have also fallen afoul of the U.S. authorities down the years range from Graham Greene to Doris Lessing to Gabriel García Márquez. Even Pierre Trudeau was barred— prior to becoming prime minister of Canada.[5]

The Bush administration also regarded lawyers working on behalf of the Guantánamo detainees as being on the wrong side of the "with us or against us" divide. One senior human-rights figure told me that he, along with representatives of five other organizations, had been summoned to a strange meeting in early 2007 with John Bellinger, the legal adviser to the secretary of state, to talk about the act. Bellinger told them these groups had a "megaphone in their hand" that would be heard in Europe and beyond; they therefore should be "sensible" in what they said. Such threats were not made lightly.

The antipatriotic and potentially subversive network therefore included not just NGOs, but lawyers, journalists, trade unionists, and academics. Even voters were not immune from pressure. Dick Cheney responded to the victory of an antiwar candidate in the primaries in one state, Connecticut, by declaring that the result would only embolden "the al-Qaeda types," who were "betting on the proposition that ultimately they can break the will of the American people."[6]

The expansion of the security state into all areas of society curtailed freedom in terms of specific civil liberties and empowered the forces of political repression. The rhetoric deployed by the administration, and echoed in most of the mainstream media, did more than reflect the new balance between security and liberty; it helped to set it. Officials viewed opposition, in any form, as undermining the "war effort"; they portrayed dissenters as either subversive or traitorous. U.S. Attorney General John Ashcroft took the lead when he testified before the Senate in December 2001 that constitutional rights could be used as "weapons with which to kill Americans." Terrorists "exploit our openness," he said. "We are at war with an enemy who abuses individual rights as it abuses jet airliners: as weapons with which to kill Americans. We have responded by redefining the mission of the Department of Justice. Defending our nation and its citizens against terrorist attacks is now our first and overriding priority." The administration set the parameters for the public discourse, expecting others to follow. All manner of groups sprang up to echo views such as Ashcroft's, such as Americans for Victory over Terrorism, which took out a full-page advertisement in the *New York Times* on March 10, 2002, to warn against external and internal threats. Lynne Cheney, the wife of the vice president, decried liberal and leftist academics as the "weak link" in the War on Terror.[7]

Right-wing bloggers and "shock jocks" praised the administration's decisions. Though the voices of condemnation were small in number, they were sometimes loud and clear, and the debate over these issues soon became a near universal cacophony. When Susan Sontag declared in the *New Yorker* less than two weeks after the attacks that they were "a consequence of specific American alliances and actions," she was condemned variously as an "America-hater," a "moral idiot," and a "traitor" who deserved to be driven into the wilderness, never to be heard from again. Former mayor of New York Ed Koch said Sontag would "occupy the Ninth Circle of Hell for her outrageous assaults on Israel."[8] Such attacks are part of what, in military parlance, is called "the demonstration effect." If you cut off a head, you set the tone. It begins with actions or statements from on high. It then becomes the consensus view, leading those who do not share it either to stay silent or risk social alienation. Fear of causing trouble becomes all-pervasive.

A culture of self-censorship gripped the nation. It was immediate and extensive. Only those unfazed by public opinion or immune to questions of career or preferment felt empowered to criticize the status quo. Noam Chomsky, with his outspoken views about neoliberal economics and U.S. foreign policy, particularly in the Middle East, is often cited internationally as an example of the breadth of the public debate in the United States. But he and others like him also epitomized its weakness—they constituted a small core passionately listened to by a minority audience, but their views are rarely aired in mainstream media. Sometimes examples are made of even the most famous.

The chilling effect extended far beyond the subject of security and affected nearly every aspect of American political discourse. During the previous few years, one of the main issues galvanizing politics in America had been globalization and the role of international institutions in forcing ultra-neoliberal policies—the so-called Washington Consensus—on other nations. The violent protests in Seattle in 1999 and Genoa in 2001 were the more visible manifestation of a broader debate about inequality and economic models. The terrorist attacks of 9/11 put an end to such vigorous public dissent. The magazine *New Republic* highlighted this trend, declaring that anyone taking part in protests against the IMF and the World Bank—which had long been planned for later that September—had "joined the terrorists in a united front."[9] A number of prominent NGOs pulled out of the march. In the United States at least, these movements were forced to keep a lower profile.

Legislation played a crucial role in curtailing liberty after 9/11, but it could only have succeeded in the context of supportive public opinion. Journalists, legislators, and judges were as caught up in the moment as anyone else. They suspended critical faculties as they were swept along by what they saw as patriotic duty. Many liberals, wittingly or otherwise, signed up to restrictions on what the press reported. Only a month after Ashcroft's testimony, Michael Kinsley, an experienced columnist and broadcaster, produced a seminal piece on the pressure toward self-censorship after 9/11, describing journalism as being replaced by an "unprecedented flood of patriotic gush and mush." People, he said, had been "listening to their Inner Ashcroft." "I know this for a fact because I'm one of them," he wrote. "As a writer and editor, I have been censoring myself and others quite a bit since September 11." This censorship took the form not of editorial judgment, but fear of the repercussions of speaking out. "Sometimes it has been a sincere feeling that an ordinarily appropriate remark is inappropriate at this extraordinary moment. Sometimes it is genuine respect for readers who might feel that way even if I don't. But sometimes it is simple cowardice." Kinsley's assessment was painfully accurate. It recalled a number of warnings from the administration, and reflected elsewhere, of an obligation journalists had to show responsibility and patriotism. In this situation of "war," said Bush's press secretary at the time, Ari Fleischer, Americans needed to "watch what they say."[10]

American journalists who caused trouble were not thrown down stairwells, as in Russia, or imprisoned, as in China, or even issued defamation orders at the stroke of a pen, as in Singapore. But the dilemma was similar: Why cause trouble when you can give yourself an easier life? Why cause trouble if, in any case, you feel you are going against the popular tide, or if you might lay yourself open to the accusation of helping terrorists?

The desire of reporters and editors to keep out of trouble was at its peak during the eighteen-month period that started with 9/11 and included the "liberation" of Afghanistan and the preparations for war with Iraq. This was not an exclusively American phenomenon, but

U.S. journalism led the way in reproducing official misinformation and failing to hold the authorities properly to account. Throughout, there were many honorable exceptions. *The Nation* played its part, as did the *New York Review of Books*, reporters on many websites, and, sometimes, the major newspapers. *The New Yorker* was one of those publications to have endorsed the war initially, but it redeemed itself with subsequent well-researched journalism, led by Seymour Hersch. As for the *New York Times*, the reporting of weapons of mass destruction by Judith Miller has been much analyzed. During the winter of 2001 and throughout 2002, the Pulitzer Prize winner produced a series of eye-catching stories about Saddam's military ambitions. It transpired that the series had been based largely on now discredited information provided by Ahmed Chalabi, a leading figure in the opposition Iraqi National Congress, which enjoyed close political and business links with the neocons. Miller's pieces helped set the tone for much of the misreporting of the run-up to the war. The *Times* sought to redeem itself afterward with much hand-wringing and deconstruction of what happened, but at the time Miller was only doing what others were doing: following their government in lowering the burden of proof in order to justify their country's actions.[11]

Journalists and the broader body politic fell for the spin and the broader rationale. It was not just the *New York Times* that fell short. Very little work was done across the media on weapons of mass destruction, on the links between the administration and U.S. oil companies, or other motivations for the invasion. The Defense Department's plans for the occupation—"invasion lite"—were barely probed. When the Bush administration famously declared in its *National Security Strategy* document of 2002 that there was now "a single sustainable model for national success: freedom, democracy, and free enterprise," its tendentious conclusion was barely challenged.[12] Analysis was thin on the ground about the causes of resentment toward the United States— it was deemed dangerously unpatriotic to bring up the subject. The willingness of commentators, initially at least, to challenge the easy truisms of the administration was limited.

During the Iraq invasion, I came across this phenomenon of voluntary gullibility firsthand. I had spent some time in March 2003 at U.S. Central Command (Centcom) reporting on news management of the war for a BBC television documentary entitled *War Spin*. In this hermetically sealed environment, hundreds of journalists were ensconced with their media minders in the unlikely setting of a hi-tech tent in a desert just outside Doha, the capital of Qatar. The Centcom strategy was to concentrate on the visuals and then to spin the message via Doha and the Pentagon. The key was to ensure the right television footage, accompanied by reports from correspondents embedded with U.S. and U.K. forces inside Iraq. No matter how professional they were, these "embeds" were naturally wary of antagonizing the soldiers who literally had their lives in their hands. In its overall strategy, the Pentagon had been influenced by Hollywood producers of action movies, notably Jerry Bruckheimer, the man behind *Black Hawk Down*. Bruckheimer explained the thinking in an interview in our film: "You have to have a bond with somebody. If you're a cheerleader of our point of view—that we deserve peace and that we deal with human dignity—then these guys [the soldiers] are really going out on a limb and risking their own lives."[13]

Reality television was being enacted in the actual theater of war. Our film became embroiled in one of the big "human interest" stories of the Iraq campaign, the discovery that the account of the release of Jessica Lynch from the clutches of malevolent Iraqis had been largely a fake. Her rescue will go down as one of the most stunning pieces of news management yet conceived—or contrived. The Pentagon's most egregious claims had been that Lynch had had stab and bullet wounds and that she had been slapped about on her hospital bed and interrogated. In fact, she had been cared for by the doctors, who looked after her long after the militia had fled. Two days before U.S. Special Forces—cameras in tow—swooped into the hospital to take Lynch to "freedom," the doctors had arranged to deliver her by ambulance to a checkpoint, only for the Americans to open fire. Those who had brought Jessica there fled, just in time, back to the hospital, taking her back with them. The Americans had almost killed their prize catch.

None of this was mentioned in the official version of events, and when I confronted the Pentagon spokesman in Washington, Bryan Whitman, about it, he declined to release the full videotape of the rescue.

I was intrigued, but not wholly surprised, by the tone of some of the American reporting of the controversy. During interviews on CNN and other networks, my allegations were met with incredulity. This is America, I was told—we don't manipulate the news—only for Lynch herself to confirm shortly afterward that the story of her "escape" had been manufactured by the Pentagon. This was the America that cheered a few weeks later when Bush triumphantly declared "mission accomplished."

The U.S. military continued its efforts to manipulate the message long after the military occupation in Iraq was clearly failing. Its approach was neither surprising nor particularly tendentious. Far more intriguing was the willingness of the media, once again, to acquiesce. Only a tiny proportion of the more than 4,000 U.S. military dead in Iraq and 600 in Afghanistan were ever seen in American newspapers or on American television. The raw numbers were released on Defense Department and other official websites, but the images of flag-draped coffins or body bags were deemed too inflammatory to be shown. The administration and the Pentagon had imposed a strict ban on pictures or footage of such things in the media. A White House spokesman, Scott McClellan, said this was in order to "show respect for those who have made the ultimate sacrifice." Almost all media dutifully obeyed. In this respect they were following custom out of a mix of patriotism and commercialism. Some editors and managers justified it on taste grounds. Almost nobody would admit that business considerations had swayed them: Graphic images of dead Americans might upset readers and scare off advertisers. The most persuasive reasons were straightforward politics— and fear. When ABC News's *Nightline* ran names and photographs of the faces of all the U.S. troops who had been killed in Iraq, conservative groups were enraged and accused the network of harming morale.[14]

It would be all too easy, and wrong, to deduce from the Bush years that there was something particularly American about the self-censorship and obeisance. The post-2001 clampdown could, in similar circumstances, have happened anywhere else. It might have been most pronounced in the United States, but it was practiced in many other countries besides. The draconian actions of the authorities, as I have set out, were not surprising under the circumstances. But why was so much of America either enthusiastic or acquiescent? To what extent did this constitute a deliberate, and voluntary, trade-off of freedom for security among the population?

"The public has bought the line that the war on terror could last decades. People accepted regulations on their movement since 9/11 with surprising ease," says Michael Kazin of Washington's Georgetown University, an expert in social movements. If congressmen had barely acquainted themselves with the details of the post-9/11 measures, including those contained in the Patriot Act, it could hardly be expected of the citizenry to do the same. "There is a difference between two lost freedoms: those people know they have given up, and those they don't know they've given up," Kazin observes.[15]

Despite the country's vaunted rhetoric about liberty, throughout American history freedom has been regularly circumscribed. Liberties do not apply so easily to noncitizens and do not apply so easily to people who deliberately vacate the mainstream of political action and discussion. American history, points out Columbia University history professor Eric Foner, is rich with incidents of "subversives" being targeted—from the McCarthy hearings in the 1950s to the detention of ethnic Japanese during World War II. These measures generally enjoyed tremendous support from the American public while they were being carried out; it wasn't until later that they were so highly criticized. By way of anecdote, Foner tells me of a recent visit to the International Spy Museum in Washington. The museum had an interactive quiz that visitors could take on computers dotted about the premises. One of the questions was about whether the government had the right to detain people hostile to America indefinitely. Of the 30,000 visitors who had registered their votes by the time of Foner's visit, some 60 percent were in favor.[16]

"There is a vigorous debate on liberty in this country, but the boundaries within this debate are strictly set," Foner says. He suggests there is a mismatch between the rhetoric and the reality. "Teaching American history after 9/11 tells us that our devotion to freedom is not as powerful as we like to think it is." Freedom, American-style, requires conformity; one must understand its limits. Again, where had I heard that before?

These liberties are rescinded around the world, again and again, with little complaint from the vast majority of people. In the United States, the security trade-off is, in fact, not a trade-off in the original sense. This is the freedom of the few—be they foreign nationals or the disenfranchised or Communists or anyone else deemed potentially dangerous—being traded for the greater good. Values might be universal in theory in the United States, but they are selective in their application. The logic of this approach reached its apogee during the Bush years, with its mix of hubris and insecurity: Voters were content with apparent contradiction, safe in the knowledge that neither they nor anyone they knew—good God-fearing, law-abiding folk—were likely to be affected by any but the most superficial of antiterrorist measures (such as enhanced airport security, which provided them with instant reassurance). Those who were affected by wiretaps or indefinite detentions probably deserved to be; and the small minority who did not deserve to be should excuse excesses in this time of war.

Corey Robin, a political scientist at Brooklyn College in New York, has written a definitive account of the role of fear in politics. He charted the various laws and actions used in America—and not just at federal level—to sow new fear or reinforce existing fears, from the Alien and Sedition Acts of 1798 to the Anarchist Act of 1918 to the Cold War. For more than half a century, police in major cities such as Chicago, New York, and Los Angeles deployed special intelligence units against Communists, anarchists, civil rights activists, women's rights activists, trade unionists, and other "subversives." These "red squads" used violence, intimidation, and bribery of witnesses to amass information on hundreds of thousands of people. They were disbanded only in 1978.[17]

Many of these repressive measures were not taken at the federal level; indeed, in some instances they were not even endorsed at the federal level. Robin provided a useful distinction between the "big actions" of authoritarian states—such as the dawn knock at the door of the dissident—and what he calls the "small coercion and petty tyranny" intermittently practiced in democracies. Indeed, civil society—at the state or, more often, the town or village or neighborhood level—can engender and reinforce that fear rather than acting as a buffer against it. The smaller the community, the harder it is to go against the grain. Conformism is a powerful weapon: the doctor ostracized because of his atheist tendencies; the local newspaper editor forced to resign for a lack of patriotism. One of the mistakes of the civil liberties community is to focus incessantly on the actions of the federal authorities, seeing civil society as innocent and the state as tyrannical. Indeed, America has a rich history of the state intervening on behalf of civil liberties, dating back to the abolition of slavery. Franklin Roosevelt's New Deal sought to gain control of labor rights back from exploitative factory owners.

Robin makes a further point about the role of the private sector in enforcing conformism and creating, or playing to, fears. "Much authoritarianism in the US is the result of outsourcing to the private sphere. The US therefore upends our traditional conceptions," he tells me.[18] This outsourcing has been exploited with most alacrity in the workplace. Many of the great constitutional guarantees applied in the state realm, not in the civic realm. The First Amendment enshrining free expression might matter when it comes to government trying to censor a newspaper, but it makes little difference when it comes to a proprietor or editor putting pressure on a reporter, or a manager putting pressure on a worker. Even at the height of the Cold War and the McCarthy era of congressional inquisitions, the number of people imprisoned for their political beliefs numbered fewer than two hundred. Yet its influence was far-reaching in offices and factories across the United States. Two in five employees were subject to surveillance, demotions, or firings. Support for labor unions was often seen as a manifestation of nonconformity and a danger to the state.

Fast forward fifty years, to the War on Terror. Americans have seen a similar effect on the workplace: Defenders of the social order claimed that any disruption—from strikers, for example—was as threatening to the war effort as opposition to the "war" itself. The red squads were back, if not in name, at least in practice. Politicians set the tone for boards and executives to follow. In January 2003, the office of Tom DeLay, then the House majority leader, sent out a fundraising letter to supporters of the National Right to Work Foundation, a business group seeking to rid America of unions. Claiming that the labor movement "presents a clear-and-present-danger to the security of the United States at home and the safety of our Armed Forces overseas," the letter denounced "big labor bosses" who were "willing to harm freedom-loving workers, the war effort and the economy to acquire more power." Why, in that context, would any company go against the grain?[19]

Pressure on academic institutions was similarly strong during this period, but it was manifested in different ways. The most obvious restriction was, as described earlier, on foreign nationals deemed too controversial to take up posts. For the most part, the incentive to conform was more subtle than during the McCarthy era, but no less pervasive. Some of it was commercial—institutions dependent on endowments from large private organizations were loath to antagonize them.

The most sensitive issue of them all was policy toward Israel. It has long been axiomatic that criticism of Israel, which would be deemed reasonable in the rest of the world, is denounced as anti-Semitic in the United States. Indeed, parts of the mainstream press in Israel itself have a better track record than the U.S. media in holding the Israeli government to account. In the United States, many journalists either instinctively accept the official Israeli point of view or are fearful of the consequences, from their editors, of speaking out of turn. Most aspiring Middle East lecturers and professors prefer to keep their powder dry. When they do not, they tend to find their career path blocked. One such individual was Juan Cole of the University of Michigan, a Middle East expert and blogger who had been a consistent advocate of Palestinian self-determination. Cole had been in line for a faculty appointment at Yale, but the offer slipped away, without explanation, following a concerted media campaign to "expose" him as an anti-Semite. Why cause trouble, the university concluded? Best to simply yield.

The issue here is not the rights and wrongs of Middle East policy—others will debate that—but the ability of mainstream American academics to buck the trend on sensitive issues. That ability, that room for maneuver, varies from college to college and from circumstance to circumstance. That is why the case of John Mearsheimer and Stephen Walt is so remarkable. These two academics, from the universities of Chicago and Harvard, respectively, were first commissioned to write a long, scholarly article on the Israel lobby by *Atlantic* magazine in 2002. They charted the role of the Israel lobby, particularly the American Israel Public Affairs Committee (AIPAC), in depth, pointing out the extent to which American and Israeli priorities had become virtually indistinguishable over the years, accelerating under Bush. The magazine's editors sat on the manuscript for months before deciding not to publish it. The article ended up in the *London Review of Books* in March 2006; the authors wrote a longer version, which was posted on the website of Harvard's Kennedy School of Government. It was roundly denounced. The biggest surprise came next, when a publishing house dared to pay the authors an advance of $750,000 to expand on the themes in a book. The result was *The Israel Lobby and US Foreign Policy*, published in August 2007.[20] Eliot Cohen, who went on to take a senior job in Condoleezza Rice's State Department, was given a prominent slot in the *Washington Post* to accuse the authors of having "obsessive and irrationally hostile beliefs about Jews."[21] Nevertheless, the book opened up, for the first time in many years, a reasonably candid debate on the issues.

Larry Wilkerson, former chief of staff to Colin Powell, secretary of state under George W. Bush, revealed that he had put the book on his students' reading list at George Washington University because it contained "blinding flashes of the obvious that people whispered in corners rather than said out loud at cocktail parties where someone could hear you."[22] At least as much caution among supporters and hostility among detractors greeted the publication by Jimmy Carter of a book deemed sympathetic to the Palestinian cause. Carter's position was a little different from Mearsheimer and Walt's. His status as a former president provided him with a certain protection. At the same time, his long-standing views about Israel had already placed him in that distinct camp of "nonmainstream" political actors—indulged by the "respectable" media but usually with a studied reserve or disdain. These episodes provide telling examples of the pressure to conform, to abide by what is considered the mainstream mood of the moment. At the same time it shows that the boundaries can be pushed if authors, journalists, editors, and their commercial backers have the courage to stand their ground. The issue is as often self-censorship, the "inner Ashcroft," rather than the imposition of legislation.

That is perhaps the most important lesson of the Bush era, particularly the first term. The state certainly did recalibrate the relationship between liberty and security, but it did so with such ease because both its rationale and its actions were so rarely challenged. This was the most voluntary of pacts. It reminds me of the remark of the Indian information minister during the emergency of 1975: "When you were only asked to bend, many of you chose to crawl."

There is no single moment when that crawling began to stop. But Bush's second election victory, in 2004, does provide a rough marker. From that moment, the administration went into a downward spiral. The public's attitude about the administration changed, and yet the fundamental terms of exchange had not changed: Liberty in return for either security or prosperity, or at least the promise to deliver one or the other, was the commodity for exchange. Bush had delivered on his economic pledge—at least to those on whom he depended for votes. He had prevented any repeat of 9/11 and had given the impression that he had neutralized the internal terrorist threat.

The picture was much clearer abroad. Internationally, America's credibility was weaker than it had been for a generation. As the self-professed leader of the free world, the United States was always subjected to particular scrutiny both at home and abroad. The administration's philosophy of preemption and primacy had turned America's global relationships on their head. Democracy promotion had been elevated to a major foreign policy goal without heed to the sensitivities of liberal democracies around the world. Francis Fukuyama, professor of international political economy at Johns Hopkins University, and one-time supporter of the war turned critic, put it to me like this: "The entire democratic process is tainted by the instrumental use of democracy, notably in Iraq. It undermined the moral authority of America to stand up against authoritarian government. The paradox is the willingness to accept torture and the erosion of civil liberties by a state that promotes itself as the bastion of freedom."[23]

Thanks to Bush, the years that followed the failed Iraq War after 2003 constituted a springtime for autocrats. An America weakened by failed diplomacy and military endeavors, and by a reeling economy, was in no position to lead others into pushing for greater social justice or human rights around the world. It was hamstrung in its dealings with Iraq. It relied on China to support its moves against North Korea. It did nothing to alleviate the suffering of Zimbabweans. More crucially, the United States had lost its powers to cajole or coerce the populist authoritarians in Russia, China, and elsewhere. They were able to swat away the complaints of the Bush White House with consummate ease.

So did it all boil down to the excesses of Guantánamo and Abu Ghraib or to the fact that weapons of mass destruction were never found in Iraq? These excesses certainly energized Bush's critics, and not just those in other countries. They allowed human rights groups and others broadly seen as on the liberal wing of politics in the United States to recapture their voice. But what would have happened if the invasion of Iraq had proven a success in military terms? U.S. forces had, after all, taken Baghdad and deposed Saddam; it was only once American forces had occupied Iraq that the blunders really began. I raise these points less to revisit issues of the war than to suggest that the collapse in Bush's personal ratings among the American public was not an inevitable consequence of his administration's pugilistic approach at home and abroad.

Ultimately, what mattered to American voters was not that the administration was unethical or hypocritical, but that it was incompetent—and was seen to be so. Even if they could not see the pictures of the body bags, they started to read about the increasing death toll among servicemen and women. And what had all these sacrifices achieved? they began to ask themselves. These ventures in Iraq and Afghanistan had not made them feel any safer. They had watched as Bush had given jobs, favors, and tax cuts to his friends. Crony capitalism—from Halliburton to other beneficiaries of the military escapades—was being exposed as corrupt and inefficient. Then the people watched with anger and embarrassment as the world's most powerful nation failed to deliver relief even during a natural disaster, Hurricane Katrina in New Orleans.

As the circumstances changed, and the Bush administration's ability to bully diminished, many influential figures in U.S. politics and the media replaced their quiescence of the 9/11 and Iraq War years with a new and fashionable vehemence. It was one thing to rail against the use of torture and the avarice of bankers in 2008, quite another to have stuck one's head out and done so in 2001. Something had changed in those seven years. The trickle of criticism gradually turned into a flood, and by the end of Bush's term, people were fed up—with the war, with Bush, and more, especially the unethical business practices of the financial elite, which had helped to cause the economic crisis. Compare and contrast the muted reaction of the government to the scandal of Kenneth Lay and the other Enron executives back at the start of the Bush era with the fury directed at Bernard Madoff for his crooked Ponzi schemes.

And yet, even when they had the power to block the excesses of the Bush regime, even when the political environment was seen to be changing, many so-called liberal politicians chose not to confront the administration or the values it espoused. When it came to performing its basic duty of providing a counterweight to executive power, Congress throughout this period was found wanting. For the first six years of Bush's presidency, Democrats complained that their hands were tied by Republican dominance in Congress. Just wait, they said, until they gained control, which they did at the end of 2006. In a defiant final act that October, the outgoing Congress passed the Military Commissions Act, which enshrined lower evidential standards for "enemy combatants." The minority Democrats, as ever, put up scant resistance. The ensuing two years, with both houses under Democrat control, saw some of the most important assaults on civil liberties of the Bush era. Time and again, when legislation was put before them, either giving an imprimatur to administration covert actions or extending them, the two chambers rolled over.

The most astonishing decision was to give political and judicial legitimacy to the secret eavesdropping that the *New York Times* had belatedly exposed in 2004. The FISA Amendments Act of 2008, amending the Foreign Intelligence Surveillance Act (FISA), was passed with substantial Democratic support, including a number of key figures in the House Democratic leadership. With the Democratic presidential nomination safely under his belt, Barack Obama, as a senator from Illinois, reversed the pledge he had made during the primaries and backed a beefed-up version of the bill. The new measure legalized vast new categories of warrantless eavesdropping. It marked the biggest revamping of federal surveillance law in thirty years. Certainly the pressure on the Democrats had been intense. The media language of patriotism was still in full flow. Christopher "Kit" Bond, a senior Republican senator from Missouri, teased his colleagues, telling them they had nothing to fear in the bill, "unless you have Al Qaeda on your speed dial." Even he was surprised at how easily the bill was passed. "I think the White House got a better deal than they even had hoped to get," he admitted.[24]

Throughout the Bush years, much of America's political elite— Democrats and Republicans alike—had refused to grapple with the broader reasons behind the widespread rejection of their country's worldview. Or if it did engage these questions, it saw in the discontent only anti-Americanism. It failed to appreciate the extent to which the failings within their own system—from electoral turnout to political participation, from corruption to an increased uniformity in global

communication—and, most importantly, the U.S.-driven recession—
had increased the attractiveness of the alternatives on offer around
the world.

The very questions about economic governance and international
institutions, about greed and globalization, that had been decreed
around the time of 9/11 to be unpatriotic and dangerous, were, once
the recession had taken hold, suddenly rendered not just acceptable,
but vital. The grand bargain that had provided a link between neoliberal free markets and Western liberal democracy—a link that American policymakers had consistently made and proselytized—began, ever
so tentatively, to be questioned.

The election campaign of 2008 rebuilt some confidence in America's democratic credentials at home and abroad. African Americans
and others who had found themselves left out of the bargain registered
to vote in record numbers, and millions voted who had not been bothered to do so previously, so great had been their apathy or antipathy.

And what of Obama himself? What will be his role in reinforcing,
or disassembling, the pact that Bush had with America before things
turned sour? In his many utterances on the campaign trail and during
his first six months in office, Obama gave the impression of having
thought long and hard about America's approach to liberty and
democracy, both domestically and in its foreign dealings. He distanced
himself from the preemption and primacy doctrines of the neoconservatives in no uncertain terms, declaring in a question-and-answer
session with the *Washington Post* in January 2009 that democracy promotion "needs to be a central part of our foreign policy. It is who we
are. It is one of our best exports, if it is not exported simply down the
barrel of a gun." He spoke at the same time of the need to build democratic institutions through civil society, and by example, going back to
Roosevelt's four freedoms.[25]

When it comes to civil liberties, many liberals assumed that under
Obama much of the legislation introduced during the Bush years
would be reversed. With his initial steps, the new president did not
disappoint. He began by issuing a string of executive orders, among

them one authorizing a review of the prison at Guantánamo with an eye to determining how to close the facility, one halting military commission trials, and one restricting interrogators to Army Field Manual techniques. This last order was, in effect, a ban on torture, something Congress had failed to enact early in 2008 when it was considering the Defense Authorization Act. These were hugely symbolic steps. At the same time, he sent out other, less promising signals. Senior members of his administration endorsed continuing the CIA's program of transferring prisoners to other countries without legal rights; they also supported indefinitely detaining terrorism suspects without trial even if they were arrested far from a war zone. What, some might ask, was the particular moral superiority of Bagram Airbase, or any other potential new prison site for the Guantánamo prisoners, over Guantánamo itself? Most worryingly, the administration left the door open to resuming military commission trials in certain extreme situations. "We are charting a new way forward, taking into account both the security of the American people and the need to obey the rule of law," said the White House counsel, Gregory Craig. "That is a message we would give to the civil liberties people as well as to the Bush people."[26] A similarly downbeat message was given to those who were expecting a shift on concerns such as surveillance and wire-tapping. Obama needed as wide a political constituency as possible for his main task of tackling the economic crisis. He had much to lose and little to gain, therefore, from providing extraneous ammunition for his Republican critics in what he regarded as second-order issues.

Then, tentatively but still remarkably, in April 2009 Obama took on the might of the security services and the fury of the many Bush supporters still in the media, releasing a series of memos detailing torture techniques approved by the CIA and allowing for the publication of scores of photographs showing abuse of prisoners held by U.S. forces around the world. In so doing, he was making clear that Abu Ghraib had been no aberration, that it had been integral to the actions of the former administration. And yet, only a few weeks later, he appeared to buckle under the pressure of the military and the security services, saying he would now try to block the release of the offending pictures. The outlook for his administration's take on such issues therefore seems mixed. But one of the most striking differences between the early Obama administration and Bush is the accent on pragmatism over easy ideology, in his international dealings as much as his domestic ones. Obama seemed implicitly to acknowledge a truth that the Bush administration had sought to deny: America was no longer in a position to impose democracy at the end of a barrel of a gun.

Therein lies the paradox of the Obama moment. The hopes vested in him are extraordinary. The demands on him are variously to protect the Americans from terrorism, to get Americans back to work and back into prosperity, to save them from environmental collapse, and to improve the standing of the United States around the world. Yet he has to do all this just at the time when liberal democracy and free markets—the twin pillars on which the post-1945 settlement rested— have been wrenched apart. Just as it is regaining its taste for liberal values, America is losing its ability to pass those values on to others.

As for the Bush administration, it is easy for American liberals to vent their fury on it and, in their opprobrium, to juxtapose it with what has followed. In so doing, they seek to absolve themselves of responsibility for what happened. Had not the Bush regime simply reflected the priorities of the moment—the supremacy of wealth creation over everything else? America's post-9/11 pact was in fact voluntary, and, for several years at least, it proved itself to be overwhelmingly popular. Bush reflected a popular mood. He did not manufacture it. That is a bitter pill to swallow.

Conclusion
People's Priorities

This was the day the world came together, declared a beaming Gordon Brown. This was the start of a "new world order." Such a grandiloquent claim had been made by Woodrow Wilson with the establishment of the League of Nations at the end of World War I. It had been decreed again by President George H. W. Bush in 1990 at the end of the Cold War. So did the London summit of the G20 in April 2009 really mark the closing of a historical chapter, the demise of an economic order that had gone unchallenged for two decades? And what about the political order that had sustained it?

In 1989, with the collapse of communism and the end of the Cold War, regimes around the world, from China and Russia to South Africa, India, and Brazil, concluded that there was no serious ideological alternative to market forces as a means of organizing productive activity. In 2009, with the collapse of the global financial order, many seemed to have reached the opposite conclusion—that unbridled free markets had led even the richest and most sophisticated societies to disaster. Many were skeptical about the atmosphere of contrition in the West, speculating that when fortunes improved again, old habits of greed would resume. But even if one accepted the admissions of guilt from the Western democracies, particularly the United States, at face value, would it mark a transformation in the *quality* of democracy, presaging the deepening and extending of basic liberties to more people?

Twenty years of globalized wealth creation had shaped an understanding of freedom in which finances were of utmost importance. The preeminent freedom had been the freedom to earn money, to keep it, and to consume. All the other freedoms were subjugated to that end, with political leaders even extolling shopping as a patriotic duty. This emphasis, combined with the dawn of the Internet and other technological advances, created a cultural homogeneity not seen before. The super-rich, the quite rich, and the aspiring rich, whether in St. Petersburg, Shanghai, São Paulo, or South Kensington, inhabited a uniform world of the same designers, the same brands, the same social-networking sites and communications tools, the same sports cars, and the same holiday destinations. A cultural conformism was born, a herd mentality that provided for those in power an easy environment in which to operate.

By the time the great bubble burst, the inequalities of the global economy had become all too apparent. In the United States, by 2007 there were 1,000 billionaires, compared with 13 in 1985, owning a staggering $3.5 trillion of wealth. According to *Forbes* magazine in March 2007, the bible of the super-rich, which every year charts their fortunes in a list, a heady cocktail of global economic growth and soaring asset prices had created 178 new billionaires in just twelve months. "This is the richest year in human history," declared the magazine's editor-in-chief, Steve Forbes. "The best way to create wealth is to have free markets and free people, and more and more of the world is realising it." The richest 1 percent received 52 percent of all the benefits of tax cuts under George W. Bush. Yet the median income of American workers had actually decreased in real terms. The most widely recognized tool for measuring inequality, the Gini coefficient, had increased in virtually every country, with China, India, and the United States leading the way. In Britain, the top 1 percent of the population was receiving more of the nation's income than at any time since the 1930s.

In 2006, the total amount paid out in bonuses was £21 billion (about $33.4 billion), about a third of the United Kingdom's education budget. The income and assets of the top 0.1 percent of the population became unmeasurable. Trying to put a figure on super-wealth was, as the director of the Institute for Fiscal Studies, Britain's most respected economic think tank, once told me, like "looking through thick fog." Such were the global flows of cash that the understaffed and demoralized tax authorities could barely keep up.[1]

Redistributive democracy had all but collapsed under the weight of unrestricted global transfers of cash. Political parties that professed to care about such issues, such as New Labour in the United Kingdom, all but gave up using political power, particularly the tax system, to challenge the excesses of the neoliberal financial orthodoxy, confining themselves to palliative mechanisms for those at the bottom of the pile. Across the world, politicians opted out of economic rule-making. It was an area into which they feared to tread. They compensated by focusing on the "other," the parts of national life over which they continued to have some control, and the one area where they could be seen to be making a difference was security.

From the early 1980s, politicians and thinkers in East and West— those who might openly identify with the Thatcher-Reagan neoliberal creed, but many more besides—argued that globalization and wealth creation could only have a positive political impact. As national economies approached a certain level of per capita income, the growing middle classes would become less submissive and less in awe of authority. They would demand legal and political power, which in turn would provide the basis for democracy. It sounds good in theory, but it has not worked out that way.

Instead, with consummate ease, the elites were bought off. They entered into the pact. Those who had only recently acquired wealth were the most susceptible to its inducements and to the political trade-off that came with it. The most innately conservative forces came from the ranks of those whose parents or grandparents were poor, who had just traded the family motorbike for a family car or swapped the flat for a house, who were worried that their gains could disappear at any time. What mattered to those with some money but wanted more, and those who had much but could never have enough, were their private freedoms. They resented the Singapore government telling them who they could sleep with; they disliked the power the Chinese authorities still had to determine foreign travel. They feared the arbitrary use of power by the Kremlin. They wanted, more than anything, an efficient state that abided by the rule of law. They needed to know that their business contracts would not be torn up retrospectively if someone close to the seat of power did not approve. They resented the sense that their money might not be safe, that their home might be taken away on a whim. They wanted modern infrastructure. They wanted low taxes, and, where possible, no taxes, in the name of encouraging "entrepreneurship." In some countries, such as the United Kingdom, that meant legal tax avoidance, encouraged by the indulgent authorities; in others, such as Italy, it meant quasi-illegal tax evasion that was ignored by the indulgent authorities. It was fundamentally the same phenomenon.

Other freedoms were regarded as either optional or unnecessary. In each country, people chose which of those freedoms they wished to keep and which they could discard in exchange for various privileges or safeguards. When it came to national security, the comfortable classes were adamant that the state should assume as many powers as possible to clamp down on any forces that might imperil their way of life. Thus, anyone deemed to be an extremist or a foreigner or a member of a minority group who did not appear respectable should face the full weight of the law. They did not begin to wonder whether the economic rules they had set up had actually exacerbated social tensions.

One of the consequences of globalization, with its merging of consumer tastes, was an increasing sense of national and local chauvinism. The lack of social solidarity produced a new atomized form of freedom. Citizens became overwhelmingly privatized in their habits, thoughts, and daily practices. They were left free to act as individual players, but they were not encouraged to go beyond that. This left a gap for charismatic leaders, for populist identity politics, to work in harmony with a mindless celebrity culture. Italy and India had much in common in this regard, each seeking to deflect voters' attention away from corroded democratic institutions and toward fear of ethnic minorities.

So what, in the end, is the definition of the modern authoritarianism in which so many acquiesced during this period? Perhaps this: state control that stops short of impeding your freedom to create wealth. The definition of the modern democracy might be this: state control that stops short of impeding your freedom to create wealth, and that maintains certain civil-liberties safeguards—for those who do not step out of the mainstream. The difference, then, between the countries that fall roughly into the "authoritarian" camp, such as Singapore, China, Russia, and the UAE, and those that pride themselves on their "democratic" values, such as India, Italy, the United Kingdom, and the United States, may just be one of degree. I have not sought to equate them, but to point out common characteristics. Even in the United Kingdom and France, where surveillance is on the rise, most individuals continue to enjoy considerable day-to-day freedoms. In the United States, for all the self-censorship in the early Bush years, for all the narrowness of the mainstream political debate, critical media self-evidently do not face anything like the sanctions of their counterparts in Singapore, Russia, and China.

All these countries have had, over the past two decades, much more in common than they would like to admit. What happened was the narrowing of the gap between democracies and autocracies. They each began to adopt manifestations of the other, each drawing the line in its own way between private and public freedoms. With free expression in the West increasingly being regarded as a problem to be managed rather than a fundamental right, with the policing of demonstrations increasingly heavy-handed, with states deeming it necessary to put a watch on more and more people, the penalties on those "causing trouble" were not so far apart any more.

What these different systems shared was the complicity of sections of the population that mattered. As was pointed out in the Introduction, the pact does not apply to out-and-out dictatorial regimes. In places such as Zimbabwe and Burma, of course, there are individuals and groups around the leader who stand to benefit, and therefore do the state's bidding; what is different about countries in which the pact is firmly in place, however, is that there is a much larger segment of the population, consisting of the middle and upper classes as well as the ruling elite, that is willing to make compromises for the sake of safety and security, not to mention prosperity. One of the achievements of the past twenty years has been the reduction in the number of states that operate as pure dictatorships. This has been an admirable achievement, which, as Freedom House and other groups have suggested, reached a peak around the turn of the millennium.[2] But along with this achievement has come a greater willingness to enter into a pact of the sort I have been discussing in this book.

It is one thing to rid a country of tyranny, quite another to allow a strong and equitable democracy to grow, particularly in conditions of instability. Among the many strong pieces of work in this area was the final report in 2006 of the Princeton Project, a nonpartisan group looking at the challenges posed to the United States in the post-Communist world. It outlined what it called the "deeper preconditions for successful liberal democracy—preconditions that extend far beyond the simple holding of elections." It concluded that "labelling countries as democracies or non-democracies, much less as good or evil, . . . needlessly complicates our relations with many nations and often undermines the very goals we seek to achieve." Such a point of view, recognizing an uneasy and precarious middle ground, was naturally targeting the simplistic worldview of the neoconservatives and their trigger-happy notions of democracy promotion.[3]

Yet such analyses continued to look upon other countries and the forms of democracy they had chosen from a position of superiority. Even if expressed with sensitivity, they still took as a given the success of the Western economic and political model. They did not acknowledge the extent to which democracy within the West itself had been undermined, not just by the double standards of Western foreign policy, but by the corrosion of its domestic political institutions.

Chris Patten, a passionate advocate of the spread of democracy, is disdainful of the claims made by many of the former Communist states. He points to terms such as "managed democracy" or "sovereign democracy," so beloved of the Russians and Chinese, noting: "It is a good rule of thumb to assume that whenever the word democracy is preceded, as a definition of a form of government, by some descriptive prefix, then one thing it is not is democratic."[4] He is surely right, but does that mean that in the West, societies have achieved the dream of democracy without prefix? I do not think so. How about "controlled democracy"? That could apply to the United Kingdom, France, and many other European states. Italy would surely qualify for the term "corrupt democracy." As for the United States, a number of unflattering prefixes could be applied.

In all of these states, except for China, to a greater or lesser degree voters endorsed the pact that was being offered to them. In Singapore and Russia, those elections might have been gerrymandered, but it is hard to deny that the leaders enjoyed high levels of popularity. In India election day is a remarkable feat of freedom; what happens over the next four years is the problem. In the United States, the election result of 2000 might have been a travesty, but, even after four years of considerably curtailed freedom, enough Americans endorsed the trade-off to give Bush another term in 2004. So great is the disdain for mainstream politics in the United Kingdom, so consistently low is the turnout, that many wonder who their members of Parliament actually represent. In many of these countries, the ballot box provides only a limited choice of outcomes; still, according to the rules, all of them have passed the constitutional test.

So what does all this say about us, the people? One could argue that perhaps people require less freedom than they would like to believe. As long as the state looks after them, keeps them safe, and allows them to lead their personal lives as they wish, perhaps that is enough; at any rate, it is a pact that a sufficient number of people are comfortable with. How many fall into the category of troublemakers? What percentage of the population consists of oppositionist politicians, activists for nongovernmental organizations, dissidents, investigative journalists, or defense lawyers for potential subversives? How many people take part in marches, attend rallies, or participate in the annual World Social Forum or other alternative gatherings to the established institutions such as the G8? Participatory democracy has all but disappeared. And even when it has occasionally broken through into the mass consciousness, such as in 2003 on the eve of the Iraq conflict, when there was a huge antiwar march in London, it made no difference. It was a supine Parliament that determined the outcome, reinforcing a sense of fatalism in people's minds about their government and their own ability to effect change. The political pact had been redefined in the narrowest sense. Do your duty every four or five years by endorsing representative democracy at the ballot box. Then leave the victor the spoils, the right to determine your liberty and your security for you, and do not seek to intervene.

Economic growth, rather than being a force for democratic involvement, reinforced the confidence of business and political elites. They thrived because they reinterpreted the basic tenets of democracy to suit their needs. These neoliberal advocates became consumed by their own intellectual overshoot and hubris, redefining democracy and liberty through notions such as privatization, profit maximization, and disdain for the needs of civil society and social justice as well as for the dangers facing the environment. In so doing, they actually made it easier for authoritarians to flourish.

The tragedy of the past twenty years is that the allure of globalized wealth served as a drug, not just for the super-rich, and as much in the West as in the East. When I used the expression "anesthetic for the brain" about Singapore, I could equally have applied it to any country, irrespective of its notional political system.

Now that the economic recession has met democratic recession, what is the future for freedom? The worst excesses of the globalized era are likely to come to an end. The banks will be more regulated; capital flows will be monitored a little; international institutions will be encouraged to pay more attention to the twin needs of poverty alleviation and the environment. The G20 summit provided de facto recognition of the new leading role being played by China, in particular, along with India, Brazil, and others in determining the future financial architecture. As Luiz Inácio Lula da Silva, the Brazilian president and former shoeshine boy, declared, to the embarrassment of his guest, British Prime Minister Gordon Brown, who was standing next to him: "This is a crisis caused and encouraged by the irrational behaviour of white people with blue eyes who before the crisis appeared to know everything, but are now showing that they know nothing."[5]

But will a new generation of world leaders produce something different and more inspiring, a post-crash version of freedom that actually addresses the many inequities around the world? People's priorities reflect the socioeconomic conditions of their time. So although it may have been the bankers and hedge-fund managers who caused the immediate mess, the bigger culprits were "we the people," particularly in the West. We allowed democracy to mutate into something it should never have become—a vehicle to deliver goods and promote consumption.

That was the pact, a pernicious one, in an era of globalized wealth that fed on technological advance and that ancient human failing—greed. Around the world, a critical mass of people vested in their leaders almost unlimited powers to determine questions of liberty. In return they were bought off by a temporary blanket of security and what turned out to be an illusory prosperity.

ACKNOWLEDGMENTS

In the course of more than a year's travels, I have received remarkable assistance from countless people who have helped me to arrange trips, been willing to discuss various topics, provided interviews and insights, or read versions of the manuscript. It would be impossible to name everyone here; I offer my apologies in advance to the many people omitted from the following list who have contributed in some way to my journey and to this book.

I am grateful to all those at the National University in Singapore, particularly Professor Kishore Mahbubani, along with professors Wang Gungwu and Chua Beng Huat. I would also like to thank some old friends, including Geh Min, Patrick and Rosa Daniel, Chelvum Raja, and Chin Seng Tan. Others have asked to remain anonymous.

In China, my thanks go to Richard Spencer, Arthur Kroeber, Randy Peerenboom, Michael Pettis, Daniel Bell, Benjamin Lim, Louis Kuijs, Chenggen Hu, Kevin Ao, K. T. Mao, Jeanne-Marie Gescher, and, especially, my researcher in Beijing, Jing Wen. In Shenzhen I had the pleasure of meeting Lancel Cui, Wang He Ping, and Edward Hoffman. Others are best left unidentified, but I am very grateful to them. In Hong Kong, I am grateful to David Zweig, Joseph Cheng, Nicholas Bequelin, Geoffrey Crothall, and Robin Munro, and in Taipei to Dennis Engbarth and Andrew Yang.

I am indebted to a great number of friends and acquaintances in Russia whom I have known over the past twenty years—too many to mention in these acknowledgments—but here I wish to include Art Troitsky,

Olga Timyanskaya, Pyotr Kochevrin, and Sergei and Lena Zhgun. I would also like to thank Lilia Shevtsova, Andrei Soldatov, and Elena Nemirovskaya for their insights. Thanks go as well to RIA-Novosti for inviting me to the Valdai discussion club meetings.

In Dubai and Abu Dhabi, thanks go to Caroline Faraj, Nick Maclean, Mark Lunn, Nic Labuschagne, Ashraf Makkar, Martin Newland, Ayman Safadi, Hasan Al Naboodah, Dr. Eckart Woertz, Bob Cowan, and Frank Kane

In India, I was inspired by meetings with Tarun Tejpal, Teesta Setalvad, Barkha Dutt, Swapan Dasgupta, Shobhaa De, Shekhar Kapur, Chiki Sarkar, Kalpana Sharma, Dina Vakil, M. J. Akbar, T. N. Ninan, William Dalrymple, Naresh Fernandes, Mala Singh, Meenakshy Ganguly, Meena Menon, Gautam Mody, Adolf d'Souza, Khozem Merchant, Rashmee Roshan Lall, Ram Reddy, and Dilip Cherian. I am grateful to Gautham Subramanyam for helping with logistics.

I am indebted to Feruccio de Bortoli, Paolo Flores d'Arcais, Ezio Mauro, Sergio Rizzo, Gherardo Colombo, and Michele Polo in Italy. Alessandro Speciale provided great help in organization.

A number of London-based colleagues and friends provided invaluable assistance and insights. These include Vivienne Lo, Tari Hibbitt, Isobel Hilton, Conor Gearty, Paul Mason, Charles Grant, James Kynge, Sir Ken Macdonald, Christopher Granville, Sir Roderic Lyne, Sir Anthony Brenton, Basharat Peer, Salil Tripathi, Kamila Shamsie, Christopher Davidson, Alexandra Pringle, Rosie Goldsmith, and Mukul Devichand. In Oxford, my thanks go to Paul Chaisty, Alex Pravda, Andrew Hurrell, Laurence Whitehead, Rana Mitter, and especially Graham Hutchings and his colleagues at the specialist international analysis service Oxford Analytica. I am grateful to Ahmad Abdallah, Philip Bobbitt, Fareed Zakaria, and Anders Aslund for their time during meetings in the United Kingdom. In Paris, my thanks go to Valerie Nataf, Frederic Niel, Yves Charpentier, and Violaine de Villemeur, and in Frankfurt to Huw Pill.

Several trips to the United States were enhanced by assistance from Eric Foner, Michael Kazin, Francis Fukuyama, Jameel Jaffer, Tom

Carothers, Arch Puddington, Corey Robin, Stephen Holmes, and Katrina van den Heuvel.

I was extraordinarily fortunate to have a group of friends and experts who, as well as helping with trips, were assiduous in reading parts or all of the manuscript in various drafts: Jonathan Steele, John Arlidge, Richard Spencer, Pankaj Mishra, Andrew Stephen, Bobo Lo, Jo Glanville, Jonathan Dimbleby, Naresh Fernandes, David Hoe, Marco d'Eramo, Maxwell Kampfner, Alan Philps, Art Troitsky, Mark Easton, and Jonathan Fenby. Two people guided me all the way through the process and provided inspiration throughout: my sister, Judith Kampfner, and my wife, Lucy Ash. I owe them an immense debt of gratitude.

For providing excellent behind-the-scenes work and organizing many of the trips, I'm very grateful to my researcher, Dr. Milly Getachew. I have been delighted to work for the first time with my U.S. agent, Emma Sweeney, and with Lara Heimert, my editor at Basic Books in New York. It has been a pleasure to work again with my agent, Bruce Hunter, and with the excellent team at Simon and Schuster in London, including Ian Chapman, managing director; Hannah Corbett, publicity director; and my editor and the editorial director for nonfiction, Mike Jones.

NOTES

Introduction

1. Francis Fukuyama, *The End of History and the Last Man*, rev. ed. (New York: Free Press, 2006).

2. Michael Novak, *The Spirit of Democratic Capitalism*, rev. ed. (New York: Madison Books, 2000).

3. Community of Democracies, "Toward a Community of Democracies, Ministerial Conference, Final Warsaw Declaration," Warsaw, June 27, 2000. See text of declaration at http://www.demcoalition.org/pdf/warsaw_english.pdf.

4. Paul Ginsborg, *Democracy, Crisis and Renewal* (London: Profile Books, 2008). Emphasis added.

5. Oswald Spengler, *Decline of the West*, abridged version (New York: Vintage, 2006).

6. Barrington Moore, *Social Origins of Dictatorship and Democracy* (Boston: Beacon Press, 1993).

Chapter 1

1. Kishore Mahbubani, interview with author, National University of Singapore, May 15, 2008.

2. See http://www.youtube.com/watch?v=17qhGIwyGj0.

3. Agence France-Presse, "Recession-Hit Singapore Takes Hard Line on Protests," March 24, 2009.

4. Sinapan Samydorai, interview with Australian Broadcasting Corporation (ABC), *The Media Report*, February 8, 2007.

5. Kishore Mahbubani, interview with author, May 15, 2008. See also Kishore Mahbubani, *The New Asian Hemisphere* (New York: PublicAffairs, 2009).

6. Lee Kuan Yew, speech, "Democracy, Human Rights and the Realities," Tokyo, November 10, 1992.

7. Amartya Sen, "Human Rights and Asian Values," *The New Republic*, July 14–July 21, 1997.

8. Uri Gordon, "Machiavelli's Tiger: Lee Kuan Yew and Singapore's Authoritarian Regime," student paper, Department of Political Science, Tel Aviv University, 2000.

9. Wang Gungwu, interview with author, National University of Singapore, May 15, 2008.

10. Chua Beng Huat, interview with author, May 15, 2008.

11. Gerrie Lim, interview with author, May 16, 2008.

12. Interview with former member of parliament, Singapore, May 14, 2008.

13. Juan Jose Daboub, "Challenges for a New Asia," speech, Lee Kuan Yew School of Public Policy, May 20, 2008.

14. John Kampfner, "The New Authoritarianism: More and More of Us Are Willing to Trade Freedom for Wealth or Security," *Guardian*, July 1, 2008, http://www.guardian.co.uk/uk/2008/jul/01/civilliberties.

15. Michael Teo, "The Singapore Model: Liberal Democracy Works for the West—But in South-East Asia, We Have Different Views," *Guardian*, July 15, 2008, http://www.guardian.co.uk/commentisfree/2008/jul/15/1.

Chapter 2

1. Lanciel Cui, interview with author, Shenzhen, November 19, 2008.

2. Deng Xiaoping, as quoted in "Mini-Singapore Project Is Off and Running in China," *New York Times*, May 21, 1994.

3. Deng Xiaoping, as quoted in Mark Leonard, "China's New Intelligentsia," *Prospect*, June 2008.

4. *Guardian*, October 31, 2005.

5. *People's Daily*, January 6, 2009.

6. *China Daily*, December 9, 2006.

7. *Hurun Report*, Shanghai, October 13, 2007.

8. *Financial Times*, June 26, 2008.

9. This meeting took place on November 18, 2008.

10. As quoted in the *New York Times*, August 2, 2007.

11. As reported in the *Los Angeles Times*, June 5, 2008.

12. Anne-Marie Brady, *Marketing Dictatorship* (Lanham, Md.: Rowman and Littlefield, 2007).

13. Andrew Nathan, "Medals and Rights," *New Republic*, July 2008.

14. Amnesty International, "What Human Rights Legacy for the Beijing Olympics?" April 1, 2008.

15. Gerhard Schröder, speaking at "China's Development and World Harmony" seminar, Beijing, November 9, 2007.

16. Pew Global Attitudes Project, July 22, 2008.

17. Yun-han Chu, Larry Diamond, Andrew J. Nathan, and Doh Chull Shin, eds., *How East Asians View Democracy* (New York: Columbia University Press, 2008).

18. Official website of the Chinese Olympic Committee, June 2, 2008.

19. Nicholas Bequelin, interview with author, Hong Kong, November 21, 2008.

20. Michael Pettis, interview with author, November 15, 2008.

21. This meeting took place on November 16, 2008.

22. Joseph Cheng, interview with author, Hong Kong, November 21, 2008.

23. Dennis Engbarth, interview with author, November 22, 2008.

24. Andrew Yang, interview with author, Taipei, November 22, 2008.

25. Bloomberg, January 5, 2009.

26. *New York Times*, February 8, 2009.

27. Human Rights in China, press release, December 9, 2008.

28. Zhou Xiaochuan, essay on the People's Bank of China website, March 23, 2009.

Chapter 3

1. *Moscow Times*, October 9, 2003.

2. Roman Shleinov, "Rules of the Game," *Index on Censorship* 36, no. 2 (2007).

3. Putin interview with *Suddeutsche Zeitung*, October 10, 2006, as quoted in *New York Review of Books*, "Who Killed Anna Politkovskaya?" November 6, 2008.

4. Shleinov, "Rules of the Game."

5. Vladimir Putin, question-and-answer session at Columbia University during his visit to New York City, November 30, 2008.

6. Interview with author, Moscow, May 24, 2008.

7. Art Troitsky, interview with author, Moscow, May 24, 2008.

8. Ivan Krastev, "'Sovereign Democracy,' Russian-Style," *Open Democracy*, November 16, 2006, http://www.opendemocracy.net/globalization-institutions_government/sovereign_democracy_4104.jsp.

9. As reported in the *Independent*, July 10, 2006.

10. "Schröder Critic Is Silenced," *New York Times*, March 23, 2006, http://www.nytimes.com/2006/03/23/business/worldbusiness/23iht-schroeder.html?_r=1.

11. "Schroeder Slams Pipeline Job Critics," March 30, 2006, http://www.upstreamonline.com/live/article107676.ece.

12. "We Are Not Afraid," *Index on Censorship*, Free Speech Blog, January 21, 2009, http://blog.indexoncensorship.org/2009/01/21/we-are-not-afraid/.

13. Ian Traynor, "Putin Urged to Apply the Pinochet Stick," *Guardian*, March 31, 2000.

14. Lilia Shevtsova, *Putin's Russia* (Washington D.C.: Carnegie Endowment, 2003), 258.

15. Lilia Shevtsova, interview with author, Moscow, May 23, 2008.

16. Shevtsova, *Putin's Russia*, 37.

17. Ibid., 50.

18. Shevtsova, interview with author, May 23, 2008.

19. Sergei Karaganov, "The World Crisis—A Time for Creation," *Russia in Global Affairs*, October-December 2008, http://eng.globalaffairs.ru/numbers/25/1235.html.

20. For a transcript of the speech, see *Wall Street Journal*, January 28, 2009, http://online.wsj.com/article/SB123317069332125243.html.

Chapter 4

1. For original article, see John Kampfner, "The West's Great New Threat Is Right at Home in the City," Guardian, July 26, 2007, http://www.guardian.co.uk/commentisfree/2007/jul/26/comment.china.

2. Ashraf Makkar, interview with author, Abu Dhabi, September 22, 2008.

3. Sheikh Zayed bin Sultan Al Nahyan, interview with *New York Times Magazine*, 1998, as quoted in official tribute to Sheikh Zayed, http://www.uae.org.br/_PDF/zayed.pdf.

4. "Buying Culture," *Newsweek*, August 6, 2007.

5. Frank Gehry, interview with the *Sunday Times*, July 13, 2008.

6. As quoted in the *Guardian*, March 8, 2007.

7. "Buying Culture," *Newsweek*, August 6, 2007.

8. Sheikh Mohammed Bin Zayed Al Nahyan, Crown Prince of Abu Dhabi, as quoted by mediaME.com, April 20, 2008.

9. Martin Newland, interview with author, Abu Dhabi, September 22, 2008.

10. "Where Does the Truth Lie on Davidson's Book?" The Emirates Economist website, September 18, 2008, http://emirateseconomist.blogspot.com/2008/09/where-does-truth-lie-on-davidsons-book.html.

11. Newland, interview with author, September 22, 2008.

12. Ayman Safadi, interview with author, Abu Dhabi, September 22, 2008.

13. Hasan Al-Naboodah, interview with author, Al Ain, September 23, 2008.

14. John Kampfner, "Abu Dhabi Do," *Guardian*, March 12, 2005, http://www.guardian.co.uk/travel/2005/mar/12/unitedarabemirates.hotels.guardiansaturdaytravelsection.

15. Soheil Abedian, founder and president of Palazzo Versace, as quoted in *The Times*, December 14, 2008.

16. *Guardian*, October 8, 2008.

17. Michael Laufer, "A. Q. Khan Nuclear Chronology," Carnegie Endowment Issue Brief, Proliferation, vol. 8, no. 8, September 7, 2005.

18. Nicholas Labuschagne, interview with author, Dubai, September 21, 2008.

Chapter 5

1. Teesta Setalvad, interview with author, Mumbai, March 4, 2009.

2. Robert D. Kaplan, "India's New Face," *The Atlantic*, April 2009.

3. Setalvad, interview with author, March 4, 2009.

4. Narasimha Rao, as quoted in Gurcharan Das, *India Unbound* (Delhi: Penguin, 2002), 215.

5. Das, *India Unbound*.

6. "The Rise of India," *Foreign Affairs*, July/August 2006, introduction to special issue (see http://www.foreignaffairs.com/features/collections/the-rise-of-india); Swaminathan Anklesaria, "The Global Indian Takeover," *Times of India*,

January 4, 2004; Jaideep Bose, "India Poised, Make 2007 the Year of India," *Times of India*, January 1, 2007.

7. Pankaj Mishra, "The Myth of the New India," *New York Times*, July 6, 2006; Arundhati Roy, "The Monster in the Mirror," *Guardian*, December 13, 2008; UNICEF report available at http://www.unicef.org/india/overview_3702.htm.

8. Shekhar Kapur, interview with author, March 4, 2009.

9. Pankaj Mishra, *Temptations of the West* (London: Picador, 2006).

10. Pallavi Aiyar, *An Experience of China* (Delhi: Fourth Estate, 2008).

11. M. J. Akbar, interview with author, Delhi, March 6, 2009.

12. Barkha Dutt, interview with author, Delhi, March 7, 2009.

13. Kalpana Sharma, interview with author, Mumbai, March 3, 2009.

14. Shobhaa De, interview with author, Mumbai, March 3, 2009.

15. See Archna Shukla, "Should Private Treaties Be Made Public to Newspaper Readers?" at http://www.livemint.com/2008/01/14234923/Should-private-treaties-be-mad.html.

16. Meenakshy Ganguly, interview with author, Mumbai, March 4, 2009.

17. See Tarun J. Tejpal, "The Tahelka Exposé: Reclaiming Investigative Journalism in India," http://www.taruntejpal.com/TheTehelkaExpose.HTM.

18. Tarun Tejpal, interview with author, Delhi, March 6, 2009.

19. Ibid.

20. Ganguly, interview with author, March 4, 2009.

21. See "Obituary: John Kenneth Galbraith, 1908–2006," http://www.domain-b.com/people/profiles/20060503_american.htm.

22. "Advanaji on the Media," http://www.lkadvani.in/eng/content/view/589/363/.

23. Swapan Dasgupta, interview with author, Delhi, March 7, 2009.

24. Pankaj Mishra, interview with author, London, March 17, 2009.

Chapter 6

1. President of Russia, Official Web Portal, "Press Statements and Answers to Journalists' Questions After a Meeting with Silvio Berlusconi," April 18, 2008, http://www.kremlin.ru/eng/text/speeches/2008/04/18/1208_type82914type82915_164102.shtml.

2. Ibid. See also "Putin Denies Secret Marriage to Russian Renowned Sportswoman," http://www.youtube.com/watch?v=wDvUloWb1ko.

3. As reported, inter alia, in the *Daily Telegraph*, April 18, 2008.

4. "'Sorry' Says Russian Tabloid for Putin's Wedding Report," April 18, 2008, http://www.expressindia.com/latest-news/Sorry-says-Russian-tabloid-for-Putins-wedding-report/298586/.

5. President of Russia, Official Web Portal, "Press Statements and Answers to Journalists' Questions After a Meeting with Silvio Berlusconi," April 18, 2008, http://www.kremlin.ru/eng/text/speeches/2008/04/18/1208_type82914type829 15_164102.shtml; "Putin Denies Secret Marriage to Russian Renowned Sportswoman," http://www.youtube.com/watch?v=wDvUloWb1ko.

6. Gianfranco Fini, interview with *La Stampa* newspaper, April 2, 1994, as quoted in the *New York Times*, April 2, 1994.

7. Ferruccio de Bortoli, interview with author, Milan, July 8, 2008.

8. "Italy Editor Was 'Forced Out,'" BBC Online, May 30, 2003, http://news .bbc.co.uk/1/hi/world/europe/2950538.stm.

9. Giovanni Sartori, column in *Corriere della Serra*, May 15, 2003.

10. De Bortoli was eventually reinstated as editor of *Corriere della Serra* six years later, after the board sought to address circulation declines. See "New Editor Named at Italy's Top Newspaper," Reuters, March 20, 3009, http://uk .reuters.com/article/idUKLU56791420090330.

11. Ezio Mauro, interview with author, Rome, July 9, 2008.

12. Gherardo Colombo, telephone interview with author, Rome, July 9, 2008.

13. Paolo Flores d'Arcais, interview with author, Rome, July 9, 2008.

14. *The Times*, June 26, 2008.

15. Silvio Berlusconi, as quoted in the *Daily Telegraph*, June 18, 2008; Angelino Alfano, as quoted by the BBC, "MPs Pass Berlusconi Immunity Bill," July 11, 2008, http://news.bbc.co.uk/1/hi/world/europe/7501825.stm.

16. *The Times*, April 17, 2008.

17. Annalisa Piras, "The Battle of the Berlusconis," May 14, 2009, BBC, http://news.bbc.co.uk/1/hi/world/europe/8044711.stm, May 14, 2009.

18. Sergio Rizzo, interview with author, Rome, July 9, 2008.

19. Gian Antonio Stella and Sergio Rizzo, *La Casta* (New York: Rizzoli, 2008).

20. *New York Times*, October 22, 2008.

21. *Guardian*, March 28, 2009.

Chapter 7

1. Brendan O'Neill, "Watching You, Watching Me," *New Statesman*, October 2, 2006.

2. Prime Minister's News Conference, 10 Downing Street, August 5, 2005, http://www.number10.gov.uk/Page8041; Frances Steed Stellars, "Grin and Bear It," *Washington Post*, July 31, 2005.

3. Report of the Interception of Communications Commissioner 2006, published January 2008, http://www.official-documents.gov.uk/document/hc0708/ hc02/0252/0252.pdf.

4. Information Commissioner's Office Annual Report 2007/2008, published July 14, 2008, http://www.ico.gov.uk/upload/documents/library/corporate/ detailed_specialist_guides/annual_report_2007_08.pdf; statistics as reported by David Leppard, "There's No Hiding Place as Spy HQ Plans to See All," *Sunday Times*, October 5, 2008.

5. Richard Thomas, interview on *The World at One*, BBC Radio 4, July 15, 2008.

6. Sir Alec Jeffreys, interview with the *Guardian*, April 15, 2009.

7. Sir David Omand, "The National Security Strategy: Implications for the U.K. National Intelligence Community," Institute for Public Policy Research, Commission on National Security in the 21st Century, February 9, 2009, http://www.ippr.org/publicationsandreports/publication.asp?id=646.

8. Ross Anderson, Ian Brown, Terri Dowty, Philip Inglesant, William Heath, and Angela Sasse, "Database State: A Report Commissioned by the Joseph Rowntree Reform Trust Ltd.," March 23, 2009, http://www.jrrt.org.uk/ uploads/database-state.pdf.

9. Charles Clarke, "ID Cards Defend the Ultimate Civil Liberty," *The Times*, December 20, 2004.

10. *Power to the People: The Report of Power, an Independent Inquiry into Britain's Democracy. The Centenary Project of the Joseph Rowntree Charitable Trust and the Joseph Rowntree Reform Trust*, March 2006, http://www.powerinquiry .org/report/documents/PowertothePeople_002.pdf.

11. Tony Blair, "I Don't Destroy Liberties, I Protect Them," *The Observer*, February 26, 2006.

12. Gordon Brown, speech on liberty, October 25, 2007, http://www.number10 .gov.uk/Page13630.

13. For more details on this case, see Rachel Ehrenfeld, "The Chill of Libel Tourism," *Guardian*, June 9, 2009, http://www.guardian.co.uk/commentisfree/ libertycentral/2009/jun/09/libel-tourism-rogues-gallery; Floyd Abrams, "Through the Looking Glass," Index on Censorship, June 15, 2009, http://www .indexoncensorship.org/2009/06/through-the-looking-glass/.

14. Denis Macshane, Labour MP for Rotherham, House of Commons, December 17, 2008. For transcript of debate, see http://www.publications.parliament .uk/pa/cm200809/cmhansrd/cm081217/halltext/81217h0001.htm.

15. Tony Blair, speech at Reuters headquarters in London on the state of the U.K. media, June 12, 2007, http://uk.reuters.com/article/idUKZWE245852200 70612.

16. John Kampfner, "A Very Corporate Loss of Nerve," *New Statesman*, October 10, 2005, http://www.newstatesman.com/200510100006.

17. For quotations from John Stuart Mill see, inter alia, "The Quotations Page," http://www.quotationspage.com/quote/32944.html.

18. Polly Toynbee, "CCTV Conspiracy Mania Is a Very Middle-Class Disorder," *Guardian*, November 7, 2006; Conor Gearty, "A Convention of Cant," *New Statesman*, March 19, 2009.

19. John Kampfner, "The New Authoritarianism: More and More of Us Are Willing to Trade Freedom for Wealth or Security," *Guardian*, July 1, 2008, http://www.guardian.co.uk/uk/2008/jul/01/civilliberties.

20. Ken Macdonald, "Give Us Laws that the City Will Respect and Fear," *The Times*, February 23, 2009.

Chapter 8

1. Chua Beng Huat, interview with author, May 15, 2008.

2. John Kenneth Gailbraith, *The Culture of Contentment* (Boston: Houghton Mifflin, 1992).

3. James Risen and Erich Lichtblau, "Bush Lets U.S. Spy on Callers Without Courts," *New York Times*, December 16, 2005; see also Eric Lichtblau, "The Education of a 9/11 Reporter," *Slate*, March 26, 2008; "The United States of America vs. Bill Keller," *New York*, http://nymag.com/news/media/20334/index5.html.

4. Jameel Jaffer, interview with author, New York, August 28, 2008.

5. Jane Lampman, "Uncle Sam Doesn't Want You," *Christian Science Monitor*, May 11, 2006. For details of both legal suits, and for details on Habib and Ramadan, see American Civil Liberties Union, "Safe and Free: Restore Our Constitutional Rights," http://www.aclu.org/safefree/exclusion/index.html.

6. Dick Cheney, interview on Fox News, October 30, 2006.

7. John Ashcroft testimony to the Senate Judiciary Committee, December 6, 2001; for transcript, see http://www.usdoj.gov/ag/testimony/2001/1206transcript senatejudiciarycommittee.htm. Lynne Cheney quoted by the American Council of Trustees and Alumni, November 25, 2001, http://www.goactablog.org/blog/archives/2006/08/correction_in_t.html.

8. Susan Sontag and others in *The New Yorker*, September 24, 2001, http://www.newyorker.com/archive/2001/09/24/010924ta_talk_wtc. For background on Ed Koch speech, see David Waldstreicher, "Final Fantasy," *The Nation*, March 17, 2008, http://www.thenation.com/doc/20080331/waldstreicher; and Madeleine Elfenbein, "The Years of Magical Thinking," *American Prospect*, October 19, 2007, http://www.prospect.org/cs/articles?article=the_years_of_magical_thinking.

9. For background, see David Sirota, "Peter Beinart Has No Clothes," *Huffington Post*, April 30, 2006.

10. Michael Kinsley, "Listening to Our Inner Ashcroft," *Slate*, January 3, 2002; for transcript of Ari Fleischer's press briefing, see "Text: White House Briefing," *Washington Post*, September 26, 2001.

11. For background, see Howard Kurtz, "Embedded Reporter's Role in Army Unit's Actions Questioned by Military," *Washington Post*, June 25, 2003, http://www.washingtonpost.com/ac2/wp-dyn/A28385-2003Jun24?language=printer, and Jack Shafer, "The Scoops That Melted," Slate, July 25, 2003, http://slate.msn.com/id/2086110/.

12. National Security Strategy, September 20, 2002, transcript from *New York Times*, http://www.nytimes.com/2002/09/20/politics/20STEXT_FULL.html.

13. *War Spin, Correspondent*, BBC Two, broadcast May 18, 2003. See http://news.bbc.co.uk/1/hi/programmes/correspondent/3007953.stm. See also John Kampfner, "The Truth About Jessica," *Guardian*, May 15, 2003, http://www.guardian.co.uk/world/2003/may/15/iraq.usa2.

14. Bill Carter, "Pentagon Ban on Pictures of Dead Troops Is Broken," *New York Times*, April 23, 2004, http://www.nytimes.com/2004/04/23/national/23PHOT.html.

15. Michael Kazin, interview with author, August 22, 2208.

16. Eric Foner, interview with author, August 28, 2008.

17. Corey Robin, *Fear: The History of a Political Idea* (New York: Oxford University Press, 2004).

18. Corey Robin, interview with author, New York, February 6, 2009.

19. Juliet Eilperin, "DeLay Lashes Out at Unions," *Washington Post*, February 8, 2003.

20. John Mearsheimer and Stephen Walt, "The Israel Lobby," *London Review of Books*, March 23, 2006, http://www.lrb.co.uk/v28/n06/mear01_.html; *The Israel Lobby and U.S. Foreign Policy* (New York: Farrar, Straus and Giroux, 2007).

21. Eliot Cohen, "Yes, It's Anti-Semitic," *Washington Post*, April 5, 2006.

22. See Andrew Stephen, "Saying the Unsayable," *New Statesman*, September 13, 2007, http://www.newstatesman.com/books/2007/09/israel-policy-mearsheimer-walt.

23. Francis Fukuyama, interview with author, McLean, Virginia, August 29, 2009.

24. Eric Lichtblau, "Deal Reached in Congress to Rewrite Rules on Wiretapping," *New York Times*, June 20, 2008, and "Senate Approves Bill to Broaden Wiretap Powers," *New York Times*, July 10, 2008, http://www.nytimes.com/2008/07/10/washington/10fisa.html?_r=1&partner=rssnyt. See also Glenn Greenwald, "Another Brutal Year for Liberty," Salon, January 1, 2009, http://www.salon.com/opinion/feature/2009/01/01/civil_liberties/print.html.

25. "Elections Aren't Democracy," excerpts from President-elect Barack Obama's meeting at the *Washington Post*, January 15, 2009, http://www.washingtonpost.com/wp-dyn/content/article/2009/01/18/AR2009011801490.html.

26. Charlie Savage, "Obama's War on Terror May Resemble Bush's in Some Areas," *New York Times*, February 17, 2009, http://www.nytimes.com/2009/02/18/us/politics/18policy.html?pagewanted=all.

Conclusion

1. Herbert Lash, "Billionaires Richer, Russia, India Rise: Forbes," Reuters, March 8, 2007, http://www.reuters.com/article/worldNews/idUSN0821626920070308; Stephen Foley, "Forbes Hails 'the Richest Year in Human History,'" March 9, 2007, Independent, http://www.independent.co.uk/news/world/americas/forbes-hails-the-richest-year-in-human-history-439462.html; statistics from Robert Chote, director of the Institute for Fiscal Studies, contained in article by John Kampfner, "The Bling Bling List," New Statesman, March 7, 2005.

2. Arch Puddington, research director, Freedom House, interview with author, New York, August 28, 2008.

3. G. John Ikenberry and Anne-Marie Slaughter, codirectors, "Forging a World of Liberty Under Law: U.S. National Security in the 21st Century. Final Report of the Princeton Project on National Security," Woodrow Wilson School of Public and International Affairs, Princeton University, September 27, 2006, http://www.princeton.edu/~ppns/report/FinalReport.pdf.

4. Chris Patten, What Next? (London: Allen Lane, 2008).

5. Reported by the BBC, inter alia, in Gary Duffy, "Brazil's Lula Raps 'White' Crisis," March 27, 2009, http://news.bbc.co.uk/1/hi/business/7967546.stm.

BIBLIOGRAPHY

Books and a Selection of Essays

Singapore

Chua Beng Huat. "'Asian Values Discourse' and the Resurrection of the Social." *Positions* 7, no. 2 (Fall 1999).

Enright, D. J. *Memoirs of a Mendicant Professor.* Manchester: Carcanet Press, 1990.

Gordon, Uri. "Machiavelli's Tiger: Lee Kuan Yew and Singapore's Authoritarian Regime." Student paper, Department of Political Science, Tel Aviv University, 2000. Available at http://unpan1.un.org/intradoc/groups/public/documents/apcity/unpan002548.pdf.

Lee Kuan Yew. *From Third World to First.* London: HarperCollins, 2000.

———. *The Singapore Story: Memoirs of Lee Kuan Yew.* Singapore: Prentice Hall, 1998.

Neo Boon Siong and Geraldine Chen. *Dynamic Governance: Embedding Culture, Capabilities and Change in Singapore.* Singapore: World Scientific, 2007.

Sen, Amartya. *Development as Freedom.* Oxford: Oxford University Press, 1999.

Verweij, Marco, and Riccardo Pelizzo. "Singapore: Does Authoritarianism Pay?" *Journal of Democracy* 20, no. 2 (April 2009).

China

Aiyar, Pallavi. *An Experience of China.* New Delhi: Fourth Estate, 2008.

Alden, Chris. *China in Africa.* London: Zed Books, 2007.

Becker, Jasper. *The Chinese.* London: John Murray, 2003.

Brady, Anne-Marie. *Marketing Dictatorship.* Lanham, Md.: Rowman and Littlefield, 2007.

Doctoroff, Tom. *Billions, Selling to the New Chinese Consumer.* New York: Palgrave, 2005.

Fenby, Jonathan. *The Penguin History of Modern China.* London: Allen Lane, 2008.

Hutton, Will. *The Writing on the Wall*. London: Little, Brown, 2007.

Kurlantzick, Joshua. *Charm Offensive*. New Haven, Conn.: Yale University Press, 2007.

Kynge, James. *China Shakes the World*. London: Phoenix, 2006.

Leonard, Mark. *What Does China Think?* London: Fourth Estate, 2008.

Mitter, Rana. *Modern China*. Oxford: Oxford University Press, 2008.

Nathan, Andrew. "Medals and Rights." *New Republic*, July 2008.

Peerenboom, Randall. *China Modernizes*. New York: Oxford University Press, 2008.

Pei, Minxin. *China's Trapped Transition*. Cambridge: Harvard University Press, 2006.

Yun-han Chu, Larry Diamond, Andrew J. Nathan, and Doh Chull Shin, eds. *How East Asians View Democracy*. New York: Columbia University Press, 2008.

Russia

Aslund, Anders. *Russia's Capitalist Revolution*. Washington, D.C.: Peterson Institute, 2007.

Colton, Timothy. *Yeltsin, A Life*. New York: Basic Books, 2008.

Figes, Orlando. *Natasha's Dance*. London: Penguin, 2003.

Franchetti, Mark. "How the Oligarchs Lost Billions." *Sunday Times Magazine*, February 22, 2009.

Hoffman, David. *The Oligarchs*. New York: PublicAffairs, 2003.

Gambrell, Jamey. "Putin Strikes Again." *New York Review of Books*, July 19, 2007.

Goldman, Marshall. *Oilopoly*. Oxford: Oneworld, 2008.

Jack, Andrew. *Inside Putin's Russia*. London: Granta, 2005.

Karaganov, Sergei. "The World Crisis: Time for Creation." *Russia in Global Affairs*, no. 4, October-December 2008.

Korinman, Michael, and John Laughland, eds. *Russia: A New Cold War?* Portland: Valentine Mitchell, 2008.

Lipman, Masha. "Russia's Free Press Withers Away." *New York Review of Books*, May 31, 2001.

Litvinenko, Alexander, and Yuri Felshtinsky. *Blowing Up Russia*. London: Gibson Square, 2007.

Lo, Bobo. "Russia's Crisis: What It Means for Regime Stability and Moscow's Relations with the World." Centre for European Reform, February 2009.

Lucas, Edward. *The New Cold War*. London: Bloomsbury, 2008.

Lyne, Roderic. "Reading Russia, Rewiring the West." *Open Democracy*, September 18, 2008.

Ostrovsky, Arkady. "Flirting with Stalin." *Prospect*, no. 150, September 28, 2008.

Politkovskaya, Anna. *Putin's Russia*. London: Harvill Press, 2004.

Remnick, David. "Echo in the Dark." *New Yorker*, September 22, 2008.

Sakwa, Richard. "'New Cold War' or 20 Years' Crisis?" *International Affairs* 84, no. 2 (March 2008).

Shevtsova, Lilia. *Putin's Russia*. Washington, D.C.: Carnegie Endowment, 2003.

———. *Russia: Lost in Translation*. Washington D.C.: Carnegie Endowment, 2007.

Shleinov, Roman. "Rules of the Game." *Index on Censorship* 36, no. 2 (May 2007).

Soldatov, Andrei. "How Britain Struggles with the Russian Mafia." *Novaya Gazeta*, June 6, 2008.

Trenin, Dmitri. *Getting Russia Right*. Washington D.C.: Carnegie Endowment, 2007.

Whitmore, Brian. "Inside the Corporation: Russia's Power Elite." Radio Free Europe/Radio Liberty, October 15, 2007.

Wilson, Andrew. *Virtual Politics*. New Haven, Conn.: Yale University Press, 2005.

United Arab Emirates

Al Abed, Ibrahim, and Peter Hellyer, eds. *United Arab Emirates: A New Perspective*. London: Trident Press, 2001.

Arlidge, John. "Dubai's Desert Dream." *Sunday Times*, January 2, 2005.

———. "The Party's Over in Dubai." *Sunday Times*, November 30, 2008.

Davidson, Christopher. *Dubai: The Vulnerability of Success*. London: Hurst, 2008.

India

Das, Gurcharan. *India Unbound*. New Delhi: Penguin, 2002.

Das, Gurcharan, et al., "The Rise of India." *Foreign Affairs*, http://www.foreignaffairs.com/features/collections/the-rise-of-india, July 2006.

Dossani, Rafiq. *India Arriving*. New York: Amacom, 2008.

Fernandes, Naresh. "The Big Sellout." *Outlook*, October 16, 2006.

Guha, Ramachandra. *India After Gandhi*. London: Macmillan, 2007.

Kamdar, Mira. *Planet India*. London: Simon and Schuster, 2007.

Kaplan, Robert. "India's New Face." *Atlantic*, April 2009.

Mishra, Pankaj. *Temptations of the West*. London: Picador, 2006.

Ninan, T. N. "Boom and Gloom." *India Seminar*, February 2003.

Roy, Arundhati. *The Shape of the Beast*. New Delhi: Viking, 2008.

Sharma, Kalpana. *Rediscovering Dharavi*. New Delhi: Penguin, 2000.

Varma, Pavan. *The Great Indian Middle Class*. New Delhi: Penguin, 2007.

Italy

Anderson, Perry. "An Entire Order Converted into What It Was Intended to End." *London Review of Books*, February 2009.

Foot, John. *Modern Italy*. London: Palgrave Macmillan, 2003.

Ginsborg, Paul. *Berlusconi*. London: Verso Books, 2008.

Jones, Tobias. *The Dark Heart of Italy*. London: Faber and Faber, 2007.

Lane, David. *Berlusconi's Shadow*. London: Penguin, 2005.

Stella, Gian Antonio, and Sergio Rizzo. *La Casta*. New York: Rizzoli, 2008.

Britain

Campbell, Alastair. *The Blair Years*. London: Arrow Books, 2008.

Davies, Nick. *Flat Earth News*. London: Vintage, 2009.

Gearty, Conor. "The Blair Report." *Index on Censorship* 36, no. 2 (May 2007).

———. *Civil Liberties*. Oxford: Oxford University Press, 2007.

———. "The Politics of Terror." *Index on Censorship* 37, no. 3 (August 2008).

Kennedy, Helena. *Just Law*. London: Vintage, 2005.

Lee, Simon. *Best for Britain? The Politics and Legacy of Gordon Brown*. Oxford: Oneworld, 2008.

Lester, Anthony. "Redefining Terror." *Index on Censorship* 36, no. 2 (May 2007).

Malik, Kenan. "Out of Bounds." *Index on Censorship* 37, no. 3 (August 2008).

———. *Strange Fruit*. Oxford: Oneworld, 2008.

Noorlander, Peter. "The New Labour Decade." *Index on Censorship* 36, no. 2 (May 2007).

Peston, Robert. *Who Runs Britain?* London: Hodder and Stoughton, 2008.

Raab, Dominic. *The Assault on Liberty*. London: Fourth Estate, 2009.

Seldon, Anthony. *Blair's Britain, 1997–2007*. Cambridge: Cambridge University Press, 2007.

United States

Daalder, Ivo. *America Unbound*. London: John Wiley, 2005.

Florida, Richard. "How the Crash Will Reshape America." *Atlantic*, March 2009.

Fukuyama, Francis. *After the Neocons*. London: Profile Books, 2007.

Gaddis, John Lewis. "Ending Tyranny." *American Interest*, September-October 2008.

Kirkpatrick, Jeane. "Dictatorships and Double Standards." *Commentary*, November 1979.

Lewis, Anthony. *Freedom for the Thought That We Hate*. New York: Basic Books, 2007.

Lichtblau, Eric. *The Remaking of American Justice*. New York: Pantheon Books, 2008.

Mayer, Jane. "The Hard Cases." *New Yorker*, February 2009.

McClellan, Scott. *What Happened*. New York: PublicAffairs, 2008.

Meersheimer, John, and Stephen Walt. *The Israel Lobby and US Foreign Policy*. London: Allen Lane, 2007.

Nye, Joseph. *The Paradox of American Power*. New York: Oxford University Press, 2003.

O'Harrow, Robert. *No Place to Hide*. London: Penguin, 2006.

Robin, Corey. *Fear: The History of a Political Idea*. New York: Oxford University Press, 2004.

———. "Was He? Had He?" *London Review of Books*, October 2006.

Stelzer, Irwin. *Neoconservatism*. London: Atlantic Books, 2005.

General

Acemoglu, Daron, and James Robinson. *Economic Origins of Dictatorship and Democracy*. Cambridge: Cambridge University Press, 2006.

Carothers, Thomas, "How Democracies Emerge." *Journal of Democracy* 18, no. 1 (January 2007).

Cooper, Robert. *The Breaking of Nations*. London: Atlantic Books, 2007.

Diamond, Larry. "The Democratic Rollback." *Foreign Affairs*, http://www.foreignaffairs.com/articles/63218/larry-diamond/the-democratic-rollback, March/April 2008.

———. "How to Save Democracy." *Newsweek*, December 31, 2008.

———. *The Spirit of Democracy: The Struggle to Build Free Societies Throughout the World*. London: Times Books, 2008.

Emmott, Bill. *Rivals*. Boston: Houghton Mifflin Harcourt, 2008.

Ferguson, Niall. *The Ascent of Money*. London: Allen Lane, 2008.

Friedman, Thomas. *The World Is Flat*. London: Penguin, 2006.

Fukuyama, Francis. *The End of History and the Last Man*, rev. ed. New York: Free Press, 2006.

———. *Trust*. New York: Free Press, 1996.

Garton Ash, Timothy. *Free World*. London: Penguin, 2005.

Ginsborg, Paul. *Democracy, Crisis and Renewal*. London: Profile Books, 2008.

Greenspan, Alan. *The Age of Turbulence*. London: Penguin, 2008.

Hardt, Michael, and Antonio Negri. *Empire*. Cambridge: Harvard University Press, 2000.

Huntingdon, Samuel. *The Clash of Civilisations*. London: Free Press, 2002.

Hurrell, Andrew. *On Global Order*. Oxford: Oxford University Press, 2007.

Kagan, Robert. *Paradise and Power*. London: Atlantic Books, 2003.

———. *The Return of History and the End of Dreams*. London: Atlantic Books, 2008.

Kempf, Hervé. *How the Rich Are Destroying the Earth*. Dartington, U.K.: Green Books, 2008.

Khanna, Tarun. *Billions of Entrepreneurs*. Boston: Harvard Business School Press, 2007.

Klein, Naomi. *The Shock Doctrine*. London: Penguin, 2008.

Krugman, Paul. *The Return of Depression Economics*. London: Penguin, 2008.

Lo, Bobo. *Axis of Convenience*. Washington, D.C.: Brookings Institution Press, 2008.

Mahbubani, Kishore. *Can Asians Think?* Hanover, N.H.: Steerforth Press, 2002.

———. *The New Asian Hemisphere*. New York: PublicAffairs, 2009.

McMahon, Robert. "The Brave New World of Democracy Promotion." *Foreign Service Journal* 86, no. 1 (February 2009).

Monbiot, George. *The Age of Consent*. London: Harper Perennial, 2004.

Moore, Barrington. *Social Origins of Dictatorship and Democracy*. Boston: Beacon Press, 1993.

Munoz, Heraldo. *The Dictator's Shadow*. New York: Basic Books, 2008.

Novak, Michael. *The Spirit of Democratic Capitalism*, rev. ed. New York: Madison Books, 2000.

Patten, Chris. *What Next?* London: Allen Lane, 2008.

Puddington, Arch. "Freedom in the World 2009." *Freedom House*, http://www.freedomhouse.org/template.cfm?page=15, January 2009.

Reich, Robert. *Supercapitalism*. Cambridge: Icon Books, 2008.

Slaughter, Anne-Marie. *A New World Order*. Princeton, N.J.: Princeton University Press, 2004.

Spengler, Oswald. *The Decline of the West*, abridged version. New York: Vintage, 2006.

Welzel, Christian, and Ronald Inglehart. "The Role of Ordinary People in Democratization." *Journal of Democracy* 19, no. 1 (January 2008).

Zakaria, Fareed. *The Post-American World and the Rise of the Rest*. London: Allen Lane, 2008.

INDEX

Abu Dhabi Investment Authority (ADIA), 134, 141

Abu Dhabi, Untied Arab Emirates, 11, 121, 122–127, 129–131, 247

Abu Ghraib prison scandal, 5, 228, 251–252

ACLU. *See* American Civil Liberties Union

ADIA. *See* Abu Dhabi Investment Authority

Advani, L. K., 167

Afghanistan, 92, 94, 138, 237, 240

AIPAC. *See* American Israel Public Affairs Committee

Aiyar, Pallavi, 154

Akbar, M. J., 155

Al Ain, United Arab Emirates, 127–128

Alfano, Angelino, 187–188

Al-Jazeera, 125

Al-Qaeda, 137, 138, 140, 235, 249

American Civil Liberties Union (ACLU), 233, 234

American Israel Public Affairs Committee (AIPAC), 245

Amnesty International, 24, 60

Andreotti, Giulio, 175–176

Andreyeva, Yekaterina, 172

Anthrax, 230

Ao, Kevin, 68–69

Ari, Waskar, 234

Ashcroft, John, 235, 237, 246

Aung San Suu Kyi, 26

Authoritarianism
  Britain and, 198, 212
  capitalism and, 5–9
  China and, 69
  Italy and, 191–192
  modern, 257
  Singapore and, 32, 38
  United States and, 242, 243

Aven, Pyotr, 110

Babitsky, Andrei, 86–87, 94

Baburova, Anastasia, 108–109

Baker, Donald, 128

BBC. *See* British Broadcasting Corporation

Beijing Olympics (2008), 51–52, 59–64, 64–65, 77–78

Bellinger, John, 234

Bentham, Jeremy, 1, 222

Bequelin, Nicholas, 65–66

Berezovsky, Boris, 84, 85, 87, 102, 104

Berlusconi, Silvio, 171–194
  corruption and, 12
  democracy and, 178, 180, 181, 185, 189–190
  expression, freedom of and, 184–186
  judiciary and, 182–183, 186
  press, freedom of and, 178–182, 184–186

283